Keeping Track

Keeping Track

How Schools Structure Inequality

SECOND EDITION

JEANNIE OAKES

Yale University Press
NEW HAVEN & LONDON

Published with assistance from the foundation
established in memory of William McKean Brown.

Designed by James J. Johnson.
Printed in the United States of America.

The Library of Congress has cataloged the previous edition as follows:
Oakes, Jeannie.
Keeping track.

Bibliography: p.
Includes index.
1. Ability grouping in education. I. Title.
LB3061.O22   1985   371.2'54   84-20931
ISBN 0-300-03725-2 (pbk.)

*The paper in this book meets the guidelines for permanence and durability of the
Committee on Production Guidelines for Book Longevity of the Council on Library
Resources.*
ISBN 978-0-300-10830-9
ISBN 0-300-10830-3 (pbk. : alk. paper)

To
Marty

Contents

Preface to the Second Edition

Why a second edition of *Keeping Track*? First, tracking has both changed and endured since the first edition, and it is time to take stock of the maturing tracking literature. Also, my own analyses of tracking did not end in 1985. I've learned a great deal more about persistent inequality and the resistance to equity reform, and I want to share what these struggles reveal about our cultural ambivalence about race and educational justice.

In the past two decades, the disadvantages suffered by students in lower tracks—documented in the first edition of *Keeping Track* and elsewhere—resonated in the thinking and passions of teachers, civil rights activists, school reformers, parents, and others. If not exactly a groundswell or paradigm shift, this previously unquestioned regularity of schooling, over a period of a few years, had become visible and subjected to pointed critique and action. Open discussions of privately observed injustices heightened the attention given to tracking. Tracking could no longer be seen as an equity-neutral, educationally well-advised school structure. Evidence that the nation's schooling history was replete with "scientific" arguments for, and philosophical defenses of, racism was not news. That children of color were consigned to lower-ability classes was obvious to anyone who had ever stepped into racially mixed schools.

By the early 1990s, policymakers and national opinion leaders were responding to the growing concern about and evidence of tracking's harms by recommending that schools abolish it. Several reform groups and some states incorporated mixed-ability grouping into their efforts to improve the quality of schooling overall and the schooling opportunities of minority students, in particular. A number of courts took a hard look at tracking as "second generation" segregation, and some mandated reforms to help desegregate schools. Groups of educators around the country began to detrack their schools.

Although many were enthusiastic about detracking, others were skeptical or hostile. The two new chapters in this edition analyze the struggles surrounding tracking when people attempted to dismantle it. Chapter 11 examines what have been called "tracking wars," battles over tracking and detracking in which serious research, including *Keeping Track*, was used as both weapon and target, alongside much rhetoric and writing based on little rigorous investigation or analysis. Chapter 12 offers stories of educators and students who, knowing how tough it is to disrupt the structural inequalities of tracking, have made impressive strides toward high-quality and equitable schooling. These stories both inspire and give pause. They underscore the salience of community participation in equity-based school reform to support particular structural changes such as detracking.

Are American schools still keeping track? The surface features of tracking have changed enough that some observers argue that the "detracking movement" has had a major impact on school reform (see, for example, Maureen Hallinan, "The Detracking Movement," *Education Next*, 2004 [*http://www.educationnext.org/20044/72.html*]). Indeed, the old rigid system of completely separate and explicit academic, general, and vocational programs, found in a few of the *Keeping Track* schools, has now largely disappeared. Students enroll in classes subject by subject, rather than in a preset program of courses. Many high schools have eliminated the dead-end, general track, and some now have multiple levels of classes that serve students bound for more and less selective types of colleges, allowing schools to claim that all of their students are college prep. In almost all schools, choice has become an increasingly salient factor in placing students into tracks, shifting the responsibility for differentiated opportunities, resources, and expectations from the school to the students. With choice, students in lower-level classes have only themselves to blame. In many respects people also think about tracking differently today than they did in the past; its defenders find different rationales for explaining what it does and why it should remain in a standards-based educational system with a commitment to leaving no child behind.

However, the deep structure of tracking remains uncannily robust. Most middle and high schools still sort students into classes at different levels based on judgments of students' "ability." This sorting continues to disadvantage those in lower-track classes. Such students have less access to high-status knowledge, fewer opportunities to engage in stimulating learning activities, and classroom relationships less likely to foster engagement with teachers, peers, and learning. The sorting and differentiated opportunities promote gaps in outcomes of every sort: achievement, graduation rates, college going, and so on. Low-income students and students of color still suffer disproportionately from these negative effects, both because they are tracked disproportionately into the lowest classes in racially mixed schools and also because they are more likely to attend racially isolated schools where lower-level classes predominate. Thus, through tracking, schools continue to replicate existing inequality along lines of race and social class and contribute to the intergenerational transmission of social and economic inequality.

Chapters 11 and 12 of this edition use what I've learned from the past two decades of research as a lens through which to view and reflect on both tracking and *detracking*. A growing number of outstanding researchers—sociologists of education, curriculum scholars, and policy analysts—have contributed enormously to the pursuit of valid and credible understanding of tracking. My own work has been guided in part by tough questions from educators and policymakers wanting to know more about how tracking actually works and why, and what alternatives schools might try. Their questions prompted a series of studies that first probed more deeply into tracking's dynamics and later examined the challenges faced by educators seeking to make change. This new research bolsters the evidence and arguments of twenty years ago.

The analyses I offer in these chapters suggest that tracking is something more than a flawed schooling practice—an anomaly that might be rooted out or reformed out of schooling's structural repertoire. Indeed, it is the social *consequences* of tracking—sorting students according to preconceptions based on race and social class and providing them with different and unequal access—as much as the organizational or pedagogical details that matter most. Moreover, it is those social consequences that make so many Americans want to cling to this type of sorting. Thus, to understand tracking, one must pay attention to a complex set of beliefs and values, while noting carefully the politics of power and privilege. The most sobering lesson is that, despite the solid evidence and considerable reform of the past twenty years, most American schools are still keeping track. The most hopeful lesson is that both research and practice make increasingly clear that it need not be so.

For me personally, the years have brought wonderful mentors, colleagues, students, and foundation officers who share a quest for a deeper understanding of social stratification and for knowledge to support those seeking racial justice in schools. It almost feels arrogant to thank them, since the work is theirs as much as mine.

First among these is Gladys Topkis, former editor at Yale University Press, whose perceptive mind and relentless pen shaped the first edition of *Keeping Track*. I had no idea at the time how rare and wonderful her editorial gifts were, and I regret that I did not thank her enough twenty years ago.

During my years at RAND, Linda Darling-Hammond insisted that I continue studying tracking, as she has ever since. Over the years, Linda has been a valued adviser, trusted colleague, and treasured friend. My able colleagues in those RAND studies included Robert Bell, Tor Ormseth, Molly Selvin, and a group of talented research assistants. The National Science Foundation and the National Center for Research on Vocational Education provided funding for the tracking studies I conducted at RAND.

At UCLA, Amy Stuart Wells was my partner as I began to examine detracking schools. Amy's penetrating use of social theory to examine school practice pushed me to look deeper into the normative and political dimensions of tracking and detracking. The team of amazing UCLA graduate students who supported the labor-intensive case studies of middle schools and high schools during the 1990s, many of whom now conduct outstanding programs of research at other universities, includes Estella Williams Chizhic, Robert Cooper, Amanda Datnow, Diane Friedlaender, Jennifer Gong, Gretchen Guiton, Diane Hirshberg, Makeba Jones, Karen Ray, Irene Serna, Ash Vasudeva, and Susan Yonezawa. I'm particularly grateful to Karen Hunter Quartz, Steve

Ryan, and Martin Lipton, my coauthors on *Becoming Good American Schools: The Struggle for Civic Virtue in Education Reform* (2000), our book reporting the middle school research. This work was generously supported for several years by the Lilly Endowment and the Carnegie Corporation of New York.

Lucky for me, Kevin Welner, attorney-turned-Ph.D. student and now a professor, at the University of Colorado, joined my research group just as my interests were turning to the role of the courts in tracking and detracking. Kevin's empirical work and analytic sensibilities have been pivotal to our scrutiny of tracking as second-generation segregation and to our examination of the limits of both the law and traditional educational change strategies in securing equity-focused reform. In my view, Kevin's book *Legal Rights, Local Wrongs: When Community Control Collides with Educational Equity* stands as the seminal examination of tracking and detracking in the legal context. A number of graduate students and colleagues at UCLA and elsewhere supported the work Kevin and I did related to tracking cases, from crunching numbers to making insightful suggestions for framing our findings. These include Gilbert FitzGerald, Haggai Kuppermintz, and Roslyn Arlin Mickelson. Several funders supported this work, including the University of California's California Policy Research Center, the Ford Foundation, and the Edna McConnell Clark Foundation.

My colleagues at UCLA's Institute for Democracy, Education, and Access (IDEA) pressed me to initiate a partnership with a local high school that would seek to disrupt tracking and the social reproduction of inequality for low-income students of color, and, of course, to document and examine the results. For eight years, UCLA professor and IDEA's associate director John Rogers has not only led this work but infused it with his powerful historical, political, and sociological acumen. An incredible team of IDEA scholars—including Susan Auerbach, Tony Collatos, Makeba Jones, Martin Lipton, Ernest Morrell, Irene Serna, Marisa Saunders, and Susan Yonezawa—invested both their minds and hearts in this work. During the years of this study, Atlantic Philanthropies and the Lumina Foundation have been extraordinarily generous in their support.

Throughout the years, the advocate and writer Anne Wheelock provided enormously helpful substantive insights and camaraderie during the tracking wars as well as reassurance that the research findings in

Keeping Track and my later studies resonated with her own considerable experience with tracking policy and practice. Her book, *Crossing the Tracks*, has provided thousands of educators with inspiration and much-needed practical advice. Attorney Tom Henderson, from the Lawyers' Committee on Civil Rights Under Law, helped sharpen my thinking with his consistently tough questions. Working with Tom taught me that controversial research—if driven by principled questions and conducted meticulously—could withstand scrutiny, even that of aggressive lawyers.

Finally, the support of family today is as pivotal as it was twenty years ago. My husband, Martin Lipton, has become a full-time colleague and coauthor. His wisdom and words always inspire and teach. Our children still cheer, and over the years they have nearly tripled the size of the cheering section. Thanks to Lisa, Steve, Alison, Carter, Tracy, Ron, Emily, Haley, Lowell, Rene, Max, Sophia, and Ethan.

Preface

Educational equality is an idea that has fallen from favor. In the eighties we have decided that excellence is what we want and that somehow excellence and equality are incompatible.

What happened to educational equality? Perhaps, in the decades following *Brown* v. *Board of Education,* we were naive enough to think that *wanting* schools to make things right was enough. It was not. We became disillusioned by the extraordinary difficulties well-intentioned school people face in trying to undo past inequalities and present injustices. We got bogged down in conceptualizing what educational equality really meant. Did we want students to have merely an equal chance at education? Did we want to guarantee equal educational resources to all children? Or did we want to ensure equal educational outcomes? We became confused when, whatever brand of equality we espoused, it eluded us. Programs failed. Children in Head Start didn't catch up. Remedial and compensatory classes didn't seem to remediate or compensate. Children making long bus rides seemed to gain nothing but bus rides. Millions were spent; achievement gaps between the haves and the have-nots remained. Something had gone wrong. Were the children of unequal circumstances more than just deprived? Were they truly deficient? Could the failure of these children to learn be attributed to a deeply rooted linguistic or cultural deficit? Or, as unthinkable as it was, could there be an unalterable genetic difference?

We were generous during the sixties and early seventies, but we got tired, and then dollars got tight. Schools were naive and extravagant, we decided, to try to remedy the complex and mysterious social ills around them. Test scores fell. We accused ourselves of fuzzy-headed liberalism. In the attempt to correct inequality, we concluded, schools had neglected to do what they were supposed to do, teach academics. Equality moved out; academic excellence moved in.

This oversimplified account of educational trends over the last two decades highlights two important lapses in our thinking about equality and excellence. The first lapse is that in our search for the solution to the problems of educational inequality, our focus was almost exclusively on the characteristics of the children themselves. We looked for sources of educational failure in their homes, their neighborhoods, their language, their cultures, even in their genes. In all our searching we almost entirely overlooked the possibility that what happens *within* schools might contribute to unequal educational opportunities and outcomes. We neglected to examine the content and processes of schooling itself for ways they might contribute to school failure. The second lapse is in our current view of educational excellence. In our quest for higher standards and superior academic performance we seem to have forgotten that schools cannot be excellent as long as there are groups of children who are not well served by them. In short, we cannot have educational excellence until we have educational equality.

What follows is about both equality and excellence. It is about tracking, the nearly ubiquitous secondary school practice of separating students for instruction by achievement or ability—a practice that seems to limit schools' attempts to be either equitable or excellent. At the heart of the discussion is an analysis of how tracking affected the education of junior and senior high school students in twenty-five of our nations' schools. This analysis is based on a comprehensive set of data collected in 297 classrooms as a part of A Study of Schooling. The data analysis is placed in a context of the social, historical, and political considerations that surround tracking and become an integral part of it.

This, however, is not intended as a technical report of my study of tracking. That may be found in the series of reports of A Study of Schooling available through the ERIC Clearinghouse on Teacher Education and in the journals in which portions of this work have previously appeared: The *American Journal of Education, Sociology of Education,* and *Teachers College Record.*

It is my hope that both the style and substance of the following discussion will be of interest to practicing schoolteachers, administrators, school board members, and concerned parents as well as to social science researchers. It is also my hope that this inquiry into school tracking and its relationship to issues of equality and excellence will attract some of the attention generated by the current schooling crisis to this fundamental feature of schooling and that it will make clear how tracking may inhibit the learning of many of our country's teenagers—especially those who are poor and nonwhite.

A study such as this one depends on the good will and support of a great many people. All deserve my thanks. First, of course, are the more than 27,000 individuals who provided data for A Study of Schooling. Without their cooperation there would have been no study. Primary, too, are the many foundations that contributed their financial resources to the project. These included the Carnegie Corporation of New York, which supported the tracking study directly, and the many others that supported A Study of Schooling: the Danforth Foundation, the Ford Foundation, International Paper Foundation, the JRD 3rd Fund, Martha Holden Jennings Foundation, Charles F. Kettering Foundation, Lilly Endowment, Inc., Charles Stewart Mott Foundation, the Needmor Fund, Pedamorphosis, Inc., the Rockefeller Foundation, the Spencer Foundation, and the U.S. Office of Education. The staff of the Institute for Development of Educational Activities, who provided a great deal of assistance in the coordination of the larger study, were very interested in the completion of this volume. They also deserve my thanks. A third important source of support and direction for the study came from the six eminent men who constituted the advisory board of A Study of Schooling—Ralph Tyler, Gregory Anrig, the late Stephen K. Bailey, Lawrence A. Cremin, Robert K. Merton, and Arthur Jefferson. Their counsel is greatly appreciated.

Several colleagues on the staff of A Study of Schooling provided me with both personal and intellectual support during the preparation of this book. They include Paula DeFusco, who helped organize the data; Bette Overman, who meticulously considered numerous memos, proposals, and data analyses that preceded any writing; and David Wright, who carefully read early drafts and provided thoughtful guidance. Two others on the Study of Schooling staff, now good friends and colleagues at the Laboratory in School and Community Education at UCLA, were unflagging in their enthusiasm and support from the first idea for the study to the final revision of the manuscript. Paul Heckman listened carefully, asked challenging questions, and always managed to protect the time and place for me to work. Ken Sirotnik not only provided me with technical help in the design and analysis phases of the study but shared with me his profound understanding of the complex substantive issues that underly methodological decisions as well. And, of course, John I. Goodlad, principal investigator of A Study of Schooling, director of the Laboratory in School and Community Education, and former dean of the Graduate School of Education at UCLA, created an atmosphere of trust and intellectual freedom in which all of us could pursue ideas and explore new directions.

Finally, I would like to thank my family who made home a friendly place to work. My daughters, Lisa and Tracy Oakes, were kind enough to consider what their mother was working on important. My husband, Martin Lipton, was a wise and gentle counselor. His insightful suggestions for both the substance and the style of this book are reflected throughout. Of course, as significant as these people's contributions were, the responsibility for the views that follow remains with me.

1

Tracking

Looking back, or looking casually from the outside in, the events of junior and senior high school appear like a complex but well-choreographed series of much-practiced and often-repeated steps. Each student performs a set routine, nearly if not completely identical to that of his schoolmates. Even the stumblings, bumpings, and confusions seem so predictable and occur with such regularity that chance alone cannot explain them. Day in and day out, the rhythm continues, the tight schedule of slow hours in class interrupted by the hurried frenzy of 5 or 7 or 9½ minutes between—a few noisy moments of juggling textbooks and notebooks stuffed with worksheets and answers to a string of questions at the end of some chapter, minutes of half-finished conversations, partly made plans—and then the rush to be somewhere else on time. In class there is the near-silent, almost attentive listening and the seemingly endless talk of teacher: "Get out your books. Yes, I said get out your books. Now open to page 73 . . . 73 . . . 73. Yes, that *was* page 73. Yes. Now, if you will take out some paper . . . yes, you'll need a pencil. No, this won't be handed in, but I'll check it at the end of the period. Page 73. Could you put away your comb, please? Now, on page 73. . . ." Heads bent over books and answer sheets, students wait for the bell or for an interruption—a forgotten announcement, a call slip from the office, a fire drill, or some other break in the constant, repetitive motion. And of course there is daydreaming, meditation to the sweep of the sprinklers outside, sidelong glances at the hint of whiskers growing imperceptibly longer on a nearby adolescent chin, and the wondering if teachers go to bars after school or quietly slip into a closet after the last period and wait until morning.

There is learning, too. It seems as though everyone plows through geometric proofs, *Julius Caesar*, the causes of the Civil War, and the elements of the scientific method, but not with too much attention until just before exams. Some of us may even remember a handful of moments—not many, to be sure—when we forgot our adolescent selves enough to be absorbed in learning until the next bell sent us running to our lockers to get our smelly gym clothes before we missed the bus. And somehow things get learned and kids get smarter, test scores get better, essays get longer, problems get solved, constitutional amendments and the three branches of the federal government get memorized, leaves get labeled, frogs cut up, and on and on.

So it goes, year after year. School counselors, only semivisible most of the time, emerge periodically to sort through the maze of classes and students until somehow everyone has a class arranged for every hour for the following year. And so the dance continues with only slight variations on the dominant theme of sameness.

Isn't and wasn't it the same for everyone? Yes . . . and no.

This book is about schools and what students experience in them. More precisely, it is about twenty-five junior and senior high schools and about some of the experiences of 13,719 teenagers who attended those schools. A sameness permeated those experiences. Yet underneath this cloak of sameness the day-to-day lives of these students were quite different in some very important ways.

This book is about some of these differences in the experiences of the students and what the differences have to tell us about how secondary schooling operates in American society. The schools themselves were different: some were large, some very small; some in the middle of cities, some in nearly uninhabited farm country; some in the far West, the South, the urban North, and the Midwest. But the differences in what students experienced each day in these schools stemmed not so much from where they happened to live and which of the schools they happened to attend but, rather, from differences *within* each of the schools.

This book is about a schooling phenomenon called tracking and how it both causes and supports differences in the lives of secondary students. Tracking is the process whereby students are divided into categories so that they can be assigned in groups to various kinds of classes. Sometimes students are classified as fast, average, or slow learners and placed into fast, average, or slow classes on the basis of their scores on achievement or ability tests. Often teachers' estimates of what students have already learned or their potential for learning more determine how students are identified and placed. Sometimes students are classified according to what seems most appropriate to their future lives. Sometimes, but rarely in any genuine sense, students themselves choose to be in "vocational," "general," or "academic" programs. In some schools students are classified and placed separately for each academic subject they take—fast in math, average in science; in other schools a single decision determines a student's program of classes for the entire day, semester, year, and perhaps even six years of secondary schooling. However it's done, tracking, in essence, is sorting—a sorting of students that has certain predictable characteristics.

First, students are identified in a rather public way as to their intellectual capabilities and accomplishments and separated into a hierarchical system of groups for instruction. Second, these groups are labeled quite openly and characterized in the minds of teachers and others as being of a certain type—high ability, low achieving, slow, average, and so on. Clearly these groups are not equally valued in the school; occasional defensive responses and appearances of special privilege—i.e., small classes, programmed learning, and the like for slower students—rarely mask the essential fact that they are less preferred. Third, individual students in these groups come to be defined by others—both adults and their peers—in terms of these group types. In other words, a student in a high-achieving group is seen as a high-achieving *person*, bright, smart, quick, and in the eyes of many, *good*. And those in the low-achieving groups come to be called slow, below average, and—often when people are being less careful—dummies, sweathogs, or yahoos. Fourth, on the basis of these sorting decisions, the groupings of students that result, and the way educators see the students in these groups, teenagers are treated by and experience schools very differently.

Many schools claim that they do not track students, but it is the rare school that has no mechanism for sorting students into groups that appear to be alike in ways that make teaching them seem easier. In fact, this is exactly the justification some schools offer for tracking students. Educators strongly believe that students learn better in groups with others like themselves. They also believe that groups of similar students are easier to teach. This book is about these ideas and how they were played out in the lives of students at twenty-five schools.

This book is also about a very American notion called equality and how this ideal seems to be unwittingly subverted by tracking in schools. Most considerations of barriers to educational equality have focused on characteristics of students themselves as the source of the problem. Seen as products of disorganized and deteriorating homes and family structures, poor and minority children have been thought of as unmotivated, noncompetitive, and culturally disadvantaged. But there is another view. For in the tracking process, it seems the odds are not quite equal. It turns out that those children who seem to have the least of everything in the rest of their lives most often get less at school as well. Explored here are the ways in which the different experiences of these students reinforce the differences they experience outside the school. Those at the bottom of the social and economic ladder climb up through twelve years of "the great equalizer," Horace Mann's famous description of public schools, and end up still on the bottom rung.

This book is also about some fundamental changes needed in schooling. For there are some people—students, parents, teachers, administrators, school board members, and even legislators—who are aware of the seeming intractability of schools. They also see the relative futility of altering only one institution in a whole constellation of social forces that conspire to keep things the way they are. Even so, they say "we must do better." For these people, this book is written.

Intents and Effects

I was talking recently with a group of teachers, school administrators, and school board members about the practice of tracking in schools. During the course of the evening we were considering some of the reasons—historical, political, and educational—that seem to support the practice. At one point, a school board member stood up and said rather defensively, but also with considerable pride, that the *only* reason they tracked students in his school district was that they believed it was in the best interests of the students to do so. "No responsible person working with children in schools could have any other reason," he concluded. I believed him. And I agree that those who work with teenagers in secondary schools in this country, with very few exceptions, intend the very best for them. I believe that they want their students to achieve academically and to develop personally and socially in positive and healthy ways. I believe that they mean their students to become responsible and productive members of society. And I believe that what they do and what they have students do in school are intended to contribute toward these ends. But I also believe the old saying about where at least one road paved with good intentions can lead.

Tracking seems to be one of those well-intended pathways that, as we shall see throughout this book, has some pretty hellish consequences for many young people in schools. How can this happen? How can well-intentioned people, trained educators, participate in a process that turns out to affect many students in ways contrary to their intentions? How can they be part of a process that turns out not to be, despite the protestations of my friend the school board member, in the best interests of the students they work with?

I think one reason is that a lot of what we do in schools is done more or less out of habit stemming from traditions in the school's culture. These traditions dictate, for the most part, the ways in which schooling is organized and conducted. Many school practices seem to be the *natural* way to conduct schooling, an integral part of the way schools are. As a result we don't tend to think critically about much of what goes on. I don't mean to imply that these ways of schooling are not taken seriously. To the contrary, I think they are taken so seriously that we can hardly conceive of any alternatives to them. We have deep-seated beliefs and long-held assumptions about the appropriateness of what we do in schools. These beliefs are so ingrained in our thinking and behavior—so much a part of the school culture—that we rarely submit them to careful scrutiny. We seldom think very much about where practices came from originally and to what problems in schools they were first seen as solutions. We rarely question the view of the world on which practices are based—what humans are like, what society is like, or even what schools are for. We almost never reflect critically about the beliefs we hold about them or about the manifest and latent consequences that result from them. And I think that this uncritical, unreflective attitude gets us into trouble. It permits us to act in ways contrary to our intentions. In short, it can lead us and, more important, our students down a disastrous road despite our best purposes.

Tracking is one of these taken-for-granted school practices. It is so much a part of how instruction is organized in secondary schools—and has been for as long as most of us can remember—that we seldom question it. We *assume* that it is best for students. But we don't very often look behind this assumption to the evidence and beliefs on which it rests.

I don't mean to imply by this that no one is concerned about grouping students. I think, in fact, that the contrary is true. School people usually spend a great deal of thought deciding what group students should be placed in. They want to make sure that placements are appropriate and fair. And futher, what appear to be incorrect placements are often brought to the attention of teachers and counselors, usually with a great deal of concern. Adjustments sometimes need to be made. This is something we seem to want to be very responsible about. But this very concern over correct and fair placements underscores my point. In some way, we all know that what group or track a student is in makes a very real difference in his education. So at some level, we know that grouping is a very serious business. What we don't seem to question very much, however, is whether the practice of grouping students itself helps us achieve what we intend in schools. Most of us simply believe, as that school board member asserted, that it does.

Several assumptions seem to lend support to this belief. The first is the notion that students learn better when they are grouped with other students who are considered to be like them academically—with those who know about the same things, who learn at the same rate, or who are expected to have similar futures. This assumption is usually expressed in two ways: first, that bright students' learning is likely to be held back if they are placed in mixed groups and, second, that the deficiencies of slow students are more easily remediated if they are placed in classes together. Another assumption is that slower students develop more positive attitudes about themselves and school when they are not placed in groups with others who are far more capable. It is widely believed that daily classroom exposure to bright students has negative consequences for slower ones. A third assumption is that the placement processes used to separate students into groups both accurately and fairly reflect past achievements and native abilities. Part of this assumption too is that these placement decisions are appropriate for future learning, either in a single class or for whole courses of study (e.g., academic or vocational). A fourth assumption is that it is easier for teachers to accommodate individual differences in homogeneous groups or that, in general, groups of similar students are easier to teach and manage.

There may be other assumptions at work here, but these are the premises in support of tracking practices I hear most often.

Well, what about these assumptions?

Because we base so much of what we do on them, it seems essential that they be carefully studied. Some can be examined by looking at empirical evidence from research studies. Others require thoughtful, reflective analyses with a historical perspective sensitive to the social and political context of school practice. All require critical examination in order to discover how our implicit thinking may be leading us to practices that are contrary to the ways in which we would *choose* to work with students. This is what we are about to do here.

Despite the fact that the first assumption—that students learn more or better in homogeneous groups—is almost universally held, it is simply not true. Or, at least, we have virtually mountains of research evidence indicating that homogeneous grouping doesn't consistently help *anyone* learn better. Over the past sixty years hundreds of studies have been conducted on the effects of ability grouping and tracking on student learning. These studies have looked at various kinds of groupings, measured different kinds of learning, and considered students at different ages and grades. The studies vary in their size and in their methodology. Some are quite sophisticated, some rather crude. The results differ in certain specifics, but one conclusion emerges clearly: *no group of students has been found to benefit consistently from being in a homogeneous group.* A few of the studies show that those students identified as the brightest learn more when they are taught in a group of their peers, and provided an enriched cirriculum. However, most do not. Some studies have found that the learning of students identified as being average or low, has not been harmed by their placement in homogeneous groups. However, many studies have found the learning of average and slow students to be negatively affected by homogeneous placements.[1]

The net result of all these studies of the relationship of tracking and academic outcomes for students is a conclusion contrary to the widely held assumptions about it. We can be fairly confident that bright students are *not* held back when they are in mixed classrooms. And we can be quite certain that the deficiencies of slower students are *not* more easily remediated when they are grouped together. And, given the evidence, we are unable to support the general belief that students learn best when they are grouped together with others like themselves.

The second assumption—that students, especially the slower ones, feel more positively about themselves and school when they are in homogeneous groups—includes a number of other premises as well. We often hear that classroom competition with bright students is discouraging to slower ones and may lead to lowered self-esteem, disruptive behavior, and alienation from school. Many who support tracking do so because they are convinced it will prevent these problems.

During the past twenty years, several researchers have investigated these claims. Once again, the evidence we have about the relationship between tracking and student attitudes and behaviors shows something quite different from what so many assume to be the case. A considerable amount of work, for example, has shown that students placed in average and low-track classes do *not* develop positive attitudes. Rather than help students to feel more comfortable about themselves, the tracking process seems to foster *lowered* self-esteem among these teenagers. Further exacerbating these negative self-perceptions are the attitudes of many teachers and other students toward those in the lower tracks. Once placed in low classes, students are usually seen by others in the school as dumb. Students in upper tracks, on the other hand, sometimes develop inflated self-concepts as a result of their track placements.[2] Closely related to students' self-evaluations are their aspirations for the future and the educational plans they make. Students in low-track classes have been found to have lower aspirations and more often to have their plans for the future frustrated.[3] It is important to keep in mind at this point that much of the work in this area has controlled for other student characteristics—social class, ability, and pretrack enrollment attitudes—that otherwise might be seen as major contributors to these effects. In other words, low-track students do not seem to have lower self-concepts and aspirations or to inspire negative judgments in their peers and teachers simply because they are poorer or less bright than students in other tracks or because they themselves had more negative attitudes to begin with. While these things might be true, a good portion of the negative attitudes displayed by low-track students is attributable to the track placement itself.

Moreover, student behaviors have been found to be influenced by track placement. Low-track students have been found to participate less in extracurricular activities at school, to exhibit more school and classroom misconduct, and to be involved more often in delinquent behavior outside of school. Lower-track students are more alienated from school and have higher drop-out rates.[4] Again, these results have been obtained in studies that controlled for other student attributes that might confound the results. So we can conclude that, rather than alleviate attitude and behavior problems, as educators intend, tracking seems at least in part to contribute to them. Like the first assumption about students learning better, the second assumption about students feeling more positive about themselves and school seems to collapse under the research evidence.

The premises that student track placements are appropriate, accurate, and fair involve some fundamental considerations. To explore these fully, it is important to look both at the research evidence about them and at the logic on which they are based. First, however, it is necessary to look at the criteria by which students are placed. Almost universally, three kinds of information are taken into consideration, although in varying degrees at different schools. These three are scores on standardized tests, teacher and counselor recommendations (including grades), and students' and their parents' choices.

It is important to realize that at least the first two pieces of information are believed to be a reflection of individual merit rather than of some inherited privilege. We want to believe that students who are placed in top groups are those who *deserve* to be there. In fact, the word *deserve* is often used when a student is seen to be misplaced or does not achieve up to what is expected in high tracks; he or she doesn't deserve to be there. So the criteria we use to classify and sort students are believed to assess their merit—their ability and especially past achievements—certainly not their race or ethnicity or socioeconomic position. And we also believe that these criteria are appropriate for students' future experience. As in the past when we have questioned the criteria for hiring or for voting to be sure they were not related to race, class, or gender but were directly relevant to the actual skills and knowledge required, we want to be sure that the criteria we use in tracking are not arbitrary and that they really relate to what students will be expected to do.

In 1970, when Findley and Bryan did a large survey of tracking practices in U.S. school districts, they found that 83 percent of the districts surveyed used achievement and/or IQ tests as a basis for sorting students.[5] Later studies have also found that aptitude and achievement test scores are a major determinant of track assignments.[6] Given this heavy dependence on test scores, it is important to examine carefully the content, administration, and consequences of testing in relationship to the issues of fairness and merit.

Standardized tests are very useful devices for sorting students into ability or achievement groups. They are constructed to do just that. The tests are comprised of items that separate people in terms of their responses. Those items that everyone answers the same way—either right or wrong—are eliminated from the tests during their construction. In other words, the things that everyone is likely to know, or not know, do not appear on tests. Only those things that some people know and others do not are there. This makes the results of the tests quite predictable. Test results, then, make a group of individuals appear to be different on whatever dimension the test is measuring—an aptitude, general intelligence, or achievement in a particular subject area. Sorting people according to their differences in these respects becomes very easy.

What needs to be remembered here is that differences that appear to be substantial according to test results may, in fact, be relatively minor given the universe of knowledge or skill a test purports to measure. Take a standardized test of seventh- and eighth-grade reading achievement, for example. In designing such a test, as many as 60 percent of the items initially considered to be good indicators of reading achievement may have to be eliminated if it turns out—as it often does—that nearly all the seventh- and eighth-graders in the pilot group can answer them. Only those items are kept that a substantial number of these students miss. We have no guarantee that those items that are kept are the best determinants of reading achievement per se. We know only that they best separate students along a continuum of low to high scores. We cannot even be sure that the content of the test matches the curricular objectives of the instruction students may encounter. Moreover, we do know that this process tends to make tests that are labeled achievement tests actually tests of general ability.

The differences in actual (not measured) reading achievement, then, may be relatively quite small. And yet we are willing to judge a student's level of achievement and, consequently, determine the kind of education he or she is provided on the basis of these test scores. Part of this willingness can be understood when we consider the self-fulfilling prophecy of the normal curve. No matter what, half of the population is below the mean, below average. We really need to rethink whether this way of looking at human learning potential squares with recent and mounting evidence that, under appropriate instructional conditions, more than 90 percent of students can master course material.[7] Nevertheless, we continue to interpret large test-score differences to mean large absolute differences which demand large educational differences. And usually this happens without our being very much aware of the process that has taken place. We need, I think, to question seriously whether these relative differences are appropriate criteria for separating students for instruction.[8]

A second issue is the fairness of tests. Are scores in fact based solely on meritocratic factors—achievement and aptitude—or are they based in part on students' race, social class, or economic position? One way to answer this question is to look at the issues of test content and test administration. Many researchers who have done so have concluded that both the substance of most standardized tests and the procedures used to standardize and administer them are culturally biased. That is, white middle-class children are most likely to do well on them because of the compatibility of their language and experiences with the language and content of test questions, with the group against which the tests were normed, with testing procedures, and with most of the adults doing the testing. Lower-class and minority youngsters are less likely to do well because of their language and experience differences. Attempts to develop "culture-fair" tests and testing procedures have not been very successful.[9]

The consequences of testing, however, constitute the most damning evidence against the fairness of tests. Poor and minority students consistently score lower than do whites. This result assumes special significance when considering tests that attempt to measure innate abilities or what we sometimes call native intelligence. We could judge such tests as fair only if poor and minority youngsters were less capable than middle- and upper-middle-class whites. And despite some claims of a small group of researchers about a relationship between race and IQ, we simply do not have evidence that such a relationship exists.[10] What we *can* be quite sure of, in fact, is that the ability to learn is normally distributed among and within social groups. This is exactly the position the courts have taken in regard to the placement of black students in spe-cial-education classes in California schools. Placement strategies that result in the disproportionate assignment of minority children to special-education programs are considered a denial of the equal protection and due process guaranteed under the Constitution.[11]

One other point should be emphasized here. This view of testing deficiencies is not a rare view held only by a few quibblers at universi-ties. Many of those people who are most centrally involved in the area of educational measurement have the same concerns. A recent issue of *Educational Measurement: Issues and Practice* was devoted to a discus-sion of problems with ability testing, especially in regard to their use in sorting students.[12] Nor are these worries merely esoteric. Principals, counselors, and teachers are, more often than not, aware of some of the deficiencies of testing. But the habit of tracking is so ingrained they shrug off the problems for lack of a better way to preserve the practice.

But tests are not the only means by which students are sorted into track levels. Most districts report that counselor and teacher recommen-dations are used either as supplements to or in place of test scores. Are these recommendations accurate, appropriate, and fair? Are they likely to counter the biases in tests? Unfortunately, we have little hard evi-dence about how these recommendations are made or about what fac-tors actually influence these subjective judgments. We expect, however, that school people will accurately judge educational capabilities—both aptitude and achievement—when making placement decisions. In fact, we expect them to do more than this. We expect them to be able to determine what life course is most appropriate for different students, and we expect them to make these difficult judgments for a great num-ber of students each year. Counselors may have 300 to 500 students to place—many of whom they barely know. Teachers often have more than 150 students to recommend. What's more, we assume that these deci-sions can be accurately made under these circumstances about children as young as eleven years in many school districts and not older than thirteen in most.

What information we do have about the process of teacher and counselor guidance leads us to believe that these judgments are cer-tainly no more accurate or fair than test scores. In 1963 a study of coun-seling practices revealed that students were often placed into groups on the basis of counselors' assessment of their language, dress, and behavior as well as their academic potential.[13] We do not know how wide-spread this practice is. But even if it is widespread, the degree to which counselors and teachers are aware of these influences has not been investigated. My hunch is that, given the circumstances of placement decisions, factors often influenced by race and class—dress, speech patterns, ways of interacting with adults, and other behaviors—often do affect subjective judgments of academic aptitude and probably academic futures, and that educators allow this to happen quite unconsciously. We know that these kinds of recommendations often result in more disproportionate placements of students from various racial groups and social classes than do placements by test scores alone. Poor and minority kids end up more often in the bottom groups; middle- and upper-class whites more often are at the top.[14] Again, we are left with serious questions about the appropriateness or fairness of one of the major criteria for student placement.

The third criterion often used is student or parent choice. Often students at the senior high school level are asked to indicate whether they prefer a curriculum leading to college entrance, one leading toward a vocation immediately following high school, or a more general course (not leading to college). Although these choices are made by students themselves, Rosenbaum has pointed out that they are not made free of influence.[15] They are *informed* choices—informed by the school guidance process and by the other indicators of what the appropriate placement is likely to be. Students and parents are informed by test scores and by the recommendations of counselors and teachers. Given what we know about these two sources of information, how can their choices possibly be seen as free or uncontaminated?

This discussion leads to the following conclusion: Thinking carefully about the processes involved in placing students in track levels and examining what evidence we have about the results must make us seriously question the traditional assumptions; we cannot safely say that track placements can be counted on to be accurate, appropriate, or even fair.

The fourth assumption—that teaching is easier (with respect to both meeting individual needs and managing classroom instruction in general) when students are in homogeneous groups—may be a little more difficult to set aside. Most teachers undoubtedly have some solid experience that tells them that this is true. And as long as we confine our considerations to the way instruction is usually conducted, I would have to agree. But I hope that by the end of this book you will be convinced of two things: First, there may be some ways of conducting instruction that make working with heterogeneous groups manageable. I cannot suggest anything quite as easy as working only with the top kids, but I think there are some instructional strategies that make heterogeneity in a classroom a positive instructional resource. Further, I hope to convince you that even if tracking students so that teachers can work with homogeneous groups *is* easier, it is not worth the educational and social price we pay for it.

The Gulf Between

We have seen some fairly convincing evidence that tracking students does not accomplish what school people intend. We have also critically examined the assumptions on which tracking is based that support these good intentions. Careful analysis calls these assumptions into serious question. At the very least, we would be foolish to continue to hold these assumptions and base our practices on them as if they were common sense. Reflection on these matters is in order and in fact long overdue.

What we have seen, in essence, is that there exists a substantial gulf between intentions and effects in the matter of tracking students in schools. Some of what comprises that gulf is explored in the remainder of this book. We will look carefully at the actual experiences students have in classes at different track levels in a group of American junior and senior high schools. We will survey what content and skills they are taught, what instructional procedures their teachers use, and what their classroom relationships are like. We will consider how they feel about themselves, their classes, the subjects they are studying, their schools, and their own educational futures. We will also consider the implications of this for questions of educational quality and equality for all American secondary school students. And we will look at some different ways of schooling, which include approaches to incorporating and accommodating individual differences in classrooms. We will consider some ways that might help us do better. But first we will consider how all this got started in American schooling—the historical events that gave rise to tracking and the explanations theorists give of these events.

2

Unlocking the Tradition

Well, you may ask, if tracking is as bad as the evidence seems to indicate, why *do* we continue to do it? One reason takes us back to the discussion in chapter 1 about the power of tradition in the decisions schools make about how to organize and conduct the business of teaching and learning. Tracking, as we noted, like many practices in schools, emerged as a solution to a specific set of educational and social problems at a particular time in history. And, like many such "solutions," it has become part of what is considered to be the ordinary way to conduct schooling. As a result, the practice has continued long after the original problems arose and long after the social context from which the solution emerged has changed considerably. In short, the practice of tracking has become *traditional*.

We need to lift tracking above this taken-for-granted level in order to reflect critically about whether it is appropriate, given today's educational problems, today's social context, and today's students—in short, we need to unlock the tradition. By placing tracking in its historical and social context, we can better understand what it is. This information, too, is essential for a careful consideration of whether it is something we want to continue.

We have to go back about one hundred years to trace the development of ability grouping and tracking in American schools. Before 1860, free public elementary schools were established in only a small portion of the country, principally in the more prosperous areas of New England

and the Middle Atlantic states. The South generally did not have free public education until the post–Civil War period. In the West public education came later too, shortly after the formal organization of the states and territories. The aim of these early "common schools" was to provide universal education that would increase opportunity, teach morality and citizenship, encourage leadership, maintain social mobility, and promote responsiveness to social progress—in short, to develop an intelligent mass citizenry.[1] The curriculum of these elementary schools was common for all students and consisted primarily of reading, writing, spelling, arithmetic, geography, and Bible reading. Pedagogy consisted largely of rote learning, recitation, and strong discipline.

School attendance before the turn of the century tended to be sporadic. Even though Massachusetts had instituted the first compulsory-education law in 1852 and twenty-five other states had such a requirement before 1890, these laws were not strictly enforced until about 1900. During the more discretionary period, public schools were populated almost entirely by white Anglo-Saxon Protestant middle-class children. Students in these schools were not grouped for instruction until late in the nineteenth century and then only by ages and grades.

Few nineteenth-century teenagers enrolled in secondary schools. Throughout most of the century, the predominant institution for secondary education was the Latin grammar school—a private school functioning primarily to prepare students for higher education. The standard course offerings included the study of Latin and Greek. But very few American youngsters attended—only the most elite and affluent Anglo-Protestants. Grouping similar students together was not a standard practice within these schools, for in many ways the students were similar to begin with.

Other young people—largely those from white middle-class families—attended secondary academies, private schools that received some public financial support. Unlike the Latin grammar schools, the academies were designed to serve social as well as academic functions and to enroll a larger, more heterogeneous, and less exclusive group of students. The curriculum of the academies was intended to include both classical and modern subjects—offering preparation for life and good citizenship as well as for higher education. By the end of the nineteenth century, however, the academies had become quite diverse. Some were exclusively college-preparatory institutions; others were only for students who would not go on to higher education. But as diverse as these schools were, the students who attended them were very much alike. Because most of the academies were located in rural areas and small towns, few of the poor or immigrant youth who were swelling the cities at the end of the century attended them. Little if any classification and grouping of students took place in these schools.

During the latter part of the nineteenth century, a third form of secondary education, the public high school, developed in response to a growing demand for secondary education, to be not only publicly financed but also publicly controlled. The earliest free public high schools were established in New England in the 1860s. By the 1880s, their populations had outstripped those of private secondary schools, and they were heralded as "the people's college." Even so, secondary education was not seen as appropriate for most young people. They were needed to help out at home or to engage in adult work. As a result, at these schools, too, the vast majority of enrolled students were middle- and upper-middle-class whites. Historian David Tyack has observed that "schoolmen . . . were sensitive to the frequent accusation that they were taxing poor people to pay for elegant schooling of the rich or the complaints of self-made men that they were turning out dandies who would scorn labor. . . . it is clear that most schoolmen before 1900 regarded the high school as a minority institution designed for the bright child whose parents were willing and able to forego his or her labor."[2] So even with the spread of the public high school, by 1890 fewer than 10 percent of the nation's fourteen- to seventeen-year-olds were attending public or private secondary schools. Further, it was a very homogeneous group of students who were enrolled. Individual differences were not an educational concern, and grouping was not an educational practice.[3]

Around 1890, however, tremendous changes began to take place. Both educational and social forces weighed heavily on the schools and led to dramatic alterations in the quantity and the quality of secondary education in this country. As we shall see, the institution of tracking and ability grouping was an integral part of these changes.

In 1892, Charles Eliot, president of Harvard University, was appointed to chair the Committee of Ten on Secondary Studies of the National Education Association. The committee was charged to make recommendations for standardizing both secondary schools' college-preparatory curricula and colleges' admission requirements. Because secondary schools had pretty much "grown like Topsy," the transition between secondary schools and colleges was unsystematic. Not only were secondary schools extremely diverse, but college entrance requirements were inconsistent and often arbitrary. With the increased population of secondary school graduates came the first push for schools to help *sort and select* students for higher education as well as to *prepare* them for it.

Eliot's committee attempted to meet the demand for a standardized precollegiate curriculum with a set of proposed changes for the whole of secondary education, not merely with the development of one part to be designated "college preparation." The Committee of Ten's recommendations reflected Eliot's belief in the remarkable human potential for learning. "It is a curious fact," he argued, "that we Americans habitually underestimate the capacity of pupils at almost every stage of education from the primary school through the university. . . . It seems to me probable that the proportion of grammar school children incapable of pursuing geometry, algebra, and a foreign language would turn out to be much smaller than we now imagine."[4] Eliot's optimism helped direct the committee to recommend the restructuring of the secondary school curriculum so that, while different programs of study would be available, those programs would not be designed for any particular group of students. It was Eliot's conviction that individual differences in intellect were not of such importance to require the designing of special programs to accommodate them. Differences among the subject fields were important to Eliot only because he sought to emphasize those in which sustained study, so he believed, could help develop the students' facility for intellectual thought.

As a result, under Eliot's influence, the Committee of Ten recommended a reconstruction of the secondary school curriculum based neither on the notion of curriculum differentiation to suit individual differences nor on the concept of a set of particular subjects as best suited for college preparation. To the contrary, the committee's report suggested four courses of study to be offered at the secondary level, *each one to be acceptable for college admission*—classical, Latin-scientific, modern languages, and English. This recommendation represents a substantial expansion of the preparation for college usually provided at the time. The committee went on record as unequivocally opposing the separation of college-bound and non-college-bound students into different programs.

Further, it was clearly opposed to viewing college preparation as the major function of secondary education. The proposed curriculum consisted of the learnings the committee saw as valuable in the process of becoming an educated person, regardless of future plans. The development and implementation of such a curriculum were seen as the primary mission of secondary schools.[5]

It is obvious as we look at schools today that Eliot's ideas and his committee's recommendations did not direct the course of school reform at the turn of the century. Other influences, social and economic as well as intellectual, steered secondary schooling in a quite different direction—one that led away from optimism about all students' intellectual capacities and the school's role in their development and toward the increased importance of schooling as preparation for the world of work and for the differences in the future lives of students. Eliot and his committee, it seems, were out of touch with the other demands that were simultaneously being placed on schools.

The country was experiencing a population explosion. Immigrants flowed into the nation through Ellis Island at the rate of nearly a million a year. Lured by promises of prosperity, they came from southern and eastern Europe—15 million of them by 1924. They were mostly poor, uneducated, and unskilled. Eager to work, the immigrants settled in newly industrialized American cities looking for a better life for themselves and their families. What they found were crowded ghetto slums filled with destitute families, ill-fed and poorly clothed. There were few jobs and most of those involved intolerable conditions. They found abundance only in squalor, sickness, and crime. But the immigrants were not alone. The promise of industrial affluence had captured the hopes of rural America as well. Young people had left the farm in droves to seek their fortunes in urban America. By 1910 the cities teemed with the hopeful but unemployed poor.

Not surprisingly, a schooling explosion paralleled this tremendous population increase. Between 1880 and 1918 student enrollment across the nation increased by over 700 percent, from about 200,000 to over 1.5 million. By 1920, more than 60 percent of America's fourteen- to seventeen-year-olds were enrolled.[6] An average of more than one new high school was built for each day of each year between 1890 and 1918. Not only did the students increase dramatically in number but the kinds of students changed profoundly as well. Especially in urban schools, the overwhelming predominance of white Anglo-Saxon middle-class young-sters disappeared. Just as the influx of poor rural families and even more destitute European immigrants had changed the character of urban populations, so too the enforcement of compulsory education and the institution of child-labor laws markedly altered the population of urban schools. By 1909, 58 percent of the students in thirty-seven of the na-tion's largest cities were of foreign-born parentage.[7] As historian Law-rence Cremin wrote:

Schools that really wanted to educate these youngsters could not get by with surface changes. The mere fact that children in a single school-room spoke a half-dozen different languages, none of them English, in-evitably altered the life of that schoolroom. And the problem went far beyond language, for each language implied a unique heritage and unique attitudes toward teacher, parents, schoolmates—indeed, toward the school itself. Not only baths, but a vast variety of other activities that could not be found in any syllabus began to appear. Manners, cleanliness, dress, the simple business of getting along together in the schoolroom—these things had to be taught more insistently and self-consciously than ever.[8]

In short, the problems of schools were horrendous.

So, at the turn of the century, secondary schooling faced a major crisis. The existing schools were diverse in both their method of gover-nance and their curricula. There seemed to be no general agreement about whom or what secondary education was for. And yet, at the same time, the numbers of students and schools were increasing with explo-sive rapidity. There was increased social pressure for schools to do more. Colleges and universities wanted a more standardized precollegiate ed-ucation. Many of the middle class called for free public education avail-able to all youth. Poor and immigrant families were eager for the eco-nomic benefits they believed schooling would provide their children. Businessmen were interested in acquiring a more productive and liter-ate work force. Organized labor was concerned about who should con-trol the training of workers. Progressive reformers sought humane so-lutions to the immense social problems confronting the burgeoning population of poor and immigrant youth. But most of the population in-creasingly feared the potential dangers that could result from what was seen as unrestrained hordes of urban immigrants, and a perception of a need for the exercise of greater social control was widespread. The pub-lic high school, already struggling, was seen as a means to all these ends.

Confronted with the day-to-day business of conducting schooling, school people were forced to find solutions to their own growing problems and responses to the increasing demands placed on them from the outside. The solution ultimately settled upon was the comprehensive high school—a new secondary school that promised something for everyone, but, and this was important, that did not promise the *same* thing for everyone. Gone was the nineteenth-century notion of the need for common learnings to build a cohesive nation. In its place was curriculum differentiation—tracking and ability grouping—with markedly different learnings for what were seen as markedly different groups of students.

The ideas undergirding this new concept of schooling did not materialize from thin air. The air was thick with theories of human evolution, of the superiority of Anglo-Saxon cultures, and of the unlimited potential of science and industry. These ideas clearly shaped the direction of school reform in the changing social milieu of turn-of-the-century America.

The application of the theories of Charles Darwin to human society—so-called social Darwinism—provided a scientific basis for seeing some groups of people as being of lesser social and moral development than others. Social and economic power was seen as being held by "great men"—those most "fit" to do so. Their survival in a competitive social environment was proof enough of their evolutionary superiority. It followed that ethnic minorities and the poor were seen as being responsible for their terrible living conditions, as inherently "less fit" and at a lower evolutionary stage than Anglo-Protestants. Their lives of squalor and seeming depravity could be traced to developmental deficiencies that were biologically determined, not to the social conditions in which they were immersed. They simply lacked the internal resources necessary to make better lives for themselves. This social Darwinist view can be easily detected in the following statement about immigrant children made by a member of the Boston school committee in 1889: "Many of these children come from homes of vice and crime. In their blood are generations of iniquity. . . . They hate restraint or obedience to law. They know nothing of the feelings which are inherited by those who were born on our shores."[9]

Historian Eric Goldman has noted that although poverty and corruption were recognized as social evils, social Darwinists believed that they could be cured only through the long evolutionary process of the survival of the fittest. These social evils were considered symptoms of the moral weakness of people at a lower stage of development. Moreover, the most conservative Darwinists maintained that even vigorous social reform would be ineffective in altering this natural process or in ameliorating the material, let alone the moral and mental, inequities among groups of people.[10] In *Social Statistics,* Herbert Spencer had proposed that "history is the progressive adaptation of constitution to conditions, or, put another way, the adjustment of human character to the circumstances of living. In the course of history human perfection is ultimately attainable, but men are infinitely more the creatures of history than its creators."[11] Given this perspective, Spencer and the conservative Darwinists held little hope, if indeed any at all, for the power of education to change social conditions. Improvement would have to await the slow and tedious evolutionary process.

But Darwinists of a more progressive persuasion held a different view. While heredity might be the dominant force in determining the fitness of individuals and groups, these things were not fixed but constantly changing. The environment could powerfully influence the direction of human evolution. Therefore the force of positive environments and increased opportunity seemed to hold out hope for the adaptation of immigrant groups to American life. As early as 1877, Richard Durgale had written about the infamous family of criminals, the Jukes: "The tendency of heredity is to produce an environment which perpetuates that heredity: thus the licentious parent makes an example which greatly aids in fixing habits of debauchery in the child. The correction is change of environment."[12] These more progressive Darwinists were perhaps best represented by Lester Frank Ward, who took a view contrary to that of Spencer concerning the potential of education for social improvement. Ward proposed that if evolution could be directed through the intentional acts of men—through alteration of the environment—then the evolutionary process could work toward constructive social purposes. In this view, then, education could play a vital role in directing the progress of mankind. Ward, in fact, saw education as essential: "The action of society in inaugurating and carrying on a great educational system, however defective we may consider that system to be, is undoubtedly the most promising form thus taken by collective achievement. It means much even now, but for the future it means nothing less than the complete social appropriation of individual achievement which has civilized the world."[13]

It was from this perspective that John Dewey later wrote: "Education is the fundamental method of social progress and reform" and that "the teacher is engaged, not simply in the training of individuals, but in the formation of the proper social life."[14]

Social Darwinism, then, provided several new premises relevant to the problems confronting schools at the turn of the century. Biological, not social, forces accounted for the inferiority of some groups. Poverty, crime, and moral depravity were indicators of this evolutionary inferiority. And while efforts expanded in social programs were unlikely to greatly alter the nature of the individuals involved, alteration of the environment could exert a positive influence on the direction of the evolutionary process.

Exactly how and why schools could play a role in all this was explicated most prolifically in the writings of psychologist G. Stanley Hall, whose theories of child development reverberated with Darwinian thought. Hall's basic notion was that the development of the individual follows the same set of stages as that of the entire race in its evolution from presavagery to civilization. An important corollary to this thesis was that differing environments—notably rural as contrasted with urban settings—could have profound effects on the progression of children through these stages. The contemporary evidence for this theory could be easily found in the vast differences between the children of the cities and those from more rural areas.

Especially vulnerable to the instability and temptations of the newly urbanized cities were adolescents, who, according to Hall's "evolutionary" developmental framework, were at the stage of savage, vagrant, and nomadic life. Only the restraints of homes where "industry, intelligence and thrift prevail, where books and magazines abound, where the library table forms the center of an interested group, where refinement of thought and life prevail"—in other words, middle- and upper-class homes—could save adolescents from depravity and delinquency. Thus the problem of immigrant youth was "scientifically" explained. The role of schools, in Hall's view, was to study the needs of various children and design curricula around the differences among them.[15]

Hall's theories, elaborated at length in his 1904 book *Adolescence*, were in part a reaction to the recommendations for secondary curricula of Charles Eliot and the Committee of Ten. Hall was especially affronted by Eliot's notions about the relative insignificance of individual differences. He accused the committee of ignoring "the great army of incapables"[16] that were increasingly attending schools. Hall used his notions of the magnitude of individual differences as a basis for a system of curriculum differentiation. Further, he attacked Eliot's beliefs that the function of schooling is "training for power and general cultivation"[17] and that this kind of education is important for all students. Hall maintained that Eliot was simply trying to fit everyone into an elite college-preparatory program.

Eliot responded to Hall's advocacy of a curriculum differentiated to meet individual differences and to prepare students for life with an expression of his hope that people "will refuse to believe that the American public intends to have its children sorted before their teens into clerks, watchmakers, lithographers, telegraph operators, masons, teamsters, farm laborers, and so forth, and treated differently in their schools according to these prophesies of their appropriate life careers. Who are we to make these prophesies?"[18]

The debate was lively and much discussed among school people. Eliot's position reflected the ideals of American schooling over the previous eighty years—the notion that from common and equal educational experiences would come an intelligent American citizenry. Hall's position represented something else entirely. But, without a doubt, Hall's words spoke most loudly to those eager to find a means of socializing all those strangers newly in school and of preparing them to fit the practical and social roles they were expected to fill in their adopted country. For, in the words of Hall, immigrant youth could be characterized as culturally neglected as well as biologically inferior. As such they were susceptible to the good works of the socially and morally advanced classes, who could provide them with character training—more important to society by far than an attempt to develop their inferior intellects.

A second notion, compatible with social Darwinist assumptions, also played a major role in determining the direction of school reform. The concept of Americanization, not new in American thought, was brought again to the forefront of the nation's consciousness with the huge influx of immigrant groups at the end of the nineteenth century. Americanization had been one of the major goals of the common school early in the century—teaching the immigrants of the 1830s and 1840s the accepted ways of thinking and acting (and, of course, speaking) in their new land. But these earlier immigrants were mostly from northwestern Europe, farmers who settled in rural America. The cultural differences between these settlers and their long-established neighbors had created some antagonisms, but there also had been a considerable degree of optimism and good will about the idea of Americanizing these newcomers, who were not after all so very different.

In the case of the new and larger waves of immigration at the end of the century, the situation was not the same. This group of immigrants was composed of more unfamiliar types. From southern and eastern Europe mostly, the new immigrants had darker skin and their languages, religions, and traditions were quite far removed from those of the "original stock." They came to work in factories, so they stayed in the cities. They came poor, and for the most part, they stayed poor.

Probably because this group of immigrants was different, the attitudes toward them were different as well. Although immigrants had never been welcomed enthusiastically or as equals, this time the social Darwinists had provided "scientific" proof that suspicion of foreigners was warranted. Eric Goldman has commented on the period:

The newest immigrants, the millions pouring into the United States from southern and eastern Europe, were finding that America was no longer in a come-one, come-all mood. Many of the older settlers, feeling crowded and cornered, had little welcome for any newcomers, and every prejudice in the American collection was roused by immigrants who were predominantly impoverished and unskilled, short and dark in appearance, Catholic or Jewish in religion. Rapidly the national speech was acquiring phrases that carried as much sneer and hiss as any in the language—"wop" and "dago" for the Italian, "bohunk" for the Hungarian, "grease-ball" for the Greek, and "kike" for the Jew.[19]

Largely because of these differences and the immigrants' overwhelming numbers and poverty, a great deal of concern was expressed about preserving the dominant WASP culture, eliminating the immigrants' "depraved" life-style, and making the cities safe. It seemed absolutely necessary to bring the foreign-born into the American cultural mainstream by teaching them the American values of hard work, frugality, modesty, cleanliness, truthfulness, and purity of thought and deed. These were the lessons of Americanization.

In 1909, the prominent educator Ellwood P. Cubberly wrote:

These southern and eastern Europeans are of a very different type from the north Europeans who preceded them. Illiterate, docile, lacking in self-reliance and initiative, and not possessing the Anglo-Teutonic con-

ceptions of law, order, and government, their coming has served to di-
lute tremendously our national stock, and to corrupt our civic life. The
great bulk of these people have settled in the cities of the North Atlantic
and North Central states, and the problems of proper housing and living,
moral and sanitary conditions, honest and decent government, and proper
education have everywhere been made more difficult by their presence.
Everywhere these people tend to settle in groups or settlements, and to
set up here their national manners, customs, and observances. Our task
is to break up these groups or settlements, to assimilate and amalgamate
these people as a part of our American race, and to implant in their
children, so far as can be done, the Anglo-Saxon conception of right-
eousness, law and order, and popular government, and to awaken in
them a reverence for our democratic institutions and for those things in
our national life which we as a people hold to be of abiding worth.[20]

Just prior to the turn of the century the journalist and photographer
Jacob Riis had written a sympathetic best-seller, *How the Other Half
Lives*, in which he described how some boys of poverty could turn to
crime and how the massive poverty of the immigrant slum might lead to
anarchy and class warfare.[21] But clearly a fear of the immigrants existed
among those who considered themselves to be of native stock, a fear that
lent a powerful self-interest to the mood of reform and Americanization.

The Americanization movement, in the sense of strict conformity to
white Anglo-Saxon mores, was camouflaged and confused by another
notion—the emerging view of America as a "melting pot." Popularized
by Israel Zangwill's 1908 play *The Melting Pot*, the idea that the contributions of many nationalities would result in the making of a new
"American" fed the hopes of many.

Goldman has written about the effects of the play's enthusiasm for
a great cultural potential in the sharing of traditions among the variety
of immigrant groups and between the newcomers and the old stock:
" 'Romantic claptrap,' the *New York Times* critic snorted, and Zangwill's
gushing prose is certainly hard to read today without wincing. But in a
more sentimental era, the play provided for thousands of progressives
an exciting expression of their desire for an attitude toward the immigrant that was more generous and hopeful."[22] In reality, what melting
was done was almost entirely in one direction. Immigrants learned Anglo ways; long-time Americans did not take on immigrant languages and
life-styles. For many immigrants, assimiliation was a strong positive value.
For others, the romantic ideal of the melting pot at least helped to make

tolerable the stripping away of their native language and culture that was prerequisite for success in the American mainstream.

So it was a mixture of idealism and fear that drove the movement to Americanize the immigrant. The hope among many was for a true American melting pot, blending old and new, foreign and familiar. The hope among most, however, seemed to be for peace only, a peace that would leave the status quo of the American social and economic hierarchy untouched and would be based on instilling the belief among immigrants that the American way was the good way. This inculcation of the American way into the minds and actions of the immigrants was to be accomplished by the American public school. And so Americanization became a major function of turn-of-the-century schools.

Social Darwinism had provided the "scientific" *justification* for the schools to treat the children of various groups differently. The Americanization movement provided much of the *content* of the schooling to be offered the children of the poor and immigrant. It was left to American industry to provide the *form* this new kind of education would take.

Turn-of-the-century Americans had fallen in love with industrial efficiency, the vision of the factory busily engaged in a neatly standardized and controlled process of mass production. In went raw materials and through the application of scientifically determined "best" methods and tools out came ready-made goods and machinery—all designed to improve the quality of American life. The essence of the factory model of production was efficiency. Unlike the older cottage-craft style of industry, the factory tolerated little waste of time and material, little duplication of effort. Human energies were controlled, coordinated, and channeled into machinelike parts, each worker constituting a small part of an efficient whole. Thus, industrial output could be maximized through efficient use of human resources.

Where did this notion come from? For one thing, there was during the period a rediscovery of Adam Smith's 1776 *The Wealth of Nations,* which, among other things, advocated the division of labor as a means of getting work done. Sociologist Max Weber's theories of bureaucracy were important, too, as they provided an explanation of how man's finite capacities could be brought together in a cooperative structure to increase productivity. Weber suggested the tremendous potential of the voluntary transformation of individuals into machinelike parts of a functioning whole. And of course, social Darwinism played a role as well, providing a justification for the exploitation of human resources in the name of increased production and efficiency.

But the notion of efficiency caught the public imagination chiefly through the writings of Frederick Winslow Taylor, an engineer who introduced the idea of efficient production through the application of scientific management techniques to industrial settings. With the publication of *Shop Management* in 1895, Taylor's notions of efficiency caught hold. On the basis of his beliefs that a great deal of waste occurred because of industrial inefficiency, that the basic cure for inefficiency was proper management, and that the best management was truly scientific in that it drew on clearly defined principles and natural laws, Taylor outlined principles of "scientific management." Known as the Taylor System, scientific management recommended time-and-motion studies to help determine standards of performance; the separation of planning from performance (so that plans based on data could be carried out by managers replacing the rule-of-thumb approach used by workers); the determination of the best methods of work through scientific study and the training and supervision of workers in these methods; the use of managers trained in scientific management and control techniques; and the structuring of the organization so that it would best aid in the coordination of activities among various specialists.[23] These features made possible a system with authority and decision making centralized at the top, with specialization and division of labor, the establishment of rules and regulations, and an attitude of impersonality toward the individual.

As scientific management gained popularity in industry, the businessmen who sat on school boards pushed for its adoption in the operation of schools and school systems. This push was not resisted by schoolmen as it placed education professionals in the role of "experts" and thus gave them more power in the battle with lay boards over control of schools.[24] In fact, schoolmen welcomed and often spearheaded the move to incorporate scientific management into schools. Schools were being widely criticized for their inefficient organization and methods and for their dubious successes. In an era of specifiable and measurable outcomes, many had come to wonder just what the measures of success of the educational enterprise were.

Criticisms of the school's inefficiency began with the publication of a series of articles in the *Forum* between 1895 and 1903 in which Joseph

Mayer Rice reported the results of tests in arithmetic and spelling that he had devised and administered to thousands of children in urban schools. He found the work of the schools to be worse than poor.[25] School critic and educator Leonard Ayers in 1909 published *Laggards in Our Schools*, reporting data collected from school records. Ayres wrote that the schools were filled with the retarded (those retained in grades longer than one year) and that most students dropped out before grade eight. The data cited indicated that "for every child who is making more than normally rapid progress there are from eight to ten children making abnormally slow progress." His conclusion was that schools had no programs suitable for the slow or average child, only programs suited to the brightest children. He suggested that the schools were proceeding inefficiently both through the use of inappropriate programs and through wasteful expenditures on the retarding of children that resulted.[26]

Public distrust of the effectiveness of education mounted as a flood of popular articles appeared, criticizing the schools' inefficiency in an era besieged by inflation and an increasing concern about the cost of public services. For example, in 1912 the *Ladies' Home Journal* published "The Case of Seventeen Million Children—Is Our Public-School System Proving an Utter Failure?" questioning the returns the public was getting for its investment in schooling. A second article on "The Dangers of Running a Fool Factory" attacked the school system as being filled with errors and hypocrisies. Finally, a commentary by H. Martyn Hart, dean of St. John's Cathedral in Denver, charged:

The people have changed but not the system; it has grown antiquated and will not meet our present needs; it has indeed become a positive detriment and is producing a type of character which is not fit to meet virtuously the temptations and exigencies of modern life. The crime which stalks almost unblushingly through the land; the want of responsibility which defames our social honor; the appalling frequency of divorce; the utter lack of self-control; the abundant use of illicit means to gain political position; all are traceable to its one great and crying defect—inefficiency.[27]

It was seductive, as schools became large, to think of them as factories that could use efficient and scientific methods to turn the raw material—children—into finished products—educated adults. The emphasis of the efficiency movement, however, was to produce educational products (students) at the lowest cost. The excellence of the product was hardly considered. Issues of educational quality or scholarship were rarely brought to bear on schooling decisions.

As we look at the ways in which schools developed after the turn of the century, we can discern the threads of these ideas woven into the institution that emerged. The ethnocentric ideas of social Darwinism, the push for Americanization to socialize newcomers to their appropriate places in society, and the model of the factory as an efficient way to mass produce an educated citizenry all converged in the concept of the comprehensive high school, complete with differentiated education and with ability grouping and tracking.

The National Education Association's 1910 Report of the Committee on the Place of Industries in Public Education clearly states the rationale publicly articulated by schoolmen for this new concept of education:

1. Industry, as a controlling factor in social progress, has for education a fundamental and permanent significance.
2. Educational standards, applicable in an age of handicraft, presumably need radical change in the present day of complex and highly specialized industrial development.
3. The social aims of education and the psychological needs of childhood alike require that industrial (manual-constructive) activities form an important part of school occupations. . . .
4. The differences among children as to aptitudes, interests, economic resources, and prospective careers furnish the basis for rational as opposed to a merely formal distinction between elementary, secondary, and higher education.[28]

This early report envisioned differences in the number of years of education as the structure of differentiation. But as the high schools became increasingly attended by non-middle-class children, within-school differentiation in the *kinds* of educational programs was developed, based on the same conceptions of differences among students—many of them class related—and replaced the idea of different *amounts* of precollegiate education for different groups.

Not surprisingly, not only the organization of schooling but what was to be taught to students in differentiated educational programs was influenced by the promise of the burgeoning industrial economy. Vocational education was seen early on as the appropriate alternative curriculum for students who were not college bound. This had not always been the case, however.

The earliest advocates of vocational education had viewed manual training as complementary to academic studies in the provision of a balanced education for *all* students. The arguments for this training emphasized the need for general education in mechanical processes rather than preparation for specific trades and the learning of principles rather than the acquisition of specific skills. It was also argued that manual training provided children with a meaningful way of learning—learning by doing—and that this was a necessary complement to the more passive lecture/recitation/book learning characteristic of a general education.[29]

However, manual education was soon seen as a way to improve the lot or at least properly socialize the new immigrant poor by teaching the dominant moral values, the virtue of hard work, and discipline. At the same time schooling could be made relevant to these childrens' future lives as workers. In 1893, Boston's superintendent of schools wrote, "The systematic introduction of Manual Training appears to be the only remedy for this enervated condition of our city population; the only universal stimulus to ambition and original effort on the part of our children."[30]

Businessmen, acting in the spirit of industrial efficiency, were eager to free practical trade training from the union-controlled apprenticeship system. They strongly advocated the use of public schools for training future industrial workers in needed technical skills. Some labor leaders were skeptical about the inclusion of specific vocational training in public schools. They worried about a rapid increase in newly trained workers and recommended that educational efforts be directed instead at workers already on the job. But by 1910 their greater fear of the business community's control over public vocational education led them to join with manufacturers to support and help coordinate specific vocational training in school.[31] Leaders of the changing agricultural industry as well supported the inclusion of agricultural education in rural schools, in the hope that it would both help establish a new "scientific" approach to farming, viewed as necessary in an industrialized nation, and encourage young people to remain on the farm in an era of urbanization.[32]

Some educators in both urban and rural areas also had other than purely educational goals in mind in their advocacy of vocational education. The new breed of efficiency-minded urban school administrators saw vocational programs as a productive mechanism for differentiating the curriculum and sorting students according to what they perceived to be the diverse needs and proclivities of the expanding high school population. As we have seen, city school administrators saw the needs and educational potential of poor and immigrant children as different from those of middle- and upper-class students. But rural educators, too, perceived benefits from the inclusion of vocational education in schools. They saw the infusion of an agricultural focus into the high school curriculum to be a means of capturing both student and parent interest in education. The traditional curriculum was viewed as overly bookish and irrelevant to rural life.[33]

Progressive reformers also encouraged the move toward vocational training programs in their attempts to democratize high school education. It was hoped that the differentiated curriculum would support a new concept of equal educational opportunity—one that took into account differences in students' interests and abilities. Through the provision of different high school curricula, opportunities for success could be equalized by offering different groups of students programs suited to their backgrounds and probable futures.

With all these forces pushing for specific skill training and occupational preparation, the notion of a balanced manual and academic liberal education for all became largely empty rhetoric. Instead, the inclusion of specific vocational training programs was widely heralded as a way of achieving a variety of goals. Among them were (1) supplying the nation with a needed corps of skilled industrial workers, (2) providing students with marketable skills and thereby enhancing their employment opportunities, (3) making the school experience more relevant to students' life experiences, and (4) equalizing educational opportunity by meeting the needs and interests of students for whom the more academic high school curriculum was seen as inappropriate. With the provision of federal funds for vocational education in the Smith-Hughes Act of 1917, the place of specific vocational training in public schools was firmly established. But, as we will see, the lofty goals set for these programs were not to be achieved.

Some cities responded to the increased size and diversity of their populations by setting up separate high schools for special programs and groups—vocational high schools for lower-class immigrant youth, academic high schools with college preparation for the middle class. Most cities, however, developed comprehensive high schools to meet the needs of the variety of students who attended. An integral aspect of comprehensive high schools became the separation of students within them for different kinds of instruction.

By 1918 the form of the new high school was emerging clearly. The Cardinal Principles of Secondary Education, put forth in a widely read report of a special committee of the National Education Association (NEA) in that year, attempted to outline a curriculum tha would provide something for everyone. Included was a delineation of recommended nonacademic programs: "Differentiation should be, in the broad sense of the term vocational . . . such as agriculture, clerical, industrial, fine-arts, and household-arts curriculums."[34] The report supported the junior high school as a place for the exploration of vocations and for guidance. Full-blown differentiation was to be delayed until senior high school. It was recommended that both junior and senior high schools be comprehensive. The junior high was to be comprehensive in order to help students acquire a wide variety of experiences as a basis for the decision to be made about their educational and vocational futures. At the high school level, housing the distinct curricula of the high school in a single building would ensure that students' choices would not be influenced by such extraveous factors as location, athletic teams, and friends.

It is interesting that the committee also saw the comprehensive high school as providing for two components of a democratic society, unification and specialization. "The purpose of democracy is to so organize society that each member may develop his personality primarily through activities designed for the well-being of his fellow members and of society as a whole."[35] Specialization was interpreted by the public schools to mean the provision of an education that would best meet individuals' future needs and thus train them to play their specialized roles in industrial America. In Weberian terms, they were to be prepared to combine their finite capacities voluntarily into an efficiently functioning social whole.

While specialization would be achieved by the differentiated curricula, unification for the attainment of common goals—Americanizing, if you will—would be achieved through the *experience* of attending common schools. Unification was to provide "common ideas, common ideals, and common modes of thought, feeling and action that made for cooperation, social cohesion, and social solidarity."[36] In other countries this occurred through the operation of common heredity, a centralized government, and an established religion. Because of American diversity, both religious and ethnic, this unification did not occur naturally; it was seen as the responsibility of the public schools. And while some of this could be accomplished at the elementary level, because social instincts were viewed as being formed primarily during adolescence the comprehensive high school was to play the critical part.

The NEA committee also proposed in its 1918 report that three elements of the comprehensive high school be addressed to unification—the teaching of the "mother tongue" and social studies; the "social mingling of pupils through the organization and administration of the school"; and extracurricular participation to develop a feeling of being part of the whole. These extracurricular activities, too, were designed according to the model provided by industry in factories in which clubs were established to bolster worker morale, to socialize them with proper attitudes, and to instill a spirit of belongingness.

To those who protested curricular differentiation as undemocratic, two kinds of responses were made by school people. One, articulated by Elwood P. Cubberly in 1909, openly acknowledged the abandonment of the ideal of equality in the urban comprehensive high school:

Our city schools will soon be forced to give up the exceedingly democratic idea that all are equal, and our society devoid of classes . . . and to begin a specialization of educational effort along many lines in an attempt to adapt the school to the needs of these many classes. . . . Industrial and vocational training is especially significant of the changing conception of the school and the classes in the future expected to serve.[37]

The other view, the one that has persisted, espouses a "new" kind of equality, taking individual needs, interests, and abilities into account in defining equal opportunity. "Until very recently [the schools] have offered equal opportunity for all to receive *one kind* of education, but what will make them democratic is to provide opportunity for all to receive education as will fit them *equally well* for their particular life work," the superintendent of Boston schools wrote in 1908.[38]

Before long this new kind of education had become thoroughly cloaked in the jargon of democracy. In 1914 a congressional Commission on Vocational Education wrote, "Widespread vocational training will democratize the education of the century . . . by recognizing tastes and abilities and by giving an equal opportunity to all to prepare their life work."[39] And in 1918, the NEA stated, "Education in a democracy . . . should develop in each individual the knowledge, interests, ideals, habits, and powers whereby he will find his place and use that place to shape both himself and society toward ever nobler ends."[40]

But absent from this view of nobler social ends was Charles Eliot's optimism of twenty-five years earlier about the potential of all human beings to learn. Gone too was the notion that secondary education is essentially a training of the intellect and that this preparation is appropriate for whatever life course a student may pursue. The debate had clearly been won by G. Stanley Hall, by science, by efficiency, and perhaps most of all by fear. At the same time, schooling became increasingly seen as a means to contribute to the expansion of the industrial economy. By selecting students for various occupations and providing them with appropriate training and skills, schools assumed an important place in the industrial order. As one educator suggested:

We can picture the educational system as having a very important function as a selecting agency, a means of selecting the men of best intelligence from the deficient and mediocre. All are poured into the system at the bottom; the incapable are soon rejected or drop out after repeating various grades and pass into the ranks of unskilled labor. . . . The more intelligent who are to be clerical workers pass into the high school; the most intelligent enter the universities whence they are selected for the professions."[41]

This curricular differentiation was made possible only by the genuine belief—arising from social Darwinism—that children of various social classes, those from native-born and long-established families and those of recent immigrants, differed greatly in fundamental ways. Children of the affluent were considered by school people to be abstract thinkers, head minded, and oriented toward literacy. Those of the lower classes and the newly immigrated were considered laggards, ne'er-do-wells, hand minded, and socially inefficient, ignorant, prejudiced, and highly excitable. These stereotypes are clearly reflected in the following statement by the superintendent of Cleveland schools: "It is obvious that the educational needs of children in a district where the streets are well-paved and clean, where the homes are spacious and surrounded by lawns and trees, where the language of the child's play fellows is pure, and where life in general is permeated with the spirit and ideals of America—

it is obvious that the educational needs of such a child are radically different from those of the child who lives in a foreign and tenement section."[42]

At first, students were openly classified into various programs by their ethnic, racial, and economic backgrounds. This procedure, supported as it was by social Darwinism and notions of the special needs of groups less fit for academic education, was considered scientific, efficient, and egalitarian. But by the end of World War I, this blatantly class-biased assignment of children to different educational programs was being called into question since it so clearly conflicted with the American rhetoric of an open and classless society.

The development of IQ tests lent an air of objectivity to the placement procedures used to separate children for instruction. With the introduction of these tests into schools, "ability" groups came into being. Because the tests were seen as scientific and used sophisticated statistical procedures, they were considered both "objective" and "efficient" means of assigning students. The testing and measurement movement, too, using the psychology of individual differences, coincided with the wish to bring the division of labor, standardization, and specialization into the schools. Test pioneer Lewis Terman wrote in 1916:

At every step in the child's progress the school should take account of his vocational possibilities. Preliminary investigations indicate that an IQ below 70 rarely permits anything better than unskilled labor; that the range from 70 to 80 is pre-eminently that of semi-skilled labor, from 80 to 100 that of the skilled or ordinary clerical labor, from 100 to 110 or 115 that of the semi-professional pursuits; and that above all these are the grades of intelligence which permit one to enter the professions or the larger fields of business. . . . This information will be a great value in planning the education of a particular child and also in planning the differentiated curriculum here recommended.[43]

The fact that about 80 percent of the immigrants tested by Terman were determined to be feeble-minded did not seem to undermine belief in the objectivity of the tests. Terman wrote:

Their dullness seems to be racial, or at least in the family stocks from which they come. The fact that one meets this type with such extraordinary frequency among Indians, Mexicans, and negroes suggests quite forcibly that the whole question of racial differences in mental traits will have to be taken up anew. . . . there will be discovered enormously significant racial differences . . . which cannot be wiped out by any schemes of mental culture.

Children of this group should be segregated in special classes. . . .
They cannot master abstractions, but they can often be made efficient
workers.[44]

Edward Thorndike's group intelligence tests provided the actual
means of classifying students in the spirit of scientific efficiency. Because Thorndike's research indicated that intelligence changed little over
time, he attributed it to heredity. And because measured intelligence
was so consistently linked with cleanliness and character, they too could
be seen as inherited traits. The hierarchy based on scores on his National Intelligence Test, in fact, replicated quite closely the social class
divisions of society. It was accepted, however, as a natural hierarchy of
intelligence. The widespread belief was that moral character, social worth,
and intelligence were interconnected and biologically rooted. The low
measured intelligence of immigrants and their children simply added
scientific confirmation to the prevailing view. These tests, then, were
used as efficient and objective measures of individual differences and as
"scientific" means to separate the rich from the poor within a common
school. Historian Clarence Karier has written of Thorndike's influence:

Few seemed troubled by the fact that the standards used were based on
white Protestant middle-class values. This was probably the secret of
Thorndike's success. His influence on American education may in part
be accounted for by the fact that he, more than most, built into his studies his own middle-class values and then dared to call them "scientific."
More important, he was saying exactly what a growing middle class
wanted to hear about itself and its schools. His positive correlations of
morality, wealth, intelligence, and social power could only endear him
to the established power structure, just as his empirical finding that "the
abler persons in the world in the long run are more clean, decent, just,
and kind" would make him a patron saint of the well-washed middle-
class American educators. Thorndike embodied the attitudes and values
which came to underlie the American public school.[45]

Part of the idea of schools as a meritocracy, in fact, stems from the
results of the early research on testing. Emerging from this work was a
clear relationship between measured intelligence and occupational attainment and an equally clear association between IQ and years of
schooling. As Cohen and Lazerson have pointed out:

These results gave an enormous boost to the notion that students who
ranked high in school would later have high-ranking jobs. If people were
poor, these tests seemed to prove that it was because they were stupid.
It occurred to few (least of all the pioneers of testing) that people might

be "stupid" because they were poor—that the tests might be biased to favor certain classes and social strata.[46]

Educational testing thus became not only a scientific but a *merito-cratic* basis for assigning students to various school curricula. Predictions about the probable future of students could be made on the basis of their scores, and then training appropriate to these futures could be provided by schools. This was seen as scientific, efficient, and also as fair. Schools could provide a means for those with ability to rise. The widely believed link between inherited social and economic status and ability—as supported by test scores—did not seem to perturb many. The accuracy and fairness of the system were not questioned. Its results only confirmed popular belief.[47]

At the same time, the school counseling movement emerged in secondary education. And despite what were probably the best of intentions, guidance programs helped bring about a subtle but important shift in grouping practices that enhanced their respectability. With appropriate guidance and counseling, student choice would come to play a role in secondary tracking practices. But, of course, given the kinds of attitudes and objective data that formed the basis of the counseling students received, such choices were made in the expected direction. Affluent whites chose academic programs; poor and ethnic minorities chose a more practical or vocational course.

These, then, are some of the most important events and ideas that shaped our current school practices. They show clearly the historical and social contexts that led to the tracking systems we have in schools today. Little has happened in the twentieth century to alter these patterns. In fact, a dominant theme in curriculum making has continued to be differentiation. Certainly, the creation of the junior high schools in the 1920s was in part inspired by the wish to determine and institute appropriate curriculum placements (vocational or academic) by the time children were twelve years old. Appropriate differentiation was also an important focus of the life-adjustment movement of the 1940s. The emphasis of this educational thrust was to help young people adjust to existing conditions in society and to lead happy and productive lives within the limits of their abilities. A resolution emanating from a 1945 conference sponsored by the U.S. Office of Education summarized this view:

It is the belief of this conference that, with the aid of this report in final form, the vocational school of a community will be able better to prepare 20 per cent of the youth of secondary school age for entrance upon desirable skilled occupations; and that the high school will continue to prepare another 20 per cent for entrance to college. We do not believe that the remaining 60 per cent of our youth of secondary school age will receive the life adjustment training they need and to which they are entitled as American citizens—unless and until the administrators of public education with the assistance of the vocational education leaders formulate a similar program for this group.[48]

In James Conant's influential report of 1959, ability grouping of students subject by subject, with special and rigorous attention accorded to the academically talented, was presented as the common sense means of shoring up American academic resources in the wake of Sputnik.[49] The criticism that Conant had failed to suggest strengthening academic programs for any but the most gifted was barely heard.[50] Once more, curriculum differentiation emerged as the reasonable and efficient way to solve educational problems. The assumptions about the native abilities and appropriate future places of the poor and minorities that so influenced the form of the high school at the turn of the century may have changed considerably, but the mechanisms we use for sorting and selecting students for school programs and instructional groups have remained much the same. So have the results.

3

Twenty-five Schools

It is clear from what we know about the development of American secondary schooling around the turn of the century and from the considerable work of contemporary researchers that tracking is *not* what it may first appear to be to the casual observer or the unquestioning student, parent, teacher, or administrator. Tracking does *not* equalize educational opportunity for diverse groups of students. It does *not* increase the efficiency of schools by maximizing learning opportunities for everyone, nor does it divide students into neatly homogeneous groups. Tracking does *not* meet individual needs. Moreover, tracking does *not* increase student achievement.

What tracking does, in fact, appears to be quite the opposite. Tracking seems to retard the academic progress of many students—those in average and low groups. Tracking seems to foster low self-esteem among these same students and promote school misbehavior and dropping out. Tracking also appears to lower the aspirations of students who are not in the top groups. And perhaps most important, in view of all the above, is that tracking separates students along socioeconomic lines, separating rich from poor, whites from nonwhites. The end result is that poor and minority children are found far more often than others in the bottom tracks. And once there, they are likely to suffer far more negative consequences of schooling than are their more fortunate peers. This much we know.

What we do not know from all this scholarship is how these eventualities are played out in schools—how the day-to-day experiences in classrooms contribute to such regrettable consequences.

For insight into these phenomena we looked to twenty-five secondary schools whose contexts and processes were studied systematically and in depth. These schools and what the students in them experienced constitute the focus of the remainder of this book. For by looking carefully at what went on in these schools, we can raise important questions about what happens in American secondary schools in general. We can begin to suggest explanations for why the results of tracking turn out as they do. And because these explanations are rooted in the daily processes of schools, we can also begin to suggest what schools could do differently.

The twenty-five secondary schools to be considered here were part of a sample of schools carefully examined in a major study in the late 1970s, A Study of Schooling.[1] Early in the decade, John Goodlad, dean of the Graduate School of Education at the University of California at Los Angeles, and a number of research associates embarked on a study aimed at finding out, in a very detailed way, what was actually happening in and around American schools. The primary assumption that guided the project was that any improvement effort first of all requires knowledge about schools and the experiences and perceptions of the people who spend their days in them. Rather than study a huge number of schools, A Study of Schooling chose to inquire in depth into the workings of a small number of schools of various types and in different areas of the country. Thirty-eight schools in all were actually studied: thirteen elementary schools, twelve junior and twelve senior high schools, and one school that spanned grades seven to twelve. The thirty-eight schools represented thirteen different communities, with elementary and secondary schools studied in each location. The particular schools were chosen because they differed in ways that, taken together, would reflect the diversity of American schools in general.

The geographic areas of the schools represented the rich variety of American communities. They included small, sparsely populated settlements in the rural South, middle America, and the Southwest; suburban areas close to major cities on both coasts; a community in the heart of an industrial city in the North Central region of the country; and sections of middle-sized cities in the Northwest, Southwest, and Midwest. The groups of people who made up these communities were in some cases largely or all white, some all or predominantly black, some mostly Mexican-American, and some mixed. Some were fairly affluent and others were quite poor. In some communities the adults were generally well educated; in others they were not. Some communities were very similar in wealth, ethnicity, and education; others were quite diverse.

The schools themselves differed in several ways as well. The largest was a senior high school with more than three thousand students, the smallest an elementary school with a student population of only forty-eight. One of the schools occupied fifty acres of land; another occupied only three. One school building was fifty-seven years old; another was nearly new. Some schools spent as much as $1,500 per pupil each year; others, as little as $300 for each child. Some schools paid their teachers well; some, poorly. Some schools were plagued with vandalism costing an estimated $12,000 to $15,000 each year in damage. Others reported no such problems. Some of the schools had high rates of transiency and daily absences. At other schools, the student population was quite stable. One of the high schools sent over two-thirds of its students to colleges and universities; another, only 5 percent. One sent nearly a quarter to vocational training schools. At a few of the schools large percentages of students dropped out altogether.

The researchers spent about six weeks in each community talking with principals and teachers; gathering school documents and materials from teachers containing information about their classes; administering lengthy questionnaires to students, parents, teachers, principals, central office administrators, school board members, and other community people; and observing and recording for many hours the daily events of classroom life in a random sample of classes at each school. This data-collection period took the better part of 1977. Over 150 researchers and data collectors were involved.

Information was collected about features that are common to schooling but might be handled differently in individual schools. These *commonplaces*, as they were called in the study, included teaching practices, subject matter content, instructional materials, physical environment, activities, human and material resources, evaluation, time, organization, communications, decision making, leadership goals, issues and problems, implicit (or "hidden") curricula, and controls, or restraints. Literally thousands of pieces of information were gathered at each school, which, in essence, reflected the perceptions of the people associated with the schools and the recorded observations of trained researchers about them. What we have from these perceptions and observations, then, is a detailed picture of what the schools were like during a brief period of time.

Following the year of data collection at the schools, nearly three years were spent in organizing and analyzing the information that was gathered. The responses to each questionnaire item were tabulated for each group of respondents at each school, as were the responses across the schools at each level—elementary, junior high, and senior high. Both simple and highly complex relationships among responses were documented, analyzed, and interpreted. School documents and curriculum materials were analyzed and described. Interview responses were compiled and categorized. Observation data were coded and profiles made for each of the more than one thousand classrooms included in the study. The information, stored on computer tapes, was used for analyses of individual perceptions, classroom phenomena, and school and community characteristics. All this work had several purposes. Not the least important was to raise thoughtful and serious questions about the conduct of American education based on what was found in the thirty-eight representative schools.[2]

Tracking became, in this study, a matter of considerable interest and concern. For despite the many differences among the communities and the schools, they all included some mechanism for sorting students. And although these mechanisms differed from place to place, the results in terms of students' experiences were surprisingly similar.

It is important to realize that tracking students in schools is *not* an orderly phenomenon in which practices, even within a single school, are consistent or even reflective of clearly stated school or district policies. To the contrary, sorting out what tracking is actually done at a school is rather like putting together the pieces of a puzzle. Only two schools of our twenty-five provided us with any documents explicitly outlining the structure of their tracking systems. Of these documents, only one was a formal policy statement; the other was a letter of explanation to teachers about the criteria they should use to place students. At the other twenty-three schools partial information from many sources had to be pieced together to get complete pictures of their use of tracking. As a result, some administrators' estimates of the percentage of courses that were tracked at their schools were quite different from the calculations we made from class schedules or the percentages found in our sample of classes. Taken together, however, these various measures provided a means of describing the type and extensiveness of tracking at each of the schools.

The difficulty of obtaining accurate descriptions of tracking in schools arises for many reasons. Even though tracking is widespread—indeed, only one school of our twenty-five evidenced *no* use of homogeneous grouping—it is a topic that school people are reluctant to discuss openly, not only with outsiders such as reseachers but with people in and around the schools themselves. This undoubtedly leads to confusion at the schools and inconsistencies between what might be policy and what becomes practice.

For example, at one large suburban junior high school, Newport (a pseudonym, as are all the school names to follow), no tracking policy was set forth in any of the written statements we examined about how the school operates (class schedules, teachers' record books, course of study outlines, etc.). From all appearances it seemed that tracking just did not happen at this school. When we talked with the head counselor, however, she revealed that the academic classes at the school *were* systematically tracked into four levels, but that the classes were labeled in writing only on the counselors' master schedule for the year. Parents were not routinely informed of the level of their children's classes, and records were not kept from year to year. The hidden nature of the tracking system at the school was due, she told us, to the controversy surrounding this kind of grouping and to the school's wish to avoid damaging children or parents by letting them see how the children were being labeled. Understandably, finding out the specifics about tracking at this school was extremely difficult.

Inconsistencies between tracking policies and practices also existed at schools whose policy was clearly stated. At one small rural high school, Euclid, there was a clearly stated policy of no tracking or homogeneous groupings. The principal, in conversation, discussed with us at length and with considerable pride the registration procedure at his school, in which any student could elect to take any class. Yet it was absolutely clear from his comments that an *informal* system existed at Euclid, whereby, during the registration procedure, students were guided into classes that the staff thought were appropriate for their futures. As a result, it turned out that nearly half the classes at Euclid were homogeneous groups of students. Clearly, tracking was a practice at this school, regardless of the policy.

In some schools, even where policy concerning tracking was clear and followed in practice, unexpected and unplanned tracking occurred in addition to the deliberate groupings. At schools where the deliberate tracking was extensive and pervaded many subject areas and where there was little flexibility in the system, classes that were not intentionally tracked became homogeneous groups because of scheduling requirements. At Bradford Junior High, for example, since students stayed together in tracks for four or five periods of academics, the schedule did not permit a wide diffusion of these students for the remainder of the school day. At Bradford, even some art, physical education, and vocational education classes were comprised of nearly all high or average or low students, although these classes were not tracked according to school policy.

There were many other examples of inconsistencies and confusion surrounding tracking at our twenty-five schools, but these should make the point. Tracking is a complex phenomenon in schools, and while it is an integral part of the organizational structure at most of them, it is obscured by a variety of factors. Even so, it is possible to describe schools on several dimensions of tracking and to make comparisons among them and between the junior and senior high levels. However, the following observations should be kept in mind. Information we gained from master schedules, teacher assignment lists, and school curriculum publications pertained to intentional or overt tracking systems; where these existed, labels were usually part of the course titles. Information from the administrators' comments and teachers' curriculum materials was often less clear. It is apparent from these latter sources of information that, in some cases, homogeneous groupings simply happened without any intentional placement or structural system operating. A consideration of both of these kinds of tracking is essential to a complete understanding of how the sorting of students occurs in secondary schools.

Further, tracking at our schools existed in two distinct but overlapping forms, although both forms did not occur at all schools. One form was the division of the total school program into academic and vocational curricula with students classified as either "vocational" or "academic" students. At some schools a third or fourth division was made. These additional tracks were academically focused but designated for students not pointed toward colleges and universities. Several of the larger high schools made these clear-cut divisions in their programs. None of the junior highs did.

A second type of tracking consisted of divisions within each of the larger curricular areas. All schools divided one or more of their academic subjects into homogeneous ability or achievement groups. At some schools this system overlapped the academic/vocational split. At others academic tracking was the only form. This was the case at all the junior highs and at many of the smaller high schools. Within vocational education programs, homogeneous groupings occurred as well. Although no school had a written policy regarding it, careful analysis of the kinds of vocational classes enrolling different groups of students revealed some significant if subtle forms of tracking here too.

Senior High Schools

Of the thirteen senior high schools, five seemed to operate quite separate vocational and academic programs. These five had tracking within academic subjects as well. The other eight high schools did not seem to have a separate vocational curriculum, although vocational courses were offered at all of them. How tracking systems were organized varied considerably from school to school, however, ranging from an almost complete separation of "vocational" and "academic" students for the entire school day to separation of students only for some academic subjects. Often this academic sorting was done subject by subject, making it possible, although not highly likely, for students to be placed at different levels in different subjects.

Fairfield High is a medium-sized rural high school. Its students— about half Mexican-American and half Anglo—were from middle- to low-income families. Not surprisingly, the Mexican-Americans tended to be poorer than the whites. The classes offered at Fairfield reflected a strong emphasis on vocational as compared to academic education. Nearly half the teachers taught vocational subjects. And, as we would expect, more than 80 percent of the teachers told us that instruction that prepares students for employment was the kind of education most emphasized at the school. About a third of the students who *graduate* were expected to go to four-year colleges or universities. But nearly half of those enrolled at Fairfield were expected to drop out of school before completing their senior year.

Two kinds of tracking operated at Fairfield. Students were placed in either an academic or a vocational curriculum. Students in the academic program took required English, math, social studies, and science courses, various electives, and physical education. They were strongly encouraged to take chemistry, a foreign language, and a fourth year of English—course work beyond the basic requirements. Vocational students took only a limited number of academics and spent the rest of their time in vocational subjects; they did not take physical education. The school counselor told us that 55 to 75 percent of the students at Fairfield were enrolled in the vocational program. Within some academic subject areas, further tracking of students by achievement or ability was done. In these subjects the vocational students were usually in the lower-level classes. Because of the separation of students both into distinct curricula and into ability and achievement groups, it is unlikely that academic and vocational students were ever together in the classroom at Fairfield.

A similar system existed at Rosemont High, a large, urban high school attended almost entirely by poor Mexican-American teenagers.

Palisades High was a large, fairly affluent suburban high school attended by whites from the immediate neighborhood and blacks bused in from across town. Six distinct curricular tracks operated at Palisades: three oriented toward college preparation, one oriented toward preparation for entry-level positions in business offices and marketing, and two general programs that, in the words of a guidance counselor, "do not necessarily prepare a student for college." One of the college-preparatory tracks and one of the general tracks emphasized the performing arts. Although the tracks were separate, the subjects and courses within them overlapped. Tracking within some of these overlapping subjects was done to the extent that more than two-thirds of all the classes at the school were homogeneous groups resulting from *deliberate* separation of students. Additional separation happened in other subject areas as well because students in each track were expected to take more courses in selected areas than were students in the others (e.g., students in the business education program took nine courses in vocational subjects, whereas students in college preparatory level I took the equivalent of one vocational course).

Tracking practices at Atwater High, a suburban middle-class school, at Bradford High, a blue-collar school in an industrial suburb, and at Dennison Secondary, a small rural school including both junior and senior high school students, were similar in organization to that at Palisades

High. At all these schools, vocational education classes represented a far smaller proportion of the total course offerings than at Fairfield. And far fewer teachers at these schools than at either Fairfield or Rosemont saw vocational instruction as the kind of education most emphasized. The students at these schools were slightly better off financially than those at Rosemont and Fairfield.

Newport High, a large metropolitan high school with a widely diverse student population, divided students only in academic subjects. These divisions were not labeled "academic" or "vocational" but were made according to the ability or achievement levels of the students—"advanced placement," "academically enriched," "average," "basic," or "remedial." Although students were tracked for each subject separately— English, math, social studies, and science—it was unusual for a student to be scheduled into classes at more than one or two levels. Further separation of students occurred at Newport because courses other than the basic requirements were designed as either appropriate for university-bound students or appropriate for those planning other kinds of futures.

Many of the other senior highs used the type of tracking that was done at Newport. Each, however, differed slightly in the number of subjects tracked, the way placement decisions were made, or the amount of movement of students up or down in track levels. Vista and Crestview, middle-sized suburban schools; Woodlake, a small suburban high school; Laurel, a very small, naturally integrated rural school; and Manchester, a large urban black senior high, had tracking of this type.

Unique among the high schools was Euclid Senior High, a small school in a rural community. As we saw earlier, no official policy or systematic tracking or grouping practices existed at Euclid. All classes were said to be open to all students. But the staff, in a very informal way, guided student placement during registration for classes, making sure that students who were presumed to be college bound took highly academic courses and that those who were not did not. The result was that there were as many tracked classes at Euclid as at many of the senior highs with more straightforward policies.

To help understand this variety of tracking policies and practices, we can consider five dimensions or common elements: *extent,* the proportion of the total number of classes that were tracked at the school; *pervasiveness,* the number of subject areas at the school that were tracked;

flexibility, whether students were tracked subject by subject or across more than one subject on the same criteria; *mobility,* the amount of student movement up and down in track levels; and *locus of control,* who makes the decisions about where students belong. By considering these dimensions, we can more easily compare the schools' tracking systems with one another.

Counselors and school administrators estimated for us the proportion of all the classes at their schools that were included in their tracking systems *(extent).* These estimates ranged from about one-third at Laurel to all the classes at Fairfield and Rosemont.

The number of subject areas in which students were sorted *(pervasiveness)* varied considerably as well. At Vista, tracking was found in four subject areas, the fewest number among our schools. At Fairfield, Rosemont, and Atwater, on the other hand, students were sorted in all eight subject areas. The other nine schools fell in between.

Pervasiveness of Tracking in Thirteen High Schools

Number of Subjects Tracked	Schools
1	———
2	———
3	———
4	Vista
5	Palisades, Dennison, Woodlake, Newport
6	Crestview, Laurel, Bradford, Euclid
7	Manchester
8	Fairfield, Rosemont, Atwater

Some subject areas are tracked in high schools far more often than others, with academic subjects most likely to be separated into homogeneous achievement/ability groups. The list below shows just how many of our high schools tracked in each subject area. Of course, these numbers include both schools that tracked in those subject areas according to policy and those schools that tracked classes in these subjects even though it was not a part of stated policy:

English—13 schools
Math—13 schools
Science—13 schoools

Vocational education—11 schools
Foreign language—11 schools
Social studies—10 schools
Arts—4 schools
Physical education—4 schools

These numbers do not mean that all the classes in these subjects were tracked. Many of the schools, in fact, had both homogeneous and heterogeneous classes within each subject area. The numbers do indicate, however, that students were being sorted in these subject areas at the number of schools listed. It is impressive to note that while some subject areas were almost always tracked and some almost never, *every subject area* was taught to a homogeneous group of students somewhere in our thirteen schools.

High school tracking systems also vary in the amount of *flexibility* in their structure. At some of our schools—Fairfield, for example—it appears that students were locked into their entire school program as a result of track placement. At other schools—Vista is a good example—students were placed into track levels subject by subject and may have had courses at more than one level and with a wide variety of other students.

The following list of the thirteen high schools tells whether students were *formally* tracked into more than one subject area by a single decision or whether formal tracking decisions were made subject by subject at each school. Euclid, the one school with an entirely informal tracking system, is included in a separate category.

Tracking Flexibility

Less Flexible— Tracking across Subjects	More Flexible— Tracking Subject by Subject	No Formal System
Fairfield	Vista	Euclid
Atwater	Crestview	
Palisades	Rosemont	
Bradford	Newport	
	Woodlake	
	Laurel	
	Manchester	

No information: Dennison Secondary School

While there appears there was some variation among the schools in the degree of *mobility*—the extent to which students change to upper or lower track levels from year to year—this existed in a context of overall stability of track placements. The general rule at most schools was that nearly all students would remain at assigned track levels from year to year. No school administrator estimated more than a 30 percent change. The following chart includes the estimates of between-track mobility for some of the senior high schools. Most schools, however, did not provide such an estimate.

Mobility of Students among Track Levels

Less than 10%	10%–20%	21%–30%
Laurel	Atwater	Crestview
Dennison		Bradford
		Rosemont

No information: Vista, Fairfield, Newport, Woodlake, Palisades, Manchester, Euclid

It is interesting that, of the three schools giving the largest estimates of movement along track levels, two reported the bulk of this movement as reassignment to a lower track level: Crestview (20 percent) and Rosemont (25 percent). At Rosemont, in fact, track movement was attributed to incorrect initial placements resulting from "student input" which necessitated the subsequent movement of a large percentage of students to lower track levels.

The locus of control regarding track decisions at most of the schools resided with the counselors. Teachers appear to have had a considerable say at many schools, parents at a few, and students at almost none.

Taking these characteristics together, it is possible to gain an impression of the relative overall amount of separation and degree of rigidity in the tracking practices at the thirteen high schools. Atwater High School appears to have had the most highly stratified and rigid system of the thirteen in that it was the only school that had all the following characteristics: the majority of classes offered at the school were grouped homogeneously, including classes in all academic subjects; students were placed in a track level for more than one class rather than having separate placement decisions made for each subject area;

Locus of Control for Placement Decisions

Counselors	Teachers	Counselors/ Teachers	Counselors/ Teachers/Parents	Counselors/Teachers/ Parents/Students
Crestview	Atwater	Vista		Rosemont
Fairfield[a]		Woodlake		Palisades
Manchester		Laurel		Euclid
Bradford				
Dennison				
Newport[a]				

[a] At Fairfield and Newport, school reports indicate that the decisions were made jointly with parents and students. Since heavy reliance was placed on aptitude and achievement tests in these decisions, it seems clear that despite the stated policy, counselors had the primary responsibility at these schools.

fewer than 20 percent of the students were estimated to change their placement level in classes from year to year; and finally, there was no indication that students had a role in track placement decisions. The tracking systems at Palisades, Bradford, Fairfield, and Rosemont were also highly stratified.

The least structured system was at Euclid, which employed no formal tracking system, but rather offered only informal guidelines at the time of registration for classes. Of the schools with structured systems, the least stratified and rigid appears to have been Woodlake, whose principal was openly opposed to tracking. Only a quarter of the classes offered were homogeneous groups, and while several academic subjects were included, many classes in each subject were heterogeneous. Placement decisions were made for each subject area separately. Students at Woodlake, however, appear not to have had a role in placement decisions. Additionally, we have no information about how much mobility occurred for those students in tracked classes. Nevertheless, the system here appears to have been the least rigid of the formal tracking systems at the high school level. The tracking systems at the other ten schools fell between these three—Atwater at one end and Euclid and Woodlake at the other—in their overall amount of rigidity and stratification.

Interestingly, among the high schools the degree of stratification and rigidity in a school's tracking system did not seem to be linked to school demographics. There were no consistent patterns of similarities or differences in tracking systems related to school size, location, student socioeconomic status, or ethnicity. We found only one indication of such a relationship. Both of the schools enrolling poor Mexican-American students had well-developed vocational programs distinct from the academic programs at the schools.

Traditionally, two of the reasons given for the use of tracking and ability grouping have been (1) that they meet individual student needs better and (2) that they ease the teaching task by reducing the range of student differences in the classroom. These rationales were the predominant ones given by the administrators and counselors at our senior high schools as well. Eleven schools made statements referring to meeting individual student needs, and five included some mention of easing the task of instruction for teachers; some of these specifically cited the reduced range of student differences toward this end. Other rationales given by schools included: (1) to allow students to be with peers of near-equal ability, (2) to segregate students by interest and effort, and (3) to encourage career education. The thirteen schools, nevertheless, did not differ markedly in the rationales they gave for the use of tracking from one another or from American secondary schools in general.

Junior High Schools

Even though none of the twelve junior high schools divided its students into distinct vocational or academic categories, the academic tracking programs at some of the schools were as rigid as at some of the high schools, but in slightly different ways.

At Bradford Junior High, a middle-sized school in an industrial working-class suburb, 80 percent of the classes were tracked as high, average, or low ability or achievement groups. Bradford's tracking was a highly stratified system that cut across subject areas. In grades seven and eight, students were grouped together in sections labeled 7-1, 7-2, 7-3, and so on, for all academic subjects. Each section was comprised of students judged to be at about the same achievement or ability level. While ninth-grade students were not grouped in sections that stayed together during the day, their classes were also tracked for a variety of achievement levels. The school counselor told us that placement in a class at one level automatically determined a student's placement in other subject areas as well.

Most typical of junior high tracking was the type found at Newport.

The head counselor here too estimated that about 80 percent of the classes were grouped by the achievement or ability levels of students. All courses in English, mathematics, social studies, science, and foreign language were tracked, as were some of the vocational classes as well. Newport, located in an ethnically diverse area, had a considerable number of special classes for non-English- and limited-English-speaking students. These classes were considered by the school to be a separate track. In the four major academic areas—English, mathematics, science, and social studies—four other levels of classes were offered as well. Students were placed in either honors, high, average, or low classes in these subjects. A student at Newport was tracked at the same level for all academic subjects unless a special exception was made. These exceptions usually resulted from teacher requests.

A similar but less rigid type of tracking existed at Vista Junior High School. Fewer academic subjects were tracked, and most student placements were made subject by subject and were based on different criteria for each course. The following excerpt from a letter from Vista Junior High to sixth-grade teachers at Vista Elementary explains the basis on which students were to be placed in seventh-grade math classes at Vista Junior High:

Seventh grade mathematics classes are divided into four levels to provide for individual differences. The materials covered in Levels I and II are similar but the level of abstraction and the rate of speed at which the material is covered will be greater in Level I. The material covered in Level III will resemble Levels I and II but will be varied depending on the ability of the students and their mastery of skills in the mathematical processes. Level IV is designed for students whose math work is below seventh grade level.

I. *Honors:* A very select group of students which you would consider the "cream of the crop" in their mathematical ability, possessing systematic and effective *habits of study, an appreciation for thoroughness and accuracy.* Habits of logical thought, a curiosity for exploring, and an enthusiasm for mathematics are characteristic of these students, along with a command of basic addition, subtraction, multiplication, and division facts of whole numbers, decimals, and fractions.

II. *Academic:* Students who have many of the characteristics of Level I except in mathematical reasoning ability and attitude. They probably approach the Honors students in capability but are *less consistent* in their performance and are probably *less motivated* to excel in math.

III. *General:* Students of average mathematical ability. They should be able to *perform well* as far as the basic facts of *addition, subtraction,* and *multiplication* of whole numbers. Some may not be able to perform well in long division problems. Characteristically, pupils of this level not only vary in mathematical abilities but also in their inclination to study it; all are considered capable of showing an interest in mathematics and able to acquire the knowledge and skill necessary to solve the mathematical problems they may encounter in everyday life.

IV. *Basic Math I:* Students placed in Level IV are those working below the seventh grade level in mathematics. These cannot perform well in basic addition, subtraction, multiplication, and division facts of whole numbers let alone fractions, decimals, and other more complex operations.

Equally detailed criteria were given for English placements.

Euclid Junior High, a small rural school, was the only school of our twenty-five where classes were deliberately grouped heterogeneously by dividing students at different achievement levels (using standardized test scores) as evenly as possible between classes.

From these four examples, the variety in the tracking systems at the twelve junior highs becomes clear. Estimates from the counselors at all the schools of the proportions of the total classes at their schools that were tracked (extent) ranged from none (at Euclid) to four-fifths (at Newport and Bradford).

The number of subject areas in which students were tracked varied as well, from none at Euclid to seven at Bradford. As with the high schools, however, we found that the fact that tracking was done in a particular subject at a school did not necessarily imply that all classes in that subject were homogeneous. At some of the junior highs Atwater, for example), only some classes in a tracked subject were homogeneous. At others (Newport, Vista, Manchester), all classes in a tracked subject were homogeneous groups. The following chart shows the number of tracked subjects at each of the twelve junior high/middle schools.

Pervasiveness of Tracking

Number of Subjects Tracked	Schools
0	Euclid
1	Crestview
3	Atwater, Vista, Woodlake, Rosemont, Palisades
4	Laurel
5	
6	Fairfield, Newport, Manchester
7	Bradford

The list below indicates the number of junior high/middle schools tracking in each subject area. These numbers include both those subjects tracked by policy and those subjects in which homogeneous groups occurred without a stated policy.

Math—11 schools
English—10 schools
Science—6 schools
Social studies—6 schools
Foreign language—5 schools
Vocational education—4 schools
Arts—3 schools
Physical education—0 schools

Taken together, these two charts indicate the pervasiveness of tracking with regard to subject areas at our junior high/middle schools. As we found at the high school level, some subjects were rarely tracked—physical education, the arts, and vocational education—and others were almost always tracked—English and mathematics.

The flexibility of tracking systems varied among the junior high schools as at the high schools. Half of the schools placed students into tracked classes subject by subject. These tended to be the same schools that tracked in the fewest subject areas. At three schools, tracking placements were made across subjects, with the most extreme form existing at Bradford, where students were grouped together for all their academic subjects. At two schools—Vista and Palisades—both types of tracking took place, with some subjects linked together and others treated separately. Below, the schools are categorized as to their degree of flexibility.

Schools differed too in the mobility that was estimated to exist for

Tracking Flexibility

Less Flexible Tracking across Subjects	More Flexible Tracking Subject by Subject	No Formal System
Newport	Crestview	Euclid
Manchester	Fairfield	
Bradford	Rosemont	
Vista	Woodlake	
Palisades	Atwater	
	Laurel	

students among track levels at the twelve junior high/middle schools. At Vista only 3 percent of the students were estimated to change track levels from year to year. At Atwater, the estimate was 4 percent. It should be noted that these two schools were among those with the fewest tracked subjects. The following are the estimated amounts of student movement among tracks at the junior high schools.

Mobility of Students among Track Levels

Less than 10%	10–20%	21–30%
Vista	Crestview	Palisades
Atwater	Rosemont	
	Newport	
	Woodlake	
	Laurel	
	Manchester	
	Bradford	

No information: Fairfield
Not applicable: Euclid

The locus of control of track decisions at most of the schools resided with counselors and teachers together. At the other schools, one of these two groups had the sole responsibility for placement decisions. At none of the junior high/middle schools did either parents or students have a role in these decisions.

As at the high school level, these dimensions can be considered together to see the overall amount of stratification and rigidity in a track-

Locus of Control for Placement Decisions

Counselors	Teachers	Counselors/ Teachers	Counselors/ Teachers/Parents	Counselors/ Teachers/ Parents/ Students
Newport	Vista	Crestview		
		Fairfield		
Atwater	Woodlake	Rosemont		
		Palisades		
		Laurel		
		Manchester		
		Bradford		

ing system at the junior highs and to make informal comparisons among schools. The most highly stratified and rigid tracking systems appear to have been those at Bradford, Newport, and Manchester. At Bradford approximately 80 percent of the courses were tracked, including all academic classes and some others. Students were kept together in track levels for all their academic classes. And neither students nor their parents were reported to have a say in student placement decisions. While Newport and Manchester did not report that tracked students were kept together as a group, in other respects their tracking systems were very similar to that at Bradford.

At the other extreme was Euclid, with neither a stated tracking policy nor evidence of homogeneous groups in academic classes in either the course offerings or in the classes we studied. Of the eleven schools with a tracking policy, Crestview appears to have had less stratification and rigidity in its tracking of students than did the other schools. Only about 17 percent of the classes were tracked, and those were in only one subject area, math. It was estimated that about 20 percent of the students at Crestview changed levels each year. Less stratified systems were also found at Rosemont and Laurel.

Interestingly, as at the senior high schools, the degree of stratification and the rigidity of the tracking system at junior high schools did not seem to be associated with school size or location, or the socioeconomic status or ethnicity of the student population. Further, the eight junior high schools that provided us with rationales for using homogeneous grouping all stated the belief that individual differences are better accommodated in tracked settings. Two of the schools specifically mentioned easing the teaching task as well. At the junior highs, the stated reasons for tracking were nearly identical to those at the senior high level.

Considering the Differences

Despite the difficulty of unraveling the specifics of how tracking operated, we can be sure that the adults and students at all but one of the secondary schools we studied were involved in and influenced by some type of tracking system. The existence of a tracking system at a school must in some way affect all the students there. It means that placement decisions are being made about all students who take a tracked subject or who ask to take a tracked subject. Furthermore, since all the schools except Euclid Junior High tracked in required academic subjects, it is a fair assumption that placement decisions were being made about all the students in the rest of the schools. From this information about our twenty-five schools, it becomes clear that tracking is a very persuasive and salient feature of secondary schooling.

What are we to make of these differences? How does the degree of structure and separation affect students within different schools? Do different kinds of tracking systems contribute more or less to the kinds of effects researchers have found associated with tracking?

In considering the information we have uncovered—the lack of overall consistency in the nature of tracking systems and the importance that differences in grouping practices at the schools make in the experiences of students—the following conclusion from Findley and Bryan's extensive review of research on tracking, *The Pros and Cons of Ability Grouping* (1975), is helpful. "At high school, assignment to a curriculum or program of study may be a part of a total ability grouping program. On the other hand, ability grouping is often accomplished to a degree by self-selection in which individual students choose their programs of study freely or with some regard to prerequisites. In essential respects, the differences between the two methods is analogous to the distinction between *de jure* and *de facto* segregation."[3] In other words, despite difference in track *systems*, tracking *effects* on students seem to be remarkably similar.

It seems that the tremendous variety in the specific mechanisms of tracking represents only minor variations of the dominant pattern. And it is the dominant pattern that is likely to result in the outcomes we noted in chapter 1 and in the differences in classroom experiences we found in our twenty-five schools. As we have said, this pattern, common to all track systems, contains a number of components. First, the presumption is made that students' related past achievements and potential for learning what will be presented in a particular secondary school course or program of courses can be accurately and fairly measured by tests or the judgments of school people. Second, it is assumed that by dividing students according to the results of whatever criteria or measures are used, groups of similar learners will be formed. Third, it is believed that by grouping like students together individual learning needs will be met and that group instruction is probably adequate for the major part of this task. Fourth, it is thought that, by arranging students in groups so that individual needs can be sufficiently met with common learning goals, instructional activities, and materials, the teaching task is made considerably more manageable for teachers. Fifth, regardless of the process used, students are publicly labeled and categorized according to the school's estimation of their potential as learners. Sixth, the classifications that result from this process are neither neutral nor equal. They form, in fact, a hierarchical system of stratification, with students in the top groups—whether they are labeled "Academic," "College Preparatory I," "Gifted," or "High"—accorded the most value and those in the bottom tracks—whether they are called "Vocational," "Low," or "Basic"—accorded the least. And seventh, as will soon become clear as we consider the everyday experiences of students in the twenty-five schools, tracking results in different and *not always equal* educational treatments being given to various groups of students.

These beliefs and features are basic to all tracking systems. They, not the particulars of how specific practices are carried out, are what make the difference in the lives of students. While the differences in tracking systems are fascinating, their chief interest is that they are not likely to make a real difference in tracking effects. There seem to be no *essential* distinctions between various types of tracking. Either schools do or do not track. As we have seen in our twenty-five secondary schools, they almost always do. The results are predictable and remarkably similar.

4

The Distribution of Knowledge

As we have seen, there has been a considerable amount of interest in tracking and some scholarly effort spent analyzing it. As a result, we know quite a bit about the outcomes of tracking—what happens to students as a result of being in one or another track, how their academic learning is affected, and what behaviors and attitudes they are likely to exhibit. Other studies have considered the factors that are important in determining who gets placed in which track level. Much of this inquiry has revolved around the question of fairness and has tried to assess the extent to which student placements are based on social class or on "merit." This question has not yet been resolved to everyone's satisfaction, because underlying the issue is a whole hotbed of other concerns: the definition of "merit," the objectivity of standardized tests, and probably the most volatile of all, the relationship between race and scholastic aptitude.

We looked at tracking from a slightly different, but not unrelated, perspective. Consistent with the focus of A Study of Schooling, we were interested in learning the content and process of classrooms under tracking systems. We wanted to know what actually goes on in classes at different track levels and how they are similar or different from one another. We wanted to know specific information about what students were being taught, how teachers carried out their instruction, what classroom relationships were like, and how involved students seemed to be in classroom learning. We also wanted to know about what kinds of student attitudes were characteristic of classrooms—attitudes students had toward themselves, their classrooms, and their schools. Essentially, we wanted to know details about what different kinds of classes were like for students and how students felt about being in them.

These aspects of tracking are not altogether removed from what most other research has considered. In fact, we hoped that by studying tracked classes themselves we could begin to suggest some explanations for why things turn out the way they do for teenagers in different tracks. And because our explanations would revolve around things that go on in schools rather than around characteristics of the students themselves, we could, in turn, suggest things schools might do differently in order to avoid some of the negative results that are related to tracking. But since our interests were somewhat different from most of those who have studied tracking, we needed to approach our study differently as well.

We bypassed, for example, the whole issue of what characteristics of students seem to most influence the decisions about which track they belong in. We did not consider whether the students in our twenty-five schools were placed "fairly." However, we were very much interested in knowing which kinds of students ended up in each track: rich or poor, white or nonwhite. We were concerned with this because we would be making judgments about the *quality* of the educational experiences in different track levels. And if it turned out, as it did, that there were differences in the quality of educational experiences, we wanted to be able to discuss these differences in terms of educational *equality* for those students who seem to benefit least from schooling—the poor and minorities. Thus we decided to leave the class/merit debate to others and make the bold assertion at the beginning of our work that regardless of how "fair" their placements might appear to be by traditional educational standards, it is never equitable to have any group of students be systematically offered less when it comes to educational quality. By looking at the distribution of various groups of students into track levels next to an assessment of the quality of education offered in those tracks, we could address the issue of equity in a new way. Does the disproportionate placement of poor and minority students in low-track classes mean that they are getting a poorer quality of education in their day-to-day experience in classrooms?

Not surprisingly, then, we were more interested in classrooms as the focus for our study than we were in individual students. Because we were less concerned with outcomes for individuals than with what students experience in groups, we decided to describe what whole classrooms were like, rather than what the individuals in them were like. Of course, we knew that the characteristics of individuals in classes contribute considerably to the classroom environment. We were most interested, however, in the result of this interaction between individuals and schools—what actually goes on in class. As a result, we used the views of individuals in classrooms collectively as a means of describing the group experience rather than individually as a way of describing students.

Because of this classroom focus, we did not study individual students classified as "academic," "general," or "vocational," as most tracking studies have done. We studied classes that were considered to be at various track levels. We could not use the traditional track labels assigned to students since they did not apply to the academic classes that were a part of the tracking systems at our twenty-five schools. For example, classes for the most highly academic tracks were variously called "advanced placement," "academically enriched," "college preparatory level I," "honors," or "gifted." What they all had in common was that they were intended for the highest achievement- or ability-level, college-bound students in the school. We simply grouped together all the tracked classes at similar levels and categorized them as "high," "average," or "low." The administrators, counselors, and teachers at the schools helped us determine which classes belonged in each category.

To discover how the track levels themselves were alike and different, we wanted to study a *representative* group of classes at each level. We wanted to be able to compare tracks fairly without being overinfluenced by class differences that were more related to differences among subjects or to differences among the schools in the number of subjects they tracked than to actual track differences. We settled on the analysis of math and English classes only. We had studied a large number of these classes—297 to be exact. These classes were fairly evenly distributed among the secondary grades. We knew that nearly all of the twenty-five schools tracked in these subjects (twenty-three in English, twenty-four in mathematics). We also knew that nearly every student at our schools took classes in these subjects; most took five or six years of English and at least four years of math. And finally, we recognized that these two subjects. although both highly academic, differed considerably from each other. We felt that by considering these subject-area differences, we would be able to identify characteristics of classroom processes that were likely to be common to certain track levels in all subjects and those that seemed to be unique to specific subjects. With our decision to study English and math classes, then, we believed that what we found out about classroom processes at various track levels would not be distorted by any particular group of schools, students, or subjects.

We ended up studying 75 high-track classes, 85 average-track classes, and 64 low-track classes that were about evenly divided between math and English. Seventy-five other classes in these two subjects were identified as heterogeneous (or not tracked). These classes proved to be useful, as we will see later, for comparing what went on in tracked and untracked classes.

Throughout this chapter, examples of student and teacher responses will be drawn from high- and low-track classes in many subject areas. These responses are illustrative of the track-level differences we found. However, when conclusions are presented, they are based on the systematic analysis of data about the 299 English and math classes. While it is likely that these conclusions apply to tracking in a general way, it is important to be clear about how they were derived.

Who Goes Where

In chapter 1 we saw clearly that there is a pattern of relationships between students' socioeconomic positions—and important in this is their ethnicity—and their chances of being placed in a particular track level. While there is certainly no automatic placement of poor and minority students in low tracks or of affluent white students in upper tracks, the odds of being assigned into particular tracks are not equal. In virtually every study that has considered this question, poor and minority students have been found in disproportionately large percentages in the bottom groups.

In our study of twenty-five schools, we found this same pattern operating. We were able to examine it directly in two ways—related to student race and ethnicity—and indirectly—related to other socioeconomic characteristics. For one thing, we were able to look closely at the schools with racially mixed populations to determine who got placed in which track levels at those schools. And second, we were able to look at vocational education programs at all the schools and assess the differences in programs taught to white and nonwhite students. While these two considerations are related directly to race and ethnicity and tracking, they relate indirectly to other socioeconomic status factors as well, for not surprisingly, the minority students in our schools tended to be poorer than the whites. Moreover, the relationships we uncovered were the strongest at schools where the minority students were at the lowest income levels.

Academic Tracking and Race

Our twenty-five schools were very diverse in a number of ways, as we have seen. But one of the most noticeable ways in which they differed was in the racial and ethnic characteristics of the students who attended them. Seven senior highs and six junior highs were attended almost exclusively by white students. These were the schools in the Vista, Crestview, Woodlake, Atwater, Bradford, Euclid, and Dennison communities. The Rosemont schools were Mexican-American, and the Manchester schools black. The other eight schools were racially or ethnically mixed: Fairfield Junior and Senior highs were about half Mexican-American and half white, the Laurel and Palisades schools about half black and half white. Laurel's schools were part of a mixed, athough hardly integrated rural community. The blacks at the two Palisades schools were bused in to this affluent white community The Newport schools, located in a highly diverse metropolitan suburb, were unique among our group. The student population at these schools represented a rich variety of ethnic and racial groups. Slightly less than half of the students at each of the schools were white; the others were Mexican-American, black, or Asian, and a scattering of students were from a number of other distinct ethnic. Together, the thirteen white schools enrolled 10,783 students; the four nonwhite schools, 8,248 students; and the eight mixed schools, 4,287 white and 4,546 nonwhite students.

The relationship between student ethnicity and tracking could be seen at six of our mixed schools: Fairfield, Laurel, and Palisades. At these schools we recorded the race or ethnic background of every student in the classes we studied.[1] By looking at how students from various groups were tracked into the English and math classes at these six schools, we could check to see if the schools followed the pattern that has been found so consistently in other research.

The white student populations at these six mixed schools ranged from a low of 46 percent to a high of 53 percent with an average for the six of 50 percent. Within these schools, an average of 62 percent of the students in high-track English classes were white, a considerably larger proportion than in the student population as a whole. Only 29 percent of the students in low-track English classes at these six schools were white, a substantially smaller percentage than in the total student population.[2]

Eight high-track and ten low-track English classes were included in the sample at these six multiracial schools. Of these eighteen classes, fourteen followed the predominant pattern in racial composition, with disproportionately large percentages of white students in high-track classes and of nonwhite students in low-track classes. Of the four classes that did not conform to this racial pattern, three were high-track classes with between 32 and 46 percent white students; the other, a low-track class, had 67 percent white students.

These four classes, however, shared some common characteristics. All four were located in the Palisades community, which, as we have seen, was a middle- to upper-middle-class suburb of a large city. The minority students were middle- and upper-middle-class blacks voluntarily bused to the school. At the other four multiracial schools, the minority populations were considerably less affluent. Additionally, three of these four nonconforming classes were elective subjects—speech, journalism, and creative writing. Only one was a standard language arts class, and that class had the largest white population of any of the three high-track classes (46 percent).

Math classes, too, evidenced this disproportionate allocation of racial groups in track levels. An average of 60 percent of the students in high-track math classes at the six schools were white, compared to only 37 percent of the students in the low-track math classes. As with the English classes, these percentages differed markedly from the percentage of white students in the total population at these multiracial schools.

Six high-track and twelve low-track math classes were studied at these schools. Of these eighteen math classes, only five did not follow the predominant pattern in racial composition—larger percentages of white students in high-track classes and smaller percentages of whites in low-track classes than in the schools as a whole. Of these five non-conforming classes, two were high-track classes—one with 44 percent white students and one with 29 percent—and three were low-track classes with a percentage of whites ranging from 55 to 65 percent. Like the exceptional English classes, three of these five math classes were located in the Palisades community, which had the more affluent black students.

From the information about these six schools, then, it is clear that in our multiracial schools minority students were found in disproportionately small percentages in high-track classes and in disproportionately large percentages in low-track classes. And, as we have seen, this pattern was most consistently found in schools where minority students were also poor. These findings are consistent with virtually every study that has considered the distribution of poor and minority students among track levels in schools. In academic tracking, then, poor and minority students are most likely to be placed at the lowest levels of the schools' sorting system.

Among vocational classes, the issue of who goes where is more complex. The relationship between students' ethnicity and their placement in vocational programs at our schools will be considered in detail in chapter 8.

Who Learns What

QUESTION: What is the most important thing you have learned or done so far in this class?

We were interested in finding out what students regarded as the most important learnings in their classroom experience. We gave them a considerable amount of empty space on their questionnaires to tell us what they thought. Students in high-track classes tended to write answers like these:

RESPONSES: I've learned to analyze stories that I have read. I can come with an open mind and see each character's point of view. Why she or he responded the way they did, if their response was stupidity or an heroic movement. I like this class because he [the teacher] doesn't put thoughts into your head; he lets you each have a say about the way it happened.
                                    High-track English—senior high

Basic concepts and theories have been most prevalent. We have learned things that are practical without taking away some in-depth studies of the subject.
                              High-track Science—senior high

Learning political and cultural trends in relation to international and domestic events.
                              High-track Social Studies—senior high

I have learned a lot about molecules and now am able to reason and figure out more things.
                              High-track Science—senior high

It teaches you how to do research in a college library.
                              High-track English—senior high

Learned to analyze famous writings by famous people, and we have learned to understand people's different viewpoints on general ideas.
                              High-track English—junior high

Things in nature are not always what they appear to be or what seems to be happening is not what really is happening.
                              High-track Science—senior high

Greek philosophy, Renaissance philosophy, humanities. How to write essays and do term papers. The French Revolution. *HISTORY!*
                              High-track social studies—junior high

We learned how to do experiments.
                              High-track science—junior high

I've really learned the whole idea and meaning behind economics and how to apply economics to my life.

The bases of our economic system and the way the business world is.
                              High-track Vocational Education—senior high

About businesses—corporations, monopolies, oligopolies, etc., and how to start, how they work, how much control they have on the economy—prices, demand, supply, advertising.

We've talked about stocks—bonds and the stock market and about the business in the U.S.A.
                              High-track Vocational Education—junior high

To infer or apply the *past* ideas to my ideas and finally to the future's ideas.
                              High-track social studies—junior high

Inductive reasoning.
High-track Math—senior high

Learned about different theories of psychology and about Freud, Fromm, Sullivan and other psychologists.
High-track Social Science—senior high

The most important thing is the way other countries and places govern themselves economically, socially, and politically. Also different philosophers and their theories on government and man and how their theories relate to us and now.
High-track Social Studies—junior high

I have learned things that will get me ready for college entrance examinations. Also, many things on how to write compositions that will help me in college.
High-track English—junior high

The thing we did in class that I enjoyed the most was writing poetry, expressing my ideas. We also had a poet come and read to us.
High-track English—senior high

I have learned quite a deal about peoples of other nations, plus the ideas of creation and evolution, ideas that philosophers have puzzled over for years."
High-track Social Studies—senior high

Many things about chemistry and experiments especially how to prove things that we learn by experiments.
High-track Science—senior high

How to read a classic novel and be able to pull out details, and write a complete and accurate report.
High-track English—senior high

We have learned the basics of the law of relativity, and basics in electronics. The teacher applies these lessons to practical situations.
High-track Science—senior high

Probably the most important thing I've learned is the understanding of the balance between man and his environment.
High-track Science—senior high

We have learned about business deals. We have also learned about contracts.
High-track Vocational Education—senior high

Learned many new mathematical principles and concepts that can be used in a future job.

> High-track Math—senior high

Learning to change my thought processes in dealing with higher mathematics and computers.

> High-track Math—senior high

How to write successful compositions, how to use certain words and their classifications. What to expect in my later years of schooling.

> High-track English—junior high

The most important thing that we have done is to write a formal research paper.

> High-track English—senior high

There is no one important thing I have learned. Since each new concept is built on the old ones, everything I learn is important.

> High-track Math—senior high

To me, there is not a most important thing I learned in this class. Everything or mostly everything I learn in here is *IMPORTANT*.

> High-track English—junior high

I have learned to do what scientists do.

> High-track Science—junior high

Students in low-track classes told us the following kinds of things:

How to blow up light bulbs.

> Low-track Vocational Education—junior high

Really I have learned nothing. Only my roman numerals. I knew them, but not very good. I could do better in another class.

> Low-track Math—junior high

I've learned how to get a better job and how to act when at an interview filling out forms.

> Low-track English—junior high

How to ride motorcycles and shoot trap

> Low-track Science—senior high

How to cook and keep a clean house. How to sew.

> Low-track Vocational Education—junior high

The most important thing I have learned in this class I think is how to write checks and to figure the salary of a worker. Another thing is the tax rate.

Low-track Math—senior high

To be honest, nothing.

Low-track Science—senior high

Nothing outstanding.

Low-track Science—senior high

Nothing I'd use in my later life; it will take a better man than I to comprehend our world.

Low-track Science—senior high

I don't remember.

Low-track Social Studies—junior high

The only thing I've learned is how to flirt with the chicks in class. This class is a big waste of time and effort.

Low-track Science—senior high

I learned that English is boring.

Low-track English—senior high

I have learned just a small amount in this class. I feel that if I was in another class, that I would have a challenge to look forward to each and every time I entered the class. I feel that if I had another teacher I would work better.

Low-track Math—junior high

I can distinguish one type rock from another.

Low-track Science—senior high

To spell words you don't know, to fill out things where you get a job.

Low-track English—junior high

Learned about how to get a job.

Low-track English—junior high

Job applications. Job interviews. Preparation for the above.

Low-track English—junior high

Learned to fill out checks and other banking business.

Low-track English—junior high

Spelling, worksheets.

Low-track Science—junior high

How to sew with a machine and how to fix a machine.

Low-track Vocational Education—junior high

Job training.

Low-track English—junior high

How to do income tax.

Low-track Math—senior high

A few lessons which have not very much to do with history. (I enjoyed it).

Low-track Social Studies—junior high

Most Americans believe that the school curriculum is fairly standard. From what we remember of our own experiences and what we see represented in the media, we have an impression of sameness. Tenth-grade English at one school seems, with only slight variations here and there, to be tenth-grade English everywhere. This seems to be so much so that we would expect a tenth-grader who moves in the middle of the year from Pittsburgh or Pensacola to Petaluma to slip quite easily into a familiar course of study—a little Shakespeare, some famous short stories, a few Greek myths, lists of vocabulary words from the College Entrance Exams, and guidelines for well-developed paragraphs and short expository themes. The same beliefs hold for most academic subjects. For example, isn't eighth-grade math everywhere a review of basic operations, an introduction to algebraic and geometric concepts, with some practice in graphing and scientific notation and a brief glimpse at function and inequalities? How much could eleventh-grade American history differ from class to class or from place to place? Or ninth-grade introductory biology?

Don't misunderstand, however. We, as a society, have no expectation that all tenth-, or eighth-, or eleventh-graders will finish these classes having *learned* all the same things. We know well that some students are more or less interested than others and that some find it more or less difficult than others do. But most of us do assume that the material itself—facts and concepts to be learned, pieces of knowledge and works of scientific literacy or cultural merit to be appreciated—is at least paraded by everyone as they proceed through school. We assume that everyone is at least *exposed*. In our study of twenty-five schools we found these assumptions and beliefs to be unsubstantiated by our observations of what actually went on in classrooms.

One of the particulars we were most interested in finding out about was whether students who were placed in different track levels in subjects had the same opportunities to learn the *content* of those subjects. Were students in different track levels being exposed to the same or similar material? If so, were the differences among tracks merely ones of mode of presentation or pace of instruction? If actual content differences did exist, were they socially or educationally important ones—that is, was what some students were exposed to more highly valued by society than what other students were presented? We also wanted to know whether students in different track levels were experiencing about the same amount of learning time. Were some groups of students getting more instruction than others? Were effective instructional techniques being used more in one track than in another? Did teachers seem to perform better with some groups of students than with others?

We studied each of these questions carefully because we knew that the implications of what we found could be far-reaching. We believe that these issues go to the very heart of the matter of educational equity. For beyond the issue of what schools students have access to is the issue of what knowledge and learning experiences students have access to within those schools. If there are school-based or system-related differences in what students are exposed to, are these differences fair? Do they interfere with our commitment to educational equality?

We have long acknowledged and perhaps even overemphasized the ways in which differences among students influence their learning in school. Cultural and socioeconomic patterns have been carefully studied with an eye toward how those patterns characteristic of poor children, and especially poor and minority children, interfere with their opportunities to achieve in school. We have also given attention to the influence of family characteristics, such as support and encouragement, on school success. Measured aptitude for learning or intelligence has received a huge share of research time and money in the search for explanations of differences in student learning outcomes. All these attributes are alike in that they are seen to reside in the student. They are clearly important in the school-learning process, but they are not factors over which schools have much control. As conceived, there is little school people can do to alter them.

We have not, however, paid so much attention to the role of school opportunities in determining what and how much students learn. For, ultimately, students can learn *in school* only those things that the school exposes them to. And this learning is restricted by the time allotted for it and the mode of instruction employed. Perhaps this is so obvious that it is clearly understood. I suspect, rather, that it is so obvious that it is usually overlooked as important. But the implications of these simple facts of schooling are tremendous. If schools, perhaps in response to differences students bring with them from home, provide them with different kinds of opportunities to learn, then the schools play an active role in producing differences in what and how much students actually learn. The different educational opportunities schools provide to students become the boundaries within which what different students learn *must* be confined. Further, if these opportunities differ in ways that may be important in influencing children's future opportunities both in and out of school, then the differences in learning that schools help produce have profound social and economic as well as educational consequences for students.

We found in our twenty-five schools that students in some classes had markedly different access to knowledge and learning experiences from students in other classes. In nearly every school, some groups of students experienced what we typically think of as tenth-grade English, eighth-grade math, eleventh-grade history, and ninth-grade science. We found also, again in nearly every school, that other groups of students encountered something quite different. And we found that these differences were directly related to the track level of the classes students were in.

In our study we used several sources of information about the 299 English and math classes to shed light on this question of differences in what was likely to be taught and learned in classes in different track levels. Teachers had compiled packages of materials for us about their classes, including lists of the instructional topics they cover during the year, the skills they teach their students, the textbooks they use, and the ways they evaluate their students' learning. Many teachers also gave us copies of sample lesson plans, worksheets, and tests. The teachers were interviewed, and as part of the interview they were asked to indicate the five most important things they wanted their students to learn during the year with them.

In analyzing all these data we looked for similarities and differences in the content of what students were expected to learn in classes at various track levels. We looked both at the substance of what they were exposed to and at the intellectual processes they were expected to use.

We analyzed these similarities and differences systematically[3] and from a particular point of view. We did not assume that all knowledge presented in schools is equally valuable in terms of societal worth, as exchange for future educational, social, and economic opportunities. On the contrary, we began with the recognition that some kinds of knowledge are far more valuable in this way than are others.

We were not thinking, of course, about the value of knowledge in a pure—that is, culture-free—sense. The issue of what is worth knowing in this abstract sense is a question philosophers will continue to grapple with. Nor were we thinking about the value of knowledge in a purely educational sense. Again, it is not clear what kinds of learnings may be better than others in the development of a person who is a learner. This is likely to vary dramatically in groups, even those composed of very similar individuals.

These two issues ignore the social and economic ties attached to learning when it becomes housed in schools. Schools, as social institutions, do far more than impart knowledge and skills to students. They do more than pass on the traditions and values, the folkways and mores of the culture, to the young. Schooling is both more and less than education in the purest sense. It includes as an important function the preparation of youth for future adult roles and for their maintenance of the social structure and organizational patterns of society. And because our social structure is a hierarchical one, with different and fairly specific criteria for entry at various levels, schooling becomes what Joel Spring has called a "sorting machine."[4] By this he meant that the form and substance of the educative process that occurs in schools also select and certify individuals for adult roles at *particular* levels of the social hierarchy. This sorting process results in part from students' access to socially meaningful knowledge and educational experiences.

We analyzed the differences in the content of classes from this perspective. We wanted to explore whether students in different track levels were systematically given access to knowledge that would point them toward different levels in the social and economic hierarchy.

We found considerable differences in the kinds of knowledge students in various tracks had access to. We found also that these differences were not merely equally valued alternative curricula. Rather than being neutral in this sense, they were differences that could have important implications for the futures of the students involved.

For example, students in high-track English classes were exposed to content that we might call "high-status" knowledge in that it would eventually be required knowledge for those going on to colleges and universities. These students studied standard works of literature, both classic and modern. Some classes traced the historical development of literature, some studied the characteristics of literary genres (the novel, the short story, poetry, the essay), and others analyzed literary elements in these works (symbolism, irony, metaphoric language). Students in these classes were expected to do a great deal of expository writing, both thematic essays and reports of library research. In some classes, too, students were taught to write in particular styles or to learn the conventions of writing in the various literary forms. These students were expected to learn the vocabulary they would encounter on the College Board Entrance (SAT) exams and practice the type of reading comprehension exercises they would find there as well. Some, although not many, of these classes studied language itself, including historical analyses and semantics.

Low-track English classes rarely, if ever, encountered these kinds of knowledge or were expected to learn these kinds of skills. Not only did they not read works of great literature, but we found no evidence of good literature being read *to* them or even shown to them in the form of films. What literature they did encounter was so-called young-adult fiction—short novels with themes designed to appeal to teenagers (love, growing pains, gang activity) and written at a low level of difficulty. These novels constituted part of the focus of low-track classes on basic literacy skills. Prominent in these classes was the teaching of reading skills, generally by means of workbooks, kits, and reading texts in addition to young-adult fiction. The writing of simple, short narrative paragraphs and the acquisition of standard English usage and functional literacy skills (filling out forms, applying for jobs) were also frequently mentioned as course content in low-track classes.

It is probably not surprising, given the differences in *what* they were learning, that the differences in the intellectual processes expected of students in classes at different levels were substantial. Teachers of the high-track classes reported far more often than others that they had students do activities that demanded critical thinking, problem solving, drawing conclusions, making generalizations, or evaluating or synthesizing knowledge. The learnings in low-track classes, in nearly all cases, required only simple memory tasks or comprehension. Sometimes low-track students were expected to apply their learnings to new situations, but this kind of thinking was required far less frequently than were memorization and simple understanding.

The teachers of classes intended for "average" students gave us information indicating that the learnings encountered in their classes were somewhere in between the high- and low-track extremes. But it is worth noting that the kinds of knowledge and intellectual skills emphasized in these average English classes were far more like those in the high track than in the low. It is more appropriate to consider these classes as watered-down versions of high-track classes than as a mixture of the other two levels. Low-track classes seemed to be distinctly different.

Math classes followed a similar pattern of differences with one major exception. The knowledge presented in high-track classes in math, as in English, was what we could call "high status"; it was highly valued in the culture and necessary for access to higher education. Topics frequently listed included mathematical *ideas*—concepts about numeration systems, mathematical models, probability, and statistics—as well as computational procedures which became increasingly sophisticated at the higher grades.

In contrast, low-track classes focused grade after grade on basic computational skills and arithmetic facts—multiplication tables and the like. Sometimes included in these classes were simple measurement skills and the conversion of the English system into the metric. Many low-track classes learned practical or consumer math skills as well, especially at the high school level—the calculation of simple and compound interest, depreciation, wages, and so on. Few mathematical ideas as such seemed to be topics of instruction in these classes. In essence, while the content was certainly useful, almost none of it was of the high-status type.

As in the English classes, the average math classes were considerably more like the high-track classes in their content than like the low. And, too, the content of average math classes can be considered a diluted version of that of the high classes. This was especially true at the junior highs and through about grade ten at the senior highs. From that point on in our schools, math was usually no longer a required subject, and only what would be considered high-track classes were offered to those students wishing to go on in math.

Math classes did differ from English classes in the intellectual processes demanded of students in classes at the various track levels. While the topics of math classes differed considerably—and the differences in the conceptual difficulty of these topics is dramatic—students at all levels of math classes were expected to perform about the same kinds of intellectual processes. That is, at all levels, a great deal of memorizing was expected, as was a basic comprehension of facts, concepts, and procedures. Students at all levels were also expected to apply their learnings to new situations—whether it was the application of division facts to the calculation of automobile miles per gallon of gasoline in low-track classes or the application of deductive logic learned in geometry to the proof of theorems and corollaries in calculus.

It is clear that both the knowledge presented and the intellectual processes cultivated in English classes and the access to mathematical content in math classes were quite different at different track levels. Moreover, these differences seem to be more than simply a result of accommodating individual needs—a major reason given for such curricular variation. The types of differences found indicate that, whatever the motives for them, social and educational consequences for students are likely to flow from them. The knowledge to which different groups of students had access differed strikingly in both educationally and socially important ways.

Much of the curricular content of low-track classes was such that it would be likely to lock students into that track level—not so much as a result of the topics that were included for instruction but because of the topics that were omitted. Many of the topics taught almost exclusively to students in low-track classes may be desirable learnings for all students—consumer math skills, for example. But these topics were taught to the exclusion of others—introduction to algebraic equations, for example—that constitute prerequisite knowledge and skills for access to classes in different, and higher, track levels. So, by the omission of certain content from low-track classes, students in effect were denied the opportunity to learn material essential for mobility among track levels. This content differentiation was found as early as grade six. Contrary to the suspicions of many, this line of thinking, however, does not imply that all students need the same things in school. Moreover, it is not in conflict with the view that schools should accommodate differences among individuals in learning speed and style, nor does it deny that some students need remediation in fundamental prerequisite skills. But it suggests, given the importance of some curricular topics for students' future educational opportunities, that individualization and remediation should take place within the context of a core of educationally and socially important learnings—thus at least providing equal access to these topics.

We make certain assumptions about what different kinds of students are able to learn. This extends not only to what we believe they are able to master in the way of skills but also to what ideas and concepts we believe are appropriate for them to be exposed to. As a result, a student with poor reading skills may never be exposed to a Shakespearean play—literature highly valued, if not widely read, in our culture. A teacher of students with low-level reading skills may be justified in not expecting these students to read with understanding the text of a Shakespeare play. On the other hand, exposure to these works seems entirely appropriate. Franco Zefferelli's film version of *Romeo and Juliet,* for example, is not only suitable for but fascinating to teenage students of every ability and achievement level. The cultural context of the work, the themes represented in the play, and examples of the often rather base comedy used as relief from the intensity of the play's tragic events are valuable and interesting topics for all English students—even for those perceived to be at the lowest ability levels, even for those not expected to go on to colleges and universities. That Shakespeare, originally written to appeal to the Elizabethan masses—far less literate than even our least skilled American teenagers—is now reserved only for the elite of our schools, those identified as having the most intellectual promise, would be silly, if it were not for the serious consequences of differentiated content for students.

Learning Beyond Content

QUESTION: What are the five most critical things you want the students in your class to learn this year? By learn, we mean everything that the student should have upon leaving the class that (s)he did not have upon entering.

We asked this question of each of the teachers during our interviews with them. Among their responses, teachers of high-track classes typically included the following kinds of answers.

RESPONSES: Interpreting and identifying.
Evaluation, investigating power
High-track Science—junior high

Deal with thinking activities—Think for basic answers—essay-type questions.
High-track English—junior high

Ability to reason logically in all subject areas.
High-track math—senior high

The art of research.
High-track English—senior high

Learn how to test and prove ideas. Use and work with scientific equipment. Learning basic scientific facts and principles.
High-track Science—junior high

Scientific reasoning and logic.
High-track Science—senior high

Investigating technology, investigating values.
High-track Social Science—junior high

Self-reliance, taking on responsibilities themselves.
High-track Science—junior high

To learn values and morals—to make own personal decisions.
High-track English—junior high

To think critically—to analyze, *ask* questions.
High-track Social Science—junior high

Individual interpretation of materials covered.
High-track English—senior high

Logical thought processes. Analysis of given information. Ability to understand exactly what is asked in a question. Ability to perceive the relationship between information that is given in a problem in a statement and what is asked.
High-track Science—senior high

Love and respect for math—want them to stay curious, excited and to keep believing they can do it.
High-track Math—junior high

To realize that all people are entitled to certain inalienable rights.
High-track Social Science—junior high

To think critically (analyzing).
> High-track English—senior high

How to think critically—analyze data, convert word problems into numerical order.
> High-track Math—senior high

To be creative—able to express oneself.
> High-track English—senior high

The most important thing—think more logically when they leave.
> High-track Math—senior high

Ability to think and use information.

Concept development.
> High-track Science—senior high

Ability to think for themselves,
> High-track Science—senior high

How to evaluate—think objectively. To think logically and with clarity and to put it on paper. To be able to appreciate a variety of authors' works and opinions without judging them by their own personal standards.
> High-track English—senior high

Confidence in their own thoughts.
> High-track English—senior high

Able to collect and organize information. Able to think critically.
> High-track Social Science—junior high

Determine best approach to problem solving. Recognize different approaches.
> High-track Math—senior high

That their own talents and thoughts are important. Development of imagination. Critical thinking.
> High-track English—senior high

Problem-solving situations—made to think for themselves. Realizing importance of their education and use of time. Easy way is not always the best way.
> High-track Science—senior high

Better feeling for their own abilities and sense of what it's like in a college course.
> High-track Math—senior high

To gain some interpretive skills.
> High-track English—senior high

Teachers of low-track classes said the following kinds of learnings were essential for their students:

Develop more self-discipline—better use of time.
Low-track English—junior high

Respect for each other
Low-track Math—junior high

I want them to respect my position—if they'll get this, I'll be happy.
Low-track Math—junior high

That they know that their paychecks will be correct when they receive them. Punctuality, self-discipline and honesty will make them successful in their job. They must begin and end each day with a smile. To be able to figure their own income tax (at the) end of the year. Properly planning to insure favorable performances.
Low-track Math—senior high

Self-discipline, cooperativeness, and responsibility.
Low-track Science—junior high

I teach personal hygiene—to try to get the students to at least be aware of how to keep themselves clean.
Low-track Vocational Education—junior high

Independence—start and complete a task on their own.
Low-track English—senior high

Responsibility of working with people without standing over them.
Low-track Science—senior high

Ability to use reading as a tool—e.g., how to fill out forms, write a check, get a job.
Low-track English—junior high

How to fill out insurance forms. Income tax returns.
Low-track Math—senior high

Understanding the basic words to survive in a job. Being able to take care of their own finances—e.g., banking, income tax, etc. Being able to prepare for, seek and maintain a job. To associate words with a particular job.
Low-track English—senior high

To be able to work with other students. To be able to work alone. To be able to follow directions.
Low-track English—junior high

Socialization—retarded in social skills.
                              Low-track English—junior high

How to cope with frustration.
                              Low-track English—junior high

Business-oriented skills—how to fill out a job application.
                              Low-track English—junior high

More mature behavior (less outspoken).
                              Low-track Science—junior high

Respect for their fellow man (students and teachers).
                              Low-track Science—junior high

Learn to work independently—use a sense of responsibility.
                              Low-track Science—senior high

Content—minimal. Realistic about goals. Develop ones they *can* achieve.
                              Low-track Science—senior high

Practical math skills for everyday living. A sense of responsibility.
                              Low-track Math—senior high

To learn how to follow one set of directions at a time, take a directive order and act upon it.
                              Low-track Social Science—junior high

Life skills. Work with checking account.
                              Low-track Math—junior high

Good work habits.
                              Low-track Math—junior high

Respect. Growth in maturity.
                              Low-track Math—junior high

It is obvious from these answers that among those learning outcomes teachers desire for their students are attitudes and behaviors not specifically related to the content areas. This is not surprising since, historically, our society has asked schools to do far more than provide academic learnings for students. Schools have been expected to transform the young into contributing members of society, imbue them with a strong commitment to our cultural ideals, increase their skills in interpersonal relationships, and contribute to their physical and mental well-being, to name only a few of their responsibilities.[5]

Knowing this, when we asked teachers during interviews to name the five most critical things they wanted their students to learn during their year with them, we expected that they would list nonacademic as well as academic learning goals. As we have just seen, many of them did. Among the senior high English classes we studied, thirty-seven teachers (45 percent) mentioned these non-subject-related behaviors as instructional goals or content and twenty-six teachers (35 percent) of junior high–middle school English classes included these types of learnings. Similar percentages of the math teachers included non-subject-related behaviors as topics of instruction or as desired learnings. At the senior high level, thirty-five teachers (49 percent) and at the junior high level, twenty-eight teachers (41 percent) included these behaviors as instructional content. Throughout the discussion of these responses it should be borne in mind that they represent only about half of the high school classes and about a third of the junior high–middle school classes we studied.

Two types of nonacademic learnings were mentioned most frequently by these teachers—one concerning desired student behaviors in the area of personal deportment, the other regarding desired behaviors considered part of the learning process or necessary to carry out class procedures. We analyzed these statements first by classifying them into one of the following categories: (1) statements indicating that the teacher was seeking student autonomy and independence (e.g., "confidence in own thoughts"); (2) statements indicating that the teacher encouraged student conformity to teacher authority and established classroom routines (e.g., "learn to follow directions accurately and promptly"); and (3) statements indicating that both types of behaviors were encouraged or statements difficult to interpret as distinctly belonging to either of the previous two categories (e.g., "self-discipline" was a response that could mean either independent or conforming behavior).

The two lists below give some examples of the kinds of learning teachers hoped for that were classified into the first two categories:

1. *independence*
   critical thinking
   work on individual projects or assignments
   self-direction
   creativity
2. *conformity*
   getting along with others
   working quietly
   improving study habits
   punctuality—both in attendance and handing in assignments

cooperation
conforming to rules and expectations

We looked then at the ways in which these non-subject-specific learning goals were distributed among track levels. We found in most of the classes we studied that students in different track levels were expected to learn different kinds of behaviors that were not actually related to the subjects they were studying.

Among the English classes, both the junior and senior high school teachers who emphasized non-subject-related learnings expected different kinds of behaviors from their high- and low-track students. We found that teachers of high-track classes were more likely to emphasize such behaviors as critical thinking, independent work, active participation, self-direction, and creativity than were other teachers. At the same time, teachers of low-track classes were more likely than others to emphasize student conformity: students getting along with one another, working quietly, improving study habits, being punctual, and conforming to classroom rules and expectations. This pattern was also found among senior high math teachers. At the junior high level, math teachers did not systematically differ in their behavioral expectations of students. From the responses of these teachers to our question, it seems that most of them wanted both independence and compliance from their students rather than strongly emphasizing one over the other. Average classes were closer to the high than to the low tracks in this respect as well as in content. Teachers of average groups (except in junior high math) tended to have "independent" student behaviors as their goals far more than did teachers of low groups. The low groups stood apart from the other kinds of classes in their teachers' emphasis on conformity and passive compliance.

Apparently many teachers were able to effect this learning in their students. At least we know that many students reported non-subject-related behaviors as the most important things they learned or did in class. And, as is clearly seen in the following responses, the pattern of differences found in teachers' learning goals for students at different track levels are also reflected in what students say they learned.

QUESTION: What is the most important thing you have learned or done so far in this class?

High-track students named the following kinds of things:

RESPONSES: I have learned to form my own opinions on situations. I have
also learned to not be swayed so much by another person's
opinion but to look at both opinions with an open mind. I
know now that to have a good solid opinion on a subject I
must have facts to support my opinion. Decisions in later
life will probably be made easier because of this.

High-track English—senior high

I've learned to study completely, and to know everything
there is to know.

High-track English—senior high

I have learned to speak in front of a group of people, and
not be scared to death of everyone.

High-track English—senior high

To know how to communicate with my teachers like friends
and as teachers at the same time. To have confidence in
myself other than my skills and class work.

High-track English—junior high

I have learned to be creative and free in doing things.

High-track English—senior high

I have learned how to make hard problems easier to solve.

High-track Math—senior high

The most important thing I have learned in this class this
quarter is how to express my feelings.

High-track English—senior high

How to organize myself and present an argument.

High-track English—senior high

I'm learning how to communicate with large groups of people.

High-track English—senior high

The most important thing I have learned or done in this
class is I now have the ability to be able to speak in front of
a crowd without being petrified, as I was before taking this
class.

High-track English—senior high

I want to be a lawyer and debate has taught me to dig for
answers and get involved. I can express myself.

High-track English—senior high

The most important thing I have learned is how to speak in
front of a group of people with confidence.

High-track English—senior high

I have learned how to argue in a calm and collected way.
High-track English—senior high

How to express myself through writing and being able to compose the different thoughts in a logical manner; this is also a class where I may express my creativity.
High-track English—senior high

Learned to think things out. Like in a book I learned to try and understand what the author is really saying to find the author's true thoughts.
High-track English—senior high

I've learned to look into depth of certain things and express my thoughts on paper.
High-track English—senior high

The most important thing I have learned in this class is to loosen up my mind when it comes to writing. I have learned to be more imaginative.
High-track English—senior high

How to present myself orally and how to listen and to think quick.
High-track English—senior high

To understand concepts and ideas and experiment with them. Also, to work independently.
High-track Science—senior high

My instructor has opened a whole new world for me in this class, I truly enjoy this class. He has given me the drive to search and find out answers to questions. If there is one thing that I have learned from this class it would have to be the want for learning.
High-track Social Studies—senior high

It taught us how to think in a logical way to work things out with a process of elimination.
High-track Math—senior high

I have learned that in high school the English classes treat you more like an adult.
High-track English—senior high

I have proved to myself that I have the discipline to take a difficult class just for the knowledge, even though it has nothing to do with my career plans.
High-track Math—senior high

I have learned that I have a wider span of imagination than

I thought. I have also learned to put how I feel and what I feel into words and explain them better.

High-track English—senior high

Many times in this class I get wrong answers, but in this class you learn to learn from your mistakes, also that even if you do have a wrong answer you should keep trying and striving for that correct answer. This, along with the subject I have learned from this class, and I think it's very important.

High-track Math—senior high

How to think and reason logically and scientifically.

High-track Math—senior high

I think the most important thing I've done in this class is exercise my brain. To work out problems logically so I can learn to work out problems later in life logically.

High-track Math—senior high

Brains work faster and faster.

High-track Math—senior high

Learning about how others respond and act—what makes them do the things they do—talking about relations, and how happenings in earlier life can affect children when they are growing up. The class discussions make it really interesting and the teacher startles us sometimes because he can really understand things from our point of view.

High-track Social Science—senior high

The most important thing that I have learned in this class is the benefit of logical and organized thinking, learning is made much easier when the simple processes of organizing thoughts have been grasped.

High-track Math—senior high

Low-track students were more likely to give answers like these:

Behave in class.

Low-track English—junior high

I have learned that I should do my questions for the book when he asks me to.

Low-track Science—senior high

Self-control.

Low-track Social Studies—junior high

Manners.

Low-track English—junior high

How to shut up.
> Low-track Vocational Education—junior high

The most important thing I have learned in this class is to always have your homework in and have materials ready whenever she is ready.
> Low-track Vocational Education—senior high

Write and getting my homework done.
> Low-track English—junior high

Working on my Ps and Qs.
> Low-track English—junior high

I think the most important is coming into class and getting our folders and going to work.
> Low-track Math—junior high

I have learned about many things like having good manners, respecting other people, not talking when the teacher is talking.
> Low-track English—junior high

Learned to work myself.
> Low-track Math—junior high

I learned about being quiet when the teacher is talking.
> Low-track Social Studies—junior high

To learn how to listen and follow the directions of the teacher.
> Low-track Math—senior high

I learn to respect the teacher.
> Low-track Vocational Education—junior high

Learn to get along with the students and the teacher.
> Low-track English—junior high

How to go through a cart and find a folder by myself.
> Low-track Math—junior high

To be a better listener in class.
> Low-track English—senior high

In this class, I have learned manners.
> Low-track English—junior high

What are the implications of these findings? Unfortunately, the data themselves don't tell us. But it seems important to consider the possible meanings of these trends. Why would teachers of adolescents considered to be of low ability or achievement consider learning to be "less outspoken," or to "cope with frustration," or to "keep themselves clean," or to "begin and end each day with a smile," or to "take a directive order and act upon it" as among the five most *critical* things students should learn during the year? Of course, not every low-track teacher said these kinds of things, but many did. And further, teachers of high-track classes tended *not* to have these kinds of goals for their students.

Are these behaviors that we know are necessary for remediating deficiencies in student achievement? That is, by acquiring these behaviors, are "slow" students more likely to catch up with their average or most able peers? I know of no evidence that suggests that these behaviors enhance students' dispositions to learn or their ability to do so.

Why, then, are these behaviors desired for slow students? And, also important, why are they *not* among the learning goals for bright ones? Do smart students already possess compliant and passive behavior patterns? If so, are these attributes a part of what makes them appear smart to school people? This also seems unlikely; we do not generally judge passive, compliant, "not outspoken" people to be bright *because* of these characteristics. And even if it were the case, why would teachers of average and especially high-achieving groups of students want what seems to be almost the opposite type of behaviors to be learned by their classes? Why instead of passivity do such teachers seek independence and autonomy in their students? Why do they hope for creativity and critical thinking?

Some possibilities come to mind. First, we might reasonably speculate that low-track students are perceived as unmanageable by their teachers. The thought of thirty or more potentially unmanageable students together in a classroom can certainly lead teachers to value control over anything else, even academic learning. And it seems clear that the behavioral goals for low classes are more closely linked to control than they are to learning. Of course, learning course content is certainly more likely in a situation that is not characterized by chaos. But are slow students in fact characteristically unmanageable? Does classroom misbehavior constitute a part of low ability or achievement? Or, and this seems more likely, are unmanageable students often labeled slow and placed in low-track classes regardless of their academic aptitude? Schools make very few efforts to distinguish between students who are poor achievers because they lack skills or even aptitude and those who are low achievers because of disruptive behavior or poor attendance. What happens, it seems, is that we may saddle those who find it hard to learn with those who find it hard to behave. What does this possibility say about the chances for slow students to learn in class? And, further, doesn't it follow that the reason high-track classes almost never have to concern themselves with issues of control may be that disruptive students are almost always selected out and sent to low classes, regardless of their "ability"?

This prospect leads us to another frightening possibility. If teachers and schools tend to associate misbehavior and nonconformity with "slowness" and place students accordingly, are these perceptions more often made about poor and minority students? We know that these students are more often found in low tracks. Could this be partly because they are perceived as less easily controlled, less conforming, and more in need of learning passivity and compliance? Could some of teachers' fears, if indeed they are at work here, be based on racial, cultural, or social-class differences? These are questions that need to be considered seriously.

A third possibility has to do with the schools' perceived mission to prepare the young for roles in adult society. Part of what students are taught in school is a set of behaviors that will make them suitable for the places they will hold in society as adults. Is it possible that the non-subject-related behaviors teachers have as learning goals for their students are the kinds of behaviors they think the students will need as adults? If this is the case, even if only partly so, the implications are serious for all students. And when we consider how students end up sorted by race and class in schools, the consequences for the futures of poor and minority students may be especially devastating.

Could it be that we are teaching kids at the bottom of the educational hierarchy—who are more likely to be from poor and minority groups—behaviors that will prepare them to fit in at the lowest levels of the social and economic hierarchy? And, at the other extreme, are we teaching kids at the top of the schooling stratification system behaviors that are most appropriate for professional and leadership roles? In essence, are we teaching kids at the bottom how to stay there and kids at the top how to get ahead?

When we look at the differences in these non-subject-related learning goals next to the differences in curricular content, we see similar patterns. Students are being exposed to knowledge and taught behaviors that differ not only educationally but in socially important ways. Students at the top are exposed to the knowledge that is highly valued in our culture, knowledge that identifies its possessors as "educated." This knowledge, too, is that which permits access to certain educational futures—specifically, college or university attendance. And, of course, the credentials resulting from higher education are required for access to upper-level social and economic positions in the adult world. Similarly, the non-subject-related behaviors that teachers have as learning goals for high-track students are those that are highly valued in our society. Behavior patterns such as independent and critical thinking, creativity, and questioning have a certain status in our culture. We see these as attributes of leaders, of decision makers; in short, we see them as qualities we admire in smart people at the top.

The knowledge and behaviors taught to low-track students are, for the most part, of another sort altogether. It's not that they are not *valued* at all but rather that they have little exchange value in a social or economic sense; they have no prestige, nor do they permit special access. Everyone, for example, needs to acquire functional literacy and computation skills, not so much for the benefit of the individual as for the functioning of society as a whole. Students who have access only to this low-prestige knowledge are being denied, by omission, access to both educationally and socially important learnings. Further, the non-subject-related behaviors that teachers expect low-track students to learn are of a similar type. While necessary to keep the social system functioning smoothly, behavior patterns such as following directions, good work habits, punctuality, being realistic about goals, and so forth are not those attributes we most admire in our leaders. They are, however, those we demand from people in lower-level occupations. Teachers say they believe tracking helps them better meet the individual needs of students. Are these the kinds of things they see as differing needs? I expect not. It is likely that teachers *intend* to adapt instruction to differences in students' learning styles and learning speeds. What they *effect* with differentiated curricular content, however, appears to be of another sort altogether.

This, of course, is somewhat speculative. But, at the same time, we would be foolish to ignore these possibilities. Whenever we sort students in schools and treat them differently, we need to examine all the possible effects of these practices. We cannot merely assume that strictly educative mechanisms and purposes are being exercised. The possibility that what goes on in classes at different track levels may have different social and economic effects is a theme we will return to repeatedly as we continue to explore these 299 classes.

5

Opportunities to Learn

Even if teenagers in classes at different track levels are exposed to identical curricular contents, differences in classroom conditions can create important differences in what they learn. Most people would readily agree that what knowledge students are exposed to is important in determining the quality of education they obtain. But probably as critical in the access students have to learning in schools are the conditions they encounter there. School and classroom situations can either enhance or restrict the chances that students will learn whatever content is presented. I am convinced, in fact, that certain critical features of the schooling context may actually constitute students' opportunities to learn.[1]

In this chapter we will look carefully at two of those classroom conditions—time to learn and quality of instruction—that appear to influence strongly whether student learning is likely to occur. We will also examine how these conditions differed in our sample of tracked math and English classes. The differences we found were marked—enough so that we believe they provided students in various track levels with greater and lesser learning opportunities.[2] And given the vast content differences we found between high- and low-track classes, these classroom differences served to further widen the gap between the prospects of various groups of students—their chances to get the best education our schools had to offer.

Before looking at these school-based differences, however, we must clarify two important premises underlying our interpretation of what we

93

found. First, the differences students bring with them to classrooms—differences in attitudes, interests, and abilities—are clearly important influences on the kind of learning experiences they have there. In fact, it seems that a great deal of what teachers do in the classroom is in response to these kinds of student characteristics. But even by early adolescence, it is almost impossible to sort out the degree to which differences among students are produced by home or cultural backgrounds, exaggerated by the schools' various responses to them, or influenced by an interaction of home and school factors. Although there are some who do not hesitate to address this question with an aura of authority, we do not claim to be able to unravel this tangle of what we believe are probably reciprocal cause-and-effect relationships. And second, while the source of individual differences is certainly an important issue, what we want to emphasize here are the educational effects of these differences. We know that the learning *opportunities* teachers are able or willing to create in classrooms are affected in some ways by their perceptions of the characteristics of the groups of students they encounter. What is often overlooked, however, is the fact that classroom differences in learning opportunities are to a large extent institutionally created and perpetuated by the process of placing seemingly similar students together for instruction—by tracking. So here, for the purpose of analyzing track-level differences and the possible inequities they reflect and produce, the issue of perceived constraints imposed by student differences is only secondary. Primary are the educational conditions that result. What happens if different kinds of classrooms systematically provide students with different kinds of learning experiences? Do these differences mean that some kinds of students have greater opportunities to learn than others? And if these differences coincide with differences in racial and social characteristics of students, what do these practices say about how our American ideal of equal educational opportunity is being played out in the schools?

In this chapter, then, we look again at the tracked English and math classes in the Study of Schooling sample, with respect to a few classroom characteristics that are emerging more and more strongly as powerful school-based determinants of student learning: how time is allocated, how students use this allocated time, and the quality of the instruction provided by teachers within it. In this chapter, too, we ask questions about the equity of what we find. And, perhaps not surprisingly, we conclude that in these rather specific ways, the important content differences discussed in the preceding chapter were matched by parallel differences in important conditions of schooling for students in different track levels. In this way, the inequality in exposure to the most highly valued school knowledge was exacerbated by unequal opportunities to learn.

Time to Learn

Time as an aspect of learning is so obvious that it has been pretty much taken for granted. Recently, however, time in classrooms has begun to emerge in the minds of many educational scholars as the pivotal element in instructional effectiveness. While certainly we have all known in some common sense way that how much someone learns is infleunced by how much time he or she spends learning it, only in the past dozen or so years has this been studied in any systematic way. As it turns out, when researchers began to define learning and classroom time precisely and study it carefully, some fairly important if predictable results were obtained.

Studies of time and its relationship to learning have ranged from looking at fairly obvious and easy to measure indicators of how much time is scheduled for instruction to researching some rather complex constructs such as how much time each student in a class spends actively engaged in learning. These latter studies have required methodological sophistication and often high levels of inference. All are important, however, as they provide insight into just how time and learning relate to one another.

Although the results of these time studies will probably not come as a great surprise, it seems useful to review what has been learned from them since they are relevant to the focus of this chapter. By doing so we will have a basis for interpreting how differences in time relate to opportunities to learn in various track levels in schools. This, however, will be only a brief review of a substantial research literature. Those who want to know more are directed to the studies listed in the notes to this chapter.

While time seems to be obviously related to learning, what we know about the nature and importance of this relationship is not entirely straightforward. It is dependent on many considerations such as how the time being studied is defined and whose time (schools', teachers', or learners') is being measured.

At probably the simplest level—scheduled school time—the actual length of school days at the elementary level and of class periods at secondary schools has been examined to determine whether any differences could be related to student achievement. First, these studies found that for subjects like reading—and we can presume for mathematics too, the most basic school subjects—the length of time scheduled by schools did not account for variations in average student achievement among the classes studied.[3]

The results, however, do not necessarily indicate that how much time students spend in school is unrelated to achievement. In studies where student attendance rates have been included along with scheduled time indicators (length of school days and length of school year), the results are not so conclusive. Some of this work has found a strong association between this kind of time and learning.

For example, Wiley and Harnischfeger found that when the average daily student attendance, length of the school day, and length of the school year were considered together in relation to student achievement, schools that provided a greater "quantity of schooling" for the typical student also had considerably higher average student achievement.[4] However, these kinds of studies have not shown consistent results.[5]

At all the schools we studied, high-track classes were of the same duration as low-track classes. Clearly, then, we cannot claim that students in one track had greater or lesser opportunities to learn because they were scheduled for longer or shorter class periods during the school day to learn what they were supposed to. But a tracking issue related to these studies is that of differences in learning among individuals who attend the same school for different amounts of time. It is very likely that the hours of instruction each year per student are systematically different for high- and low-track students as a result of their attendance patterns. Some studies have indicated that minority children get less schooling than do whites because of their lower attendance rates and high incidence of dropping out of school altogether.[6] Here again, however, we run into the sticky issue of who is responsible for this variation. But the fact remains: those who need school the most are likely to be getting the least of it in terms of quantity of schooling. Number of hours spent may at least partially account for differences in achievement outcomes.

The inconsistencies in these studies of scheduled time lead us to another not too startling hypothesis: what makes a difference in student learning is not so much how much time is set aside for learning a subject but, rather, how the available time is spent. Studies have been made of the proportion of available class time allocated by the teacher to learning as opposed to classroom routines such as preparation, roll taking, and clean-up; socializing; and getting students to behave; as well as the amount of time when virtually nothing is going on—what we might call wasted time. These studies have produced some interesting, if predictable, findings. In some studies actual class time devoted to reading and math activities as opposed to nonacademic concerns has been found to be related to student learning in these subjects.[7] However, other studies of this type have found the mere number of minutes allocated to instruction in subjects within classes to be an insignificant factor in explaining differences in actual learning.[8]

But time allocated to learning within classes does turn out to be quite important when the concept of time is taken one step further—that is, when we look at the actual amount of class time in which students are engaged in or attending to academic tasks. In this concept of time and learning, the only time that counts for student learning is that in which students are *actively involved* in the process. Several recent research efforts have yielded some important findings. Not surprisingly, academic learning time, time-on-task, or student-engaged time, as it is variously called, has been found to have a strong and consistent relationship with student learning. In fact, some have called it the critical instructional variable in accounting for differences in student learning.[9]

This, of course, does not mean that allocated instructional time is an unimportant factor in learning. To the contrary, the number of students' engaged minutes is limited by and restricted at the maximum to the number of minutes allocated to learning activities by the teacher. In most research on active learning time in classrooms, it has been found that the greater the time allocated to learning, the greater the amount of student-engaged time that occurs.[10] So while allocated instructional time in itself may not be sufficient to provide for student achievement, it is certainly necessary.

There are some fairly obvious, yet difficult, problems with ascertaining the amount of time students spend actually engaged in academic tasks or actively learning. First, what may look to the teacher or an outside observer as attention to task—reading, completing a worksheet, listening to a teacher or another student—may, in fact, constitute a very different activity for a student. For some, their full attention may be concentrated on the academic task; for others, such behaviors may really indicate only partial attentiveness; and for still others, academic posturing in some of these activities may conceal minds wandering far from the task at hand. Even with the same student, observable engaged behaviors may at different times represent different degrees of attentiveness. So there are some measurement problems associated with this academic-learning-time variable. Even so, it, along with content covered in class, currently hold the most promise for predicting what and how much will be learned by students.

In A Study of Schooling we looked at time in a number of ways that relate to classroom differences in different tracks—one of them, as noted earlier, the length of secondary class periods. Because they varied by school rather than by track—except in vocational education classes, as we will see later—we concluded that, at the secondary school level at least, students in various tracks were expected to spend about the same amount of time in English and math classes.

A second way we looked at time and learning was through the perceptions of teachers. Each teacher was asked how much of the total class time was spent in each of the following activities: (1) instruction or learning activities, (2) student behavior and discipline, (3) classroom routines, and (4) purely social activity. These estimates probably reflect both what teachers intended to have happen and what they perceived as the realities of their classrooms. The estimates were important to us because they represent an informed judgment that took into consideration day-to-day variations over the course of the entire school year. Teachers reported that the following percentages of time were spent on instruction in their classrooms:

	Instruction
High-track English	82%
High-track Math	77%
Low-track English	71%
Low-track Math	63%

Taken together, teachers of high-track classes estimated that about 80 percent of the class time was spent on instruction, and teachers of low-track classes, about 67 percent. Although 13 percentage points does not seem like a very large difference, the disparity becomes clearer if we convert these percentages to actual class time. If we assume that the average class period is 50 minutes in length, high-track students, according to their teachers, spent about 40 minutes in instruction in each of the two subjects. Given an average of 180 school days per year, this totals about 14,400 minutes per year, or about 240 hours. The figures for the low track, on the other hand, are 33½ instructional minutes per day in each subject, a total of 12,060 minutes per school year or about 201 hours. Taken together, then, students who are placed in high-track classes over their six years of secondary schooling—and we know that most placements are stable—would experience 1,400 hours of classroom instruction in the two most basic subjects. Students in low tracks, in contrast, would experience, on the average, 1,206 hours. The difference, nearly 240 hours of classroom instruction, is what most colleges constitute as 12 semester units of study—not an inconsequential amount.

Of course, these are merely approximations for what actually happens. Not everyone goes to school every day. Not everyone takes six years of English; fewer still study six years of math. But we know already that low-track students—especially minorities—have lower attendance rates and are more likely to drop out before high school graduation. We know too that high-track students, most of whom are fulfilling entrance requirements for colleges and universities, are far more likely to take six years of English and math than are even those in low-track classes who finish their high school education. Low-track students probably take just enough to meet graduation requirements, usually five years of English, but often only three years of math beyond grade six. So while the differences in our estimates of time spent in classroom instruction in English and math over students' secondary school careers are merely that, estimates, they are probably conservative ones. In all likelihood the quantity of instruction differences for high- and low-track teenagers is greater than these figures indicate.

Another look at classroom time was made by trained observers used in the Study of Schooling classrooms.[11] Among other things, they recorded the "actual" proportion of time allocated to instruction, behavior, routines, and social activities. The observers' focus was on the teacher, and their reports indicate how much time teachers spent in each of the four kinds of classroom processes. Focusing on the teacher might result in overestimating the amount of instructional time, since students may not always be paying attention during instruction. On the other hand, this teacher focus could be expected to underestimate instructional time since some students may be engaged in learning when the teaching is involved in something other than instruction.[12] We might suspect that this kind of overestimation of time would be more likely to occur in low-track classes and underestimation more likely in high-track classes, making the two track levels seem more similar than they might actually be in learning time. But when comparing classes, especially differences among *groups* of classes, both of these kinds of errors may occur simultaneously within a class or cancel each other out across groups. Therefore, we can probably use these observations as a reasonable, if conservative, measure for assessing classroom and track-level differences in *allocated* instructional time. Later we will consider some factors that will bring us closer to estimates of the relative time students spend actually engaged in learning.

The proportions of time *observed* to be devoted to instruction also differed with track level. Taken over three days of observation in each classroom studied, these observer perceptions help substantiate the reports of the teachers:

	Instruction
High-track English	81%
High-track Math	81%
Low-track English	75%
Low-track Math	78%

These observers' reports point to differences in the same direction as the teachers' perceptions, although the differences are considerably smaller. Even during our observation period—when it is not unlikely that teachers were attempting their instructional best—low-track students were getting less.

We measured one other dimension of allocated instructional time in A Study of Schooling: teachers' expectations of how much time students in their classes should spend on homework. This out-of-school learning time should add to the understanding of how much total learning time is allocated to students in English and math. Track-level differences in these teacher expectations help complete the picture of differences in the amount of allocated time for learning. Teachers of the four groups of classes reported expectations for homework time that were consistent with their allocation of instructional time in the classroom.

Average Expected Homework Time

High-track English classes	42 minutes
High-track Math classes	38 minutes
Low-track English classes	13 minutes
Low-track Math classes	27 minutes

Again the pattern of difference is clear, although more so in English than in math classes—more time for fast students, less time for slow.

These three measures of allocated time—teachers' estimates over the entire year, observers' records over three class periods, and teachers' expectations for time spent on homework—make clear the differences in one of the conditions necessary for student learning. As we saw earlier, other studies have established that those classes where more time is *allocated* to learning are also those in which more active student learning takes place. So we know from these statistics that the proportion of time in which students were actually *engaged* in learning is likely to differ in the same direction.

Two other pieces of information about A Study of Schooling classes help to establish the probable existence of engaged-time differences among track levels. First, we have an assessment made by the classroom observers of the average percentage of students who, although expected to be involved in an instructional activity, were in fact off-task. By off-task we mean that students were engaged in some *observable* activity not related to learning. Again, this is undoubtedly a conservative estimate, since many students whose minds are far from the learning activity at hand can appear to observers to be engaged. These figures, therefore, include only those students who were conspicuously off-task.

	Average % Off-task
High-track English	2%
High-track Math	1%
Low-track English	4%
Low-track Math	4%

These differences, while quite small, add to the accumulating evidence of less learning time for low- than for high-track students. For if less time is allocated, and within that time fewer students are displaying outward signs of attentiveness, we can be certain that less active learning time occurs in low-track classes. Admittedly, these off-task percentages are small in all four groups. At least three explanations for this are possible. First, we might speculate that nearly all students in the Study of Schooling classrooms were attentive during periods of instruction because this was their usual pattern of behavior. Second, it is possible that students were more likely to display attentive behaviors in class while our observers were present. And third, it may be that inattentiveness is difficult to observe because it is more often a passive withdrawal from the activity, really an inner state more than overt behavior. In fact, our observers were asked to look only for such overt activities as reading comic books or teasing neighbors as indications of students being off-task. While all three of these are possible explanations for our small percentages, my hunch is that the last two are the most likely. We can probably be confident of the relative differences among the groups of classes. Small as the percentages are, in both subject areas a greater proportion of students were observed to be off-task in low- than in high-track classes.

Possibly a more accurate view of the differences in students' engagement in learning in classes at different track levels can be gained from the perceptions of students themselves about what they do in their classes. As a part of the survey we gave the students we asked them the following question:

In this class, how much time is usually taken by the following three things?

(1) Daily routines (passing out materials, taking attendance, making announcements)
(2) Learning
(3) Getting students to behave

Students were asked to rank the three types of activity in terms of the amount of time they occupied. While this is obviously not a direct measure of active student learning, it does give us some evidence as to how the students believe they spend their time in class. This is useful because it reflects the attitudes of the learners themselves.

We aggregated these responses (coding "most time" as 3, "next most" as 2, and "least" as 1) at the class level and then averaged across classes within tracks for each activity. A score of 2.5 to 3 indicates that the average response was "most time," a score of 1.5 to 2.4 "next most," and a score of 1 to 1.5 "least." Track-level averages were as follows:

	Average Responses for Learning
High-track English classes	2.80
High-track Math classes	2.77
Low-track English classes	2.44
Low-track Math classes	2.53

The high-track students, without a doubt, saw learning as the activity that occupied most of their class time. And, while not as unequivocally, so did low-track math classes. However, taking the two subjects together, the two tracks seem distinctly different—high-track classes saying that learning usually takes up most of their class time, low-track classes reporting that learning is second to something else. What that something else is likely to be in low-track classes becomes clearer when we look at the responses students made for "getting students to behave."

	Average Responses for Behavior
High-track English classes	1.48[a]
High-track Math classes	1.43
Low-track English classes	1.83
Low-track Math classes	1.81

[a] It should be remembered that because we are using aggregated data it is possible to have more than one activity fall within the same range, even though each student was to rank order the three activities.

These responses indicate that while high-track students believed getting students to behave took the least time, low-track students saw it as taking the "next most" amount of time—not quite as much as learning but within the same range. Interpreted broadly, this means that students in low-track classes perceived that more time was taken away from learning to deal with student behavior problems in class than did high-track students. For this to be the case we can assume a greater incidence of off-task behavior in these classes. We might, then, interpret these responses as low-track students telling us that students are inattentive in class and that time is spent on getting them to behave (which we might translate as "become engaged in learning") rather than on learning itself. Students in high-track classes do not seem to be reporting this same set of circumstances.

Taken together, these various measures show that, without question, low-track classes have considerably less of both the necessary and the sufficient elements of classroom time for student learning. Regardless of the causes of these differences, regardless of whether the students or the teachers or something else entirely is to blame, the actual circumstances of schooling are such that these differences, in themselves, constitute an educational injustice if we believe that active student learning time is one of the most critical school-based contributions to achievement outcomes.

But further, most scholars and teachers recognize that the absolute amount of engaged time itself does not constitute the whole explanation for differences in student learning. Most recognize that the time needed to learn skills and concepts (what is sometimes called learning rate) varies considerably among students. It is interesting that Benjamin Bloom, using mastery learning techniques, has found that these differences among students in learning rate decrease dramatically as slow learners experience success.[13] Nevertheless, these differences do exist, and probably the more accurate explanations of classroom learning take them into account. For example, Carroll's model of learning suggests that the amount of learning is a function of both the time actually spent on the task and the time needed by the learner to master it.[14] Carroll and others hypothesize that the time needed is influenced by a learner's general aptitude, his or her ability to understand instruction, and the quality of the instruction itself. The first two factors are characteristics of the learner, but not necessarily independent of schools. The culture of the school, reflecting white middle-class language and behavior patterns, often is not congruent with the language and cultural patterns familiar to other groups. This cultural mismatch may be reflected in the school's assessment of poor and minority students' general aptitude or ability to understand instruction as much as any innate capacity to learn. In turn, this mismatch may also explain why many poor and minority children may need more time to learn skills and concepts in school than do middle-class white children. They may need to make a cross-cultural translation of language and behavior as well as engage in the usual learning processes. For some, this translation is probably never made successfully. And, of course, students who are perceived to be of lower general aptitude, with less ability to understand instruction—in short, slow—are those who are placed in low-track classes.

We can speculate, then, that these low-track students are placed in an educational double bind. Within schools, students cannot learn concepts, topics, and skills fully if they are allocated less time than they need. Further, if the time needed is longer for students who are usually placed in classes where the actual learning time is less, the chances for these students to achieve at a rate comparable to their peers are diminished. In fact, these circumstances are far more likely to widen the achievement differences among students than to narrow them.

But the characteristics of the students, in these learning models, are not the only determinants of the amount of time needed for learning. Both the student's ability to understand instruction and the quality of instruction provided—Carroll's second and third components of needed time—are characteristics that are either determined or influenced by schools themselves. The ability of students to understand instruction seems most likely a product of the interaction between what is presented in classrooms and students' perceptions of it. It can be argued that instruction can be made comprehensible and that the ability of various students to understand is closely related to whether instruction is made understandable to all kinds of students. This, of course, is related to Carroll's third determinant of learning time needed—the quality of instruction. This factor is clearly a property of teachers, classrooms, and schools and is entirely within the realm of their manipulation and control.

Quality of Instruction

Until recently, much of the thinking and research about instructional quality or effective teaching has focused almost exclusively on attributes and behaviors of teachers. Effective instruction has been seen as those teaching behaviors associated with student achievement, the tacit assumption being that if the two are found together consistently the behaviors are likely to have *caused* the learning. The cumulative result of a considerable body of research of this type is a list of about a half dozen teaching behaviors, each of which seemed to be positively related to increases in learning. Characteristics and behaviors typically included as effective instructional behaviors are: (1) clarity in teachers' presentation of lessons; (2) teachers' use of variety during lessons—including variety in the types of activities, materials, tests, and instructional procedures; (3) enthusiasm conveyed by teachers during instruction; (4) teachers being task oriented, achievement oriented, and businesslike; (5) teachers' avoidance of the use of strong criticism of students; and (6) teachers giving students exposure to the material that they were expected to learn, in other words, making the content of instruction consistent with the learning objective.[15] Unfortunately, although seemingly related to learning, none of these teacher behaviors has been shown to account for a very substantial proportion of the differences in student outcomes. And because this work simply identified relationships, we cannot be sure that these behaviors actually cause learning at all.

The seeming futility of this type of work—i.e., the lack of strong relationships or any substantial evidence of causality—has led to a rethinking of how instructional quality might be viewed. As a result, more recent work on factors relating to learning have looked at what students actually do in class rather than at how teachers behave. The time-on-task studies stemmed from this new focus. So, too, did our consideration in chapter 4 of what kinds of knowledge students encounter in their classrooms. What teachers do—instruction—is still seen as important in the learning process but in a somewhat different way. Teachers are seen as having a direct influence on learning through their allocation of classroom time and an indirect influence through the motivational effects of their own time usage on students' involvement with learning tasks.[16] In other words, what teachers do is likely to influence strongly what proportion of allocated instructional time students actually use as academic learning time. This student use of time, in turn, is what is directly related to learning. In this view, teaching behavior is seen as part of a more complex process—one in which students, under appropriate conditions, translate instructional stimuli into learning. Variations in student learning are explained by differences in this translation process among different students. The translation process is at least partly influenced by the kind of instructional condition students experience, part of which are teacher behaviors.[17] While this may seem overly complicated, the essential differences between the old and new views of the importance of teaching behaviors are these. We used to look at the direct link between teaching behaviors and learning outcomes—chiefly test scores. It was almost as if we believed that the behaviors caused the scores directly. Now the process is treated as more complex; the newer view attempts to account for what was previously overlooked—how students turn teacher behaviors into the learning that is reflected in outcome measures such as tests.

This newer concept of how teaching influences learning may help explain both the consistent relationships between the list of teaching behaviors presented above and student achievement, and the weakness of these relationships (i.e., their inability to explain a very substantial portion of the variation in student learning). These behaviors—clarity, variability, enthusiasm, task orientation, lack of strong criticism—may be *among* those features of a complex learning environment that motivate active student learning. And as we concluded earlier about allocated instructional time, these behaviors may in themselves be *necessary* but far from *sufficient* to provide the appropriate conditions for the degree or intensity of student engagement (and the translating processes that constitute it) necessary for markedly greater student achievement outcomes. Many other essential elements of the instructional context are undoubtedly at work as well.

Even given these limits on what we can conclude about the effects of teacher behaviors in classrooms, it is interesting to note that most of them seem to have been present in greater degrees in high-track classes than in low. By looking carefully at how these teaching behaviors differed among track levels, we can begin to see a pattern—a combination of factors—that adds greatly to our understanding of just how low-track students get less from school: less instructional time allocated, fewer teaching behaviors within the allocated time likely to motivate these students to translate allocated time into active learning time, and less time in which students are engaged in learning processes.

We measured some of these effective teacher behaviors in classrooms by having students note their level of agreement or disagreement with a series of statements describing their classrooms and teachers. The responses to statements relating to teacher enthusiasm, clarity (both verbal and organizational), variability, and punitiveness (criticism) were averaged within classes to obtain a "class score," or more properly a score given to the teacher on each of these behaviors by the class.[18]

Some other measures used in the study also shed light on the extent to which teachers exhibited these and other effective behaviors.[19]

We called the students' responses to the following three statements a "teacher enthusiasm" score:

This teacher seems to like being a teacher.
This teacher seems to enjoy what he or she is teaching.
The teacher seems bored in the classroom.

Interestingly, while all types of classes on the average saw their teachers as enthusiastic, scores were significantly higher in high- than in low-track classes. High-track classes expressed strong agreement; low-track classes only mildly agreed that their teachers were enthusiastic.

The following statements were used to measure whether teachers' verbal messages were clear to students:

This teacher uses words I can understand.
The teacher gives clear directions.
The students understand what the teacher is talking about.
I understand what the teacher is talking about.

On this most basic level of clarity, simple understanding of teachers' statements, there was little difference in responses among track levels. While high-track classes expressed *slightly* strong agreement with the statements, both groups expressed mild agreement. This was not the case, however, for perhaps a more essential kind of clarity in instruction—being clear about what is to be learned and what may be done in class. Students were asked to respond to the following: "This teacher tells us ahead of time what we are going to be learning about" and "Everyone in this class knows what we may or may not do." To both of these statements concerning the clarity of learning goals and classroom processes, high-track classes in English and math expressed significantly higher levels of agreement.

A third kind of clarity—regarding the organization of the classroom instructional process—also differed considerably between high- and low-track classes. The statements measuring this construct are very similar to what is often called *task orientation* in the teacher-effectiveness research. The scores of negative statements were reversed so that the higher the score, the more positive the response about the teacher or class.

We know exactly what we have to get done in this class.
We know why the things we are learning in this class are important.

The grades or marks I get in this class help me to learn better.

We don't know what the teacher is trying to get us to learn in this class.

Many students don't know what they're supposed to be doing during class.

This class is disorganized.

The grades or marks I get in this class have nothing to do with what I really know.

We have to learn things without knowing why.

Students know the goals of this class.

Things are well planned in this class.

Our teacher gives us good reasons for learning in this class.

This group of statements indicates the extent to which the classroom is organized by the teacher in a clear and task-oriented way. On this set of statements there were substantial differences in the responses of students in high- and low-track classes, with high-track classes agreeing more strongly that their teachers were clear and task oriented in their classroom processes.

We also asked students to respond to statements indicating how punitive teachers were in class. These statements constituted a "punitiveness" scale that allowed us to examine a teacher's use of what has been called strong criticism in traditional studies of teacher effectiveness and the occurrence of other very related negative teacher behaviors.

The teacher makes fun of some students.

This teacher hurts my feelings.

I'm afraid of this teacher.

The teacher punishes me unfairly.

The teacher makes fun of me.

The teacher gets mad when I ask a question.

While on the average none of the groups of students agreed that their teachers were terribly punitive, there were again distinct track-level differences on this dimension of the instructional environment. The level of disagreement with these negative statements about their teachers was significantly stronger among high-track students than among low. Since the teacher's use of strong criticism has been consistently found in other work to be negatively associated with student achievement, the relationship found in our data on teacher punitiveness is parallel to those found between track levels and the other teacher behaviors. Those characteristics that seem to be connected with student learning were much more evident in the high-track classes we studied than in the low.

Only the results for teacher variability were unclear. Responses to the statement "This teacher is willing to try different ways of doing things" and reports from students, teachers, and observers about the variety of materials, activities, and groupings of students used in class did not vary consistently with track levels. It appears that low-track classes may have experienced a greater variety of *materials* and high-track classes a greater variety of *activities,* but the results from our work are not entirely clear.

Nevertheless, the direction of nearly all the differences in teacher behaviors we measured was the same. The instructional environments of high-track classes were more characterized by a whole set of teacher behaviors thought to promote learning than were those of low-track classes. We suggested earlier that, given the most recent thinking about what elements of the classroom are essential in producing student learning, each of these teacher behaviors is probably important because it is likely to motivate students to spend the *allocated* instructional time in classrooms engaged in learning activities. The cumulative motivational effect of differences across this set of teacher behaviors could, in fact, be considerable.

These behaviors are not only likely to be motivators in the usual sense of the word—making students *want* to learn. It seems that at least some of these behaviors, especially clarity and task orientation, would affect the time students *need* to learn. Going back to Carroll's model of school learning, we recall that the ability to understand instruction is viewed as a factor in the time a student needs to learn. One of the ways teachers can make instruction understandable is by being clear about what is to be learned and about the classroom procedures to be followed. Both of these teaching behaviors were more characteristic of high- classes than of low. Thus it seems possible that teaching behaviors influenced student learning in two ways: as motivation for students to use allocated instructional time as engaged time, and as influences on the amount of time students needed to learn the material at hand. In both ways, high-track students appear to have benefited more than low from the behaviors of their teachers.

What about the kids in the middle, those placed in classes called average? We found, not unexpectedly, that on most of these dimensions of learning opportunity they tended to be somewhere between the high and low groups, usually about equally spaced between them. On one very important dimension, however, the average group was much more like high-track classes than low—teacher's expectations for homework time.

What does all this add up to? I stated at the outset of this chapter the conviction that certain critical features of the classroom context may actually constitute students' opportunities to learn whatever content is presented to them. Two of these critical features are the provision of time to learn and the quality of the instruction provided by teachers during this time. We have seen that these features of classrooms differed considerably in high and low tracks in the Study of Schooling secondary schools. And the direction of these differences was such that students in high-track classes seemed to have greater opportunities to learn than those in low-track classes.

We have seen that these differences taken together form a cycle of conditions that enhance opportunities for high-track students—more time set aside for learning by teachers, more actual class time observed to be taken up with learning activity, more time expected to be spent on homework, fewer students observed off-task, students' perceptions of learning as the thing they do most in class, and more of the kind of instructional practice that is likely to motivate students to learn and decrease the time needed to do so. We have also seen that conditions were such that low-track students' opportunities were more restricted in all these ways.

These differences in opportunities are compounded by the likelihood that the students who get less are those who need more time to learn. They are also those whose cultural and socioeconomic backgrounds require the best instructional quality to help bridge the gaps between school and home in language, behavior patterns, and attitudes—certainly one very important aspect of motivation. Students who are poor are the least likely to have educated parents and, therefore, the least likely to bring to school notions of how to do well there. They and minority students are the least likely to share the white middle-class culture of their teachers. They are, however, most likely to be found in low-track classes.

Students bring differences with them to school. Schools, most specifically through counselors and teachers, respond to these differences. These responses are such that the initial differences among students are likely to widen. Students seen as different are separated into different classes and then provided with vastly different kinds of knowledge and with markedly different opportunities to learn. It is in these ways that schools exacerbate the differences among the students who attend them. And it is through tracking that these educational differences are most blatantly carried out.

6

Classroom Climate

Certainly a great deal more happens in secondary school classrooms than the presentation of curricular content and the creation of opportunities for students to learn. Day after day thirty or so teenagers are grouped together in a relatively small boxlike space. One adult, the teacher, is charged with an almost unbelievably difficult task. He or she must first of all keep the group physically confined to its space. There must be order and usually quiet. And further, the teenagers there are expected to spend their time learning—learning what someone else has decided is important for them. Often what is to be learned would not rank high on a list of what the teenagers themselves would say is interesting or important to them. They might not choose to consider the topics and skills of their courses at all if left to their own devices.

We usually take all this for granted. Rarely do we step back to consider what a huge and difficult task teachers are expected to do. Nor do we think much about the substantial degree of cooperation and willingness to go along with what others expect of them adolescents demonstrate in their participation in classrooms. Essentially, we have in every classroom, even in "high-achieving" classrooms, a mutual process of teacher coercion and student compliance. But, as we all know, this process is manifested in very different ways in different classrooms. Some teachers coerce in subtle, almost invisible ways—which quickly give way to mutual, cooperative, positive interrelating—and others in an obviously authoritarian style. Some groups of students seem to be eager and enthusiastic participants. Others are clearly recalcitrant.

Involved in this process, certainly, is the quality of the relationships that develop between students and their teacher. Part of it too is the way the students feel about being with one another in class. And clearly the kind of roles students are expected to play in the learning process—whether they are expected to be actively engaged or passively receptive in their compliance with the learning activity—is involved as well. All these elements help to create the feeling tone of the classroom, the general atmosphere—what many have called the classroom climate.

A great deal of student and teacher attention and energy is spent on these aspects of classroom life—the feelings students have about what's going on, the kind of involvement they have with learning activities, and the kinds of relationships that develop among those who are together day after day. These elements may not be as obviously related to learning outcomes as is the knowledge that is presented or the time spent in learning activity or the quality of instruction in a classroom. But we all have an intuitive sense of how important feelings, involvement, relationships, and other elements of our environments are to all of us. The climate or atmosphere of the places we inhabit strongly influences what most of us do in them. This is certainly no less true in classrooms than it is anywhere else.

This chapter will consider some aspects of classroom climate—why they are important and how they were manifested in different track levels at our twenty-five schools. As with the curricular contents and the kinds of learning opportunities students had available to them, considerable differences were found in the quality of relationships and type of student involvement that characterized high- and low-track classes. In addition to describing these differences, we will look closely at what they are likely to mean to students in terms of their learning outcomes, how they might influence the ways students come to see themselves in relationship to social institutions, and how they are likely to affect the quality of everyday school life for students. These things will be related, as were students' access to knowledge and learning opportunities in earlier chapters, to the larger question of educational and social equality. For here again, what we discovered about how the quality of classroom life differed for high- and low-track classes in our sample adds to the growing picture of unequal educational experiences in these twenty-five American schools.

About the Climate of Classrooms

Realizing that the quality of life in institutional environments is likely to be important in terms of both what is accomplished and how people feel about being in those environments, some social scientists have begun to study institutional climates. A substantial amount of this work has focused on education environments—on both schools as educational institutions and classrooms as learning environments.

The climate of classrooms has been thought of by many of these researchers as the social and psychological forces that influence the social environment of the whole group and subgroups within classes.[1] These social and psychological forces have been seen as comprising three distinct but interacting dimensions. First are the relationships that develop in classroom life. This dimension includes how supportive teachers are of students, how students work together, the degree of affiliation or friendship they feel for one another, and finally, the way students participate in classroom activities. The second dimension is the goal-orientation and personal-development features of environments, which are generally thought of in classrooms as the task or academic orientation that exists there. The third dimension, the system-maintenance and change dimension, includes the degree to which classrooms are orderly and organized, how control is maintained in them, how much students are involved in classroom planning, and the amount of unusual and varying activities that occur there.[2]

We considered some of these features of class climate in chapter 5. Certainly the clarity of classroom organization and procedures and the task orientation of both teachers and students, which differed so markedly in high- and low-track classes, are a part of classroom climate. In this chapter our focus will turn to the relationship dimension of classrooms and to the kinds of involvement students have in their learning experiences. Before we look at the data, however, we need to consider the research done on the impact of climate on students. What evidence or theory do we have about its importance generally? Does it *really* matter what relationships in classrooms are like? What difference is it likely to make if students are more or less involved in what goes on? We will look at these questions in two ways. First we will consider how different classroom climates relate to academic student outcomes; then we will consider how different climates might affect the quality of life in schools for teenagers and in the adult social settings they may encounter in the future.

There is considerable evidence that differences in classroom climates do account for substantial differences in student learning. Several studies in a variety of subject areas have clearly established the relationship between particular psychological and social aspects of classroom life and student achievement in those subjects. For example, one rather comprehensive study of secondary classrooms in several subject areas (including physics, chemistry, biology, geography, mathematics, English literature, history, and French) found that, even when the measured intelligence of students was controlled, more learning took place in classes with a greater degree of intimacy among all classroom participants and an accompanying lack of cliquishness and friction among them. Also important in student learning were a lack of perceived teacher favoritism and the existence of a generally democratic atmosphere. Additionally, students in the classes where more learning occurred were considerably less apathetic about their class experiences.[3]

What might account for these results? Going beyond our intuitive notion that how we feel about the people and places that surround us must influence what we do, R. P. McDermott, in a provocative *Harvard Educational Review* article a few years ago, suggested some useful explanations for just how and why classroom interactions—one important aspect of climate—may serve to either enhance or limit students' learning.[4]

McDermott's explanations are not mere speculation but are based on an intensive study of classrooms in a variety of school systems. He first reminds us that, as was discussed in the previous chapter, environments that most enhance learning are those in which children are clear about what they are to do and have enough time to complete learning tasks. McDermott suggests that the interactions and relationships that are present in the classroom affect both the availability of time and students' understanding of tasks. The kinds of interactions that take place determine whether students and teachers develop what he calls "trusting relations," relations in which both teacher and students interpret what others in the classroom do as being "directed to the best interests of what they are trying to do together and [understand] how they can hold each other accountable for any breach of the formulated consensus."[5] In other words, trusting relations exist when teachers and students see one another as mutually involved and working at the project of learning. In classrooms where trusting relations exist, students will spend their time and energy on learning. Where they do not exist, a great deal of time will be spent trying to get organized and negotiating relationships. Much of the teacher's time and energy is likely to be devoted to establishing rewards and punishments to get students to attend to tasks. Much of the students' time and energy is likely to be devoted to not working and disrupting what the teacher is attempting to do. If McDermott is correct, his propositions go a long way toward explaining why students' perceptions of teacher support and concern are related not only to organized, task-oriented classrooms but to learning outcomes themselves.

It seems reasonable to extend McDermott's conceptualization of trusting relations and their impact on learning to involve all the inhabitants of the classroom. If the students in the classroom trust one another as cooperating participants in the learning enterprise, they will be likely to spend more of their time together on intellectual taks than on relationship issues among them. This certainly is consistent with the findings cited earlier, that classrooms in which there is a high degree of affiliation and a lack of friction seem to be those in which students learn more.

This line of thinking is especially useful because it enables us to conclude with some confidence that positive classroom relations are something more than a nice accompaniment to learning. Good classroom relations enhance student learning. This is not to say that the quality of everyday life in classrooms is important only insofar as it affects learning. Indeed, the kinds of relationships students experience daily in schools are tremendously important in themselves. But it certainly helps us to understand the interrelatedness of all aspects of schooling to see how classroom relationships may be directly connected to the learning process.

Of course, academic achievement is not the only kind of student outcome likely to be influenced by the classroom atmosphere. We would certainly expect that the climate of classes, and particularly the relationship dimension, would strongly influence outcomes in the affective area as well, such as how students feel about themselves and their school experience. Some research has been done in these areas that suggests that student satisfaction is likely to be higher in classrooms where students are more involved, where students actively participate in a variety of activities, and where personal relationships are positive. Further, there is some indication that in classes with less friction and student apathy interest in the subject area is increased.[6] We will look in depth at student attitudes such as these in chapter 7. At that point, we will be able to suggest some relationships between classroom environments and student outcomes in the affective area from the data collected about our twenty-five schools. Generally, however, the evidence we have from other work that has been done suggests most strongly that "satisfying human relationships tend to facilitate personal growth and development. . . . Objective behavioral and performance effects seem to depend on a combination of warm and supportive relationships, an emphasis on specific directions of personal growth, and a reasonably clear, orderly and well-structured milieu."[7]

There is another type of student outcome that has been speculated about but not thoroughly investigated in relationship to specific aspects of the classroom environment. This concerns the socialization of students for participation as adults in the larger society. To explore this aspect further we need to turn for a moment to a much discussed interpretation of the function of schooling in relation to the preservation of the structure of economic and social life in the United States.

In 1976, two political economists, Samuel Bowles and Herbert Gintis, published an explosive book, *Schooling in Capitalist America*, which put forth a radical criticism of the U.S. education system.[8] A key part of this critique was a hypothesis about how the sorting and selection among students that go on in schools in this country and the differences that students experience in the kinds of educational environments that result can be directly linked to the preservation of the social, economic, and political inequality that exists in our society.

In their analysis of schools as agents in the reproduction of the inequalities in the American economic system, Bowles and Gintis focus a major part of their dicussion on the school's reinforcement of the social-class differences children bring with them to school and on the different kinds of socialization children from various social classes receive there. An essential element in their perspective of schooling is that groups of students, sorted (as we have seen) largely on race and class differences, receive different treatments that result in differences not only in academic outcomes but in nonacademic outcomes as well. In fact, to Bowles and Gintis, even more important than the differences expected in the type and quantity of knowledge acquired by students in various educational settings are the differences expected in students' attitudes towa institutional structures, toward themselves, and toward their anticipa roles in adult society. In other words, in preparing students for their lives in the real world, schools must socialize students in very particular ways. This socialization must include how students feel about themselves, about schools, and what they can expect in the future. Also important, not all students can feel that they are competent, that they have unlimited potential, and that they can play a leadership role in the institutions they encounter. Some students must come to feel in quite the opposite way. These differences in attitudes, Bowles and Gintis believe, make possible the continuance of a social and economic system in this country that is characterized by unequal and undemocratic structures which go largely unquestioned.

By socializing children differently, largely reinforcing the values and personality characteristics of the social class of their families, schools, Bowles and Gintis assert, prepare students to meet the demands of the occupations they are expected to assume within the existing class structure. Lower-class students are expected to assume lower-class jobs and social positions as adults. Middle- and upper-class children are likewise expected to follow in their parents' footsteps. This socialization is accomplished through what Bowles and Gintis label "the close correspondence between the social relationships which govern personal interaction in the work place and the social relationships of the educational system."[9] The social relationships and interactions in schools and classrooms, by imitating the social relationships in various work settings, produce different kinds of future workers by fragmenting students into stratified groups wherein capabilities, attitudes, and behaviors that are appropriate for different work environments are rewarded. These school and classroom relationships serve to tailor "the self-concepts, aspirations, and social class identifications of individuals to the requirements of the social division of labor."[10] Thus, they claim, the educational system turns lower-class children into lower-class workers. These workers will be subordinate to external control and alienated from the institutions but willing to conform to the needs of the work place, to a large extent because of the way they were treated in school. Additionally, Bowles and Gintis suggest that the absence of close interpersonal relationships is characteristic of both lower-class work environments and classroom environments for lower-class children. In contrast, upper- and middle-class students, destined for upper-status and middle-level positions in the economic hierarchy, are more likely to experience social relationships and interactions that promote active involvement, affiliation with others, and the internalization of rules and behavioral standards. Self-regulation is the goal here rather than the coercive authority and control seen as appropriate for the lower class.

Recently, others have elaborated this "correspondence" view in work that begins to explain more precisely how classroom interactions may lead to these ends.[11] Rather than seeing students as basically passive, submissive recipients of school socialization, these closer looks at classroom interaction point out that students, especially lower-class students, often actively resist what schools try to teach them. These students openly reject both the behaviors schools expect and the content they value. By doing so, students challenge the control schools have over them. The existence of student resistance, however, does not contradict Bowles and Gintis's view of the role and function of schools in reproducing the work force. To the contrary, it explains how this happens in a way consistent with what we know about how many low-achieving students behave. The act of resisting what schools offer is part of how social and economic reproduction occurs.

For example, Paul Willis's ethnographic account of working-class boys in an English comprehensive secondary school, *Learning to Labour: How Working Class Kids Get Working Class Jobs*, shows in interesting detail how this struggle between school and students takes place. By finding ways to leave the classroom, to smoke, to divert or subvert teachers' agendas, to disrupt routines and break rules, the boys in Willis's study assert some measure of control over the school and classroom environment. But with their rejection of the values and expected behaviors of their school, the boys also reject school learning—or any form of "mental" as opposed to "manual" work. Thus they see industrial work as desirable and appropriate for them. Willis also suggests that the resistance behaviors are an important part of learning to become low-level workers as these behaviors are what will make work life tolerable for them in the future.

The production of lower-class workers from lower-class students, then, can be seen as more complicated than the simple kind of correspondence between the school environment and the work place Bowles and Gintis's work might suggest. It stems not only from the differential treatment the school offers students but also from the kinds of responses students make to it. This interaction becomes the reproductive force through which the differential socialization of students is accomplished.

Following Bowles and Gintis and Willis, classes at different track or ability levels, because of the different kinds of students they serve in terms of their backgrounds, would be the logical places to accomplish this differential socialization. We wanted to look at our data in light of this possibility, to explore whether what happens in low-track classes functions to socialize students from lower groups toward passivity; institutional relationships characterized by dominance, coercion, and distance; and alienation from the educational environment. Conversely, we wanted to examine whether relationships and interactions in high-track classes were of the type that might help to socialize students toward more active involvement, institutional relationships characterized by greater warmth and concern, and greater affiliation with the learning experience. If these conditions did exist, that would suggest that tracking in schools does serve to reinforce and reproduce the inequities in the larger society by limiting some students' participation in the educational experience.

There is an interesting similarity between those classroom characteristics that Bowles and Gintis suggest promote socialization for upper-status positions and those that others have found are related to greater student learning. Those aspects of classroom climate that appear to lead to socialization for lower-class occupations also seem to be those found in classes where students learn less. Taking the research and theory together, then, we can begin to appreciate the importance of the psychosocial dimensions of classrooms. Once again, differences in these dimensions seem very likely to be linked to tracking and ultimately to unequal educational experiences for students in various tracks—with environments for students at the bottom less conducive to student learning and more likely to channel students into the lowest social and economic positions as adults. With these powerful possibilities in mind, we turn now to the data we have about the climates of our Study of Schooling classrooms.

Relationships and Involvements in Twenty-five Schools

The study collected data on several important aspects of classroom relationships and student involvement from student questionnaires, teacher questionnaires, and the reports of outside observers. From the student questionnaires, scales were developed that measured such features as the teacher's concern for students, the teacher's punitiveness, the amount of disruption and dissonance in the classroom, student apathy, and the regard students had for one another, to name just a few. Both the teacher questionnaires and the observation reports gave us information about the time teachers spent disciplining students and the kind of involvement students were likely to have in classroom activities. All these data help us to unravel what the quality of classroom environments was like. And of course, we were most curious to see whether track levels were different along these lines. Our analyses showed that indeed they were.

Additionally, when we interviewed the teachers about their classes, we asked them to describe the climates they perceived. Their answers were varied as the teachers tended to interpret *climate* in a number of ways. Many teachers' comments, however, did speak to the issues we are concerned with here. Some of them were quite consistent with what the students in various groups said about their classes.

Teacher-Student Relationships

There is a tremendous rapport between myself and the students. The class is designed to help the students in college freshman English composition. This makes them receptive. It's a very warm atmosphere. I think they have confidence in my ability to teach them well, yet because of the class size—32—there are times they feel they are not getting enough individualized attention.

Teacher, High-track English—senior high

I had *one* worse class than this.

Teacher, Low-track Science—senior high

This is an *especially* warm and congenial group—towards each other and towards me. Logically because of age. Warmth towards them shows— we tease each other—I give much praise, extra credits, etc. If you are open and warm with them it is returned to you. Students and teachers are together trying to change a crowded, noisy, unattractive classroom into a nice place. Working on it together. Very high student enthusiasm—very involved.

Teacher, High-track Math—junior high

This is my worst class. Kids very slow—underachievers and they don't care. I have no discipline cases because I'm very strict with them and they are scared to cross me. They couldn't be called enthusiastic about math—or anything, for that matter.

Teacher, Low-track Math—junior high

Overall a good feeling between teacher and pupils—type of students you can joke with. When you get serious 95% respond. Very few discipline problems—eager to learn for most part.

Teacher, High-track Math—junior high

They don't like me in a position of authority. These children don't like anybody in authority.

Teacher, Low-track English—senior high

Bright, enthusiastic, I had them two years ago for French and that helped. Relaxed, informal atmosphere about it. I like it because I don't have to be mean to keep them under control. In some other classes I have to keep it structured all period long, every day.

Teacher, High-track Foreign Language—junior high

My students are *made* to respect me and obey me. I make them work and learn or get out of the program.

Teacher, Low-track Vocational Education—junior high

We carefully analyzed all our information that concerned relationships between teachers and students in our 299 English and mathematics classes. We looked first at how teachers' concern for students was perceived by the students. To measure this dimension we asked the students to indicate their agreement or disagreement with a series of eight statements:

The teacher makes this class enjoyable for me.
The teacher listens to me.
The teacher lets me express my feelings.
I like the teacher in this class.
I wish I had a different teacher for this class.
I feel the teacher is honest with me.
This teacher is friendly.
The teacher is fair to me.

The teacher-punitiveness scale and the measures used to assess how much class time was spent on teachers getting students to behave were also used to get a picture of what teacher-student relationships were like in the classrooms. The punitiveness scale, as you will recall from chapter 5, included statements about the teacher making fun of students, hurting students' feelings, punishing unfairly, and creating fear in students.

The measures used to assess time were reports by teachers, students, and observers about how time was spent. We also were interested in what evidence observers could find of overtly negative or positive interactions of teachers and their students. On the positive side, this evidence included teachers' use of humor, positive touching, or expressions of enthusiasm. On the negative side, observers noted when teachers made demeaning, punishing, or angry remarks, used negative touching, or gave other overtly negative expressions.

Taken together, this information gives us an overall look at teacher-student relationships at various track levels. The following patterns emerged. Both the students' perceptions of their relationships with teachers and the measures of time spent on discipline or behavior problems turned out to be different in important ways in classes at different track levels. High-track classes saw their teachers as more concerned about them and less punitive toward them than did classes in the low track. And, as we saw clearly in chapter 5, teachers, students, and observers in high-track classes all reported that less time was spent on behavior and discipline than did those in low-track classes. Average classes were almost halfway between the high and low tracks on this set of measures. Interestingly, observers saw almost no evidence of teachers being either openly negative or openly positive in any of the track levels.

It's important to be aware that students in every track level tended to agree at least mildly that their teachers were concerned about them. Similarly, teachers in general were not seen as very punitive. Consistent with this finding is that classroom observers saw little evidence of overtly negative behavior on the part of teachers. Classrooms were for the most part what we might call flat in their emotional tone. They appeared, in large part, to be pretty neutral places. Yet even within this overall flatness, our time and student-perception data show that something markedly different was occurring in different track levels. And these track-related differences were fairly consistent across classes within each of the track levels. Relationships between teachers and students were definitely more positive in high-track classes; relationships were clearly more negative in the low.

Student-Peer Relationships

Students interact warmly and cooperation exists—few conflicts in class.
                    Teacher, High-track Vocational Education—junior high

They can be friends one day and seemingly hate each other the next. They tattale on each other—put the other person down.

Teacher, Low-track English—junior high

Very good climate. Good rapport among students. Students have a lot of fun in class.

Teacher, High-track Science—senior high

They pick on each other more than kids in average classes. They are more prone to violence—I observe—but I've not had trouble.

Teacher, Low-track English—junior high

The black and white kids do not get along in this class. They sit on different sides of the room. They attack each other verbally and they're not kidding around. Basically the blacks call the whites rednecks—poor crackers—put them down. The blacks control the class. They are in the majority—about 20, only 10 or 11 white. Sometimes they will start fighting and I have to break it up. The whites are lower socioeconomic and the blacks are too. This is deep seated and comes from home and I'm sure they don't associate in any other classes or anywhere in school. Their achievement levels are about the same.

Teacher, Low-track Science—junior high

Class is close-knit group (many know each other). Not a formal atmosphere.

Teacher, High-track Math—junior high

Generally, they have low self-esteem. They take it out on each other.

Teacher, Low-track English—senior high

Students have a lot of conflicts in their interactions and when a student is upset they vocalize it.

Teacher, Low-track Science—junior high

The climate is superb. Peer-to-peer climate is great. I get on with these children and have no problems. There is a lot of understanding and support at this particular class.

Teacher, High-track Math—junior high

Kids can't stand each other, too many emotional problems to listen.

Teacher, Low-track Science—junior high

We used five different pieces of information to find out about the relationships students had with one another and how they felt about being with their classmates. First, we used four of the scales that measured students' perceptions of their classrooms. All looked at relationships among students directly, but each focused on a slightly different aspect of those relationships.

Student agreement or disagreement with the following seven statements helped us determine how much they seemed to like and help one another. Taken together, these statements may be seen as a measure of peer esteem:

I help my classmates with their work.
If I am absent, my classmates help me to catch up on what I missed.
I like my classmates.
I like working with other students in this class.
In this class, people care about me.
If I had trouble with my work, most of my classmates would help me.
My classmates like me.

Three sets of statements helped us get an idea of how students got along in the classroom. First, three statements were used as a measure of classroom dissonance:

The students in this class fight with each other.
The students in this class argue with each other.
Students in this class yell at each other.

Second, three statements measured the degree of cliquishness among students in classrooms:

Some groups of students refuse to mix with the rest of the class.
Certain students stick together in small groups.
When we work in small groups, many students work only with their close friends.

And third, four statements were used to help us find out how much competition was a part of student relationships in their classrooms:

There is a lot of competition in this class.
In this class, students compete with each other for good grades.
When I'm in this class, I feel I have to do better than other students.
Students in this class feel they have to do better than each other.

One other statement elicited students' responses about how friendly they thought their classmates were:

Students in the class are unfriendly to me.

Among these indicators of the kinds of relationships students had, only the measures of cliquishness among students revealed no important differences among track levels.

Most important of the differences at different track levels were the feelings reported about the friendliness among students in class. Students in low-track classes, far more than those in the high tracks, told us that they felt that other students in the class were unfriendly to them.

Large differences were also found in the amount of angry and hostile interactions that were reported among students in class. Low-track students indicated that considerably more arguing, yelling, and fighting with one another took place in their classes. Substantial differences were also found in the warm, helpful feelings students had about one another. High-track students far more often agreed that their classmates really liked one another and were willing to extend help. Low-track students told us that these kinds of things were much less a part of their classroom experience. Again, average classes fell between the high and low tracks on these characteristics.

There were track-level differences in the competitiveness of classes as well, but these differences were much smaller and less consistent. For example, in English classes both high- and low-track classes indicated that a moderate degree of competition occurred, and average classes reported slightly less. In math classes, high-track classes were the most competitive, average classes the next most, and low classes the least. While these differences in competitiveness were statistically important, they were much less so than the other differences in student relationships. What stands out as most dramatic are the people-to-people interactions that took place. Clearly, the classes in the lowest track were considerably more hostile and unfriendly places. Students could not count to the same extent on help from others or even on their general good will. Overtly hostile exchanges were certainly more frequent.

Student Involvement

We wanted to investigate as many aspects of the involvement dimension of class climate as possible. How involved did students seem to be in what was happening in class? How *involving* were the learning activities that were available to them? Were students expected to be active or passive participants in what went on in class? What were the impressions of trained observers about how involved students were?

We gathered students' perceptions of their own involvement and feelings about it with three measures. One was the following set of statements, which indicated their willingness to go along with what was happening in class—in essence, their degree of compliance with what was expected of them:

I usually do my homework.
I usually do the work assigned in this class.

The students in this class usually do the work assigned.
I usually do everything my teacher tells me to do.

A second set of statements told us how much students seemed to care about how well they did in class. This set asked them to tell us about their *feelings*, whereas the previous set focused on their *behaviors*. We considered this set of statements a measure of student apathy:

Failing in this class would not bother most of the students.
Most of the students pay attention to the teacher.
Students don't care about what goes on in this class.
I don't care about what goes on in this class.

A third measure we used was the following statement:

I feel left out of class activities.

This helped us gain insight into how much students might feel *excluded* from involvement. It also gave us clues about feelings of hurt or alienation students might have experienced in their classes.

We used information from the teacher survey to determine whether students were being given opportunities to be actively involved in their learning. We divided a list of possible classroom activities into active and passive types. It was our belief that students would feel more involved if learning activities elicited active rather than passive participation from them. We categorized the following activities as more active: going on field trips; doing research; writing reports, stories, or poems; having class discussions; building or drawing things; acting things out; and making films or recordings. The following activities were categorized as more passive: listening while the teacher talks or demonstrates how to do something; listening to student reports; listening to speakers who come to class; writing answers to questions; taking tests or quizzes; and reading. We knew already that nearly all classes, expecially in English and mathematics, are far more passive than active when looked at in this way. But we were interested in the *relative* differences among track levels on this dimension. We also asked the students what kinds of activities they did in class and the observers what activities they saw taking place.

We considered the observers' reports of several other kinds of student involvement in classrooms important: an estimate of students' interest level; the percentage of time students spent off-task; the opportunities students had to answer open-ended questions; the existence of cooperative small groupings of students for learning; and the opportunities students had to direct classroom activity.

Finally, we used two indicators of how much students seemed to participate in classroom decision making. One was the students' responses to the following series of statements:

We are free to talk in this class about anything we want.
Students help make the rules for this class.
We are free to work with anyone we want to in this class.
We can decide what we want to learn in this class.
Students help decide what we do in this class.
Different students can do different things in this class.
Sometimes I can study or do things I am interested in even if they are
    different from what other students are studying or doing.
I help decide what I do in this class.

The second was the observers' reports of who—the teacher or students—made classroom decisions during the time they were in class. We felt that all this information together would give us insight into the degree of student involvement in classrooms.

The most significant thing we found is that generally our entire sample of classes turned out to be pretty noninvolving places. As we expected, passive activities—listening to the teacher, writing answers to questions, and taking tests—were dominant at all track levels. And, also not unexpected, the opportunities students had in any group of classes to answer open-ended questions, to work in cooperative learning groups, to direct the classroom activity, or to make decisions about what happened in class were extremely limited. In most classes these things just did not happen at all.[12] Any statements that can be made about differences between tracks in this respect must be seen in this context.

Having said this, we may look at some important *relative* differences in the opportunities students had to be involved in their classes at various track levels. Even though all students were primarily passive participants in the classroom as a result of the few opportunities they had to be otherwise, high-track students seemed to have somewhat more active learning activities available to them than others. They were more likely to go on trips, to do research, to do narrative or expository writing, to act things out, or to make films or recordings. On the other hand, while all students had extremely limited opportunities to make decisions, low-track students seemed to have had more than others. On the basis of these last data, certainly, we cannot say with confidence that the different learning experiences students had available to them in different track levels created the likelihood that students would be more or less involved in class.

The other indicators of involvement revealed important track-level differences. First of all, as we saw in chapter 5, the percentage of students not *attending* to learning activities was much greater in low- than in high-track classes. Further, the classroom observers estimated that a considerably greater percentage of high-track students were interested in what was going on in class. These two observations are consistent with what students themselves reported about their own involvement— the most substantial differences we found.

Marked differences were apparent on all three measures of how students perceived their involvement. Students in high-track classes saw themselves as being more involved in their classes than low-track students. Students in low-track classes reported that they were far less concerned about completing classroom tasks—doing the assigned work, the homework, or what the teacher told them to do. They also reported far greater degrees of apathy—not caring about what goes on in class or even being concerned about failing. Further, students in low-track classes reported far more often that they felt excluded, left out of class activities. Interestingly, the average classes did not follow their usual pattern in this area. While average English classes were quite like the high track, average math classes were more like the low.

What do all these pieces of information tell us about student involvement in different track levels? First, when we look just at what we might think are involving activities, track levels don't seem to differ much. None of the groups of classes seemed to generate a high level of active student involvement. In the absence of a large number of *activities* that involve students in learning, greater weight must be given to the subtler interactive methods of involvement that are more likely to reflect teacher/school attitudes, values, and expectations for different groups of students. Both the observers' reports and the responses of students tell us that students in high-track classes were far more involved than were students in the low group.

Clearly, there is something more than class activities that influences student involvement. We could speculate about what these other things might be. Many, for example, would suggest that a lack of involvement or interest in school or learning is a characteristic trait of those students who end up in low tracks and has little to do with what happens to them in the school setting. This is a difficult assumption to sustain since, as we have indicated earlier, students' characteristics are closely intertwined with what happens to them at school from the time they begin. It is nearly impossible to sort out these complex factors to produce neat causal explanations for how students end up in a low track in high school. It is probably safe to assume that an interaction of student characteristics and school experience, or even school treatment, has produced a student who tends to be off-task, uninterested, noncompliant, and apathetic and that such a student is also a low achiever or low in basic intelligence or whatever it is that gets him or her placed in low-track classes. To this assumption may be added the likelihood that the current classroom experience is so powerful that it can generate the low-track set of responses in students. This, of course, is exactly what Willis and others suggest. In earlier chapters, we have seen a great deal of evidence that the students in the classes we studied were having very different educational experiences. These differences should be borne in mind when we consider why low-track students were so much less involved than students in the high track. The substantial differences in the content they were experiencing and the learning opportunities that were available to them may have contributed to the lesser involvement of low-track students. Tracking from the earliest grades will undoubtedly result in different educational outcomes. But so can tracking in a given school year.

To see how this might be the case, it is worthwhile to look again at McDermott's conception of how relationships can influence learning and how student involvement with and time spent in learning activities are mediated by the relationship of teachers and students. Our data are consistent with McDermott's explanations of how relationships influence both students' understanding of what is to be done and their attending to it. Students' perceptions of how concerned their teachers were about them lead us to believe that "trusting relations" were far more likely in high-track classes than in low. Further, the much higher level of teacher punitiveness that was reported in low-track classes reminds us of McDermott's finding that trusting relations did not exist in classes where punishment was relied upon to attempt to coerce students into compliance. A higher degree of punitiveness, a lower degree of trusting relationships, and less involvement in class activities are related to lower educational outcomes and are more associated with low-track classes. The time measures help to fill out this pattern in that more teacher time and energy were spent on getting students to behave in low-track classes. Some of our student-involvement measures support this picture as well. Rather than participate cooperatively in what the teacher wanted them to do—as they would be likely to do if they viewed the teachers' directions as in their own best interests—low-track students tended to be noncompliant and apathetic. Apparently more of their time and energy was spent interfering with their teachers' plans.

If we consider students' relationships with one another as also important in creating a trusting environment where everyone works on a common project of learning, we see large discrepanices among track levels. Trust, cooperation, and even good will among students were far less characteristic of low-track classes than of high. More student time and energy were spent in hostile and disruptive interchanges in these classes. Clearly, the students' time and energy spent in negotiating relationships and maintaining a combative stance toward those who do not appear to be working in their best interests are time and attention taken away from learning activity. And, as McDermott suggests, this diversion of time and attention is likely to have a negative influence on academic outcomes.

We know from the research on classroom climate that the characteristics of classrooms in which students learn more include warm and positive relationships, task orientation, and student involvement. We know from our research that these features are also more characteristic of high-track classes than low. McDermott's explanations of how relationships may mediate learning help us understand how these characteristics made a difference in student learning. We see in our data just those combinations of classroom features that McDermott suggests.

Again we find a pattern of classroom experiences that seems to enhance the learning possibilities for those students already disposed to do well—those in high-track classes. We see even more clearly a pattern likely to inhibit the learning of those at the bottom. Once again, we find that those students who need the most help from the school environment are getting the least.

Turning to the issue of student socialization, it is apparent too that the differences in the relationship and involvement dimensions of classroom climates are consistent with the different kinds of socialization that Bowles and Gintis and more recent writers suggest take place in schools and classrooms. Our findings support the theory in that classes where poor and minority students are most likely to be found—low-track classes—were more characterized by alienation, distance, and authority than were high-track classes. Also supporting this view were the greater proportion of time teachers spent on discipline and student behavior, students' perceptions of their teachers as more punitive and less concerned about them, the more negative feelings and behaviors students reported they exhibited toward one another, and the more negative student attitudes expressed toward classroom experiences that were found in low-track classes. At the same time, the proportionately less time spent on behavior by teachers, students' perceptions of teachers as less punitive and more concerned about them, the lower levels of student hostility toward peers and apathy toward the classroom situation, and the less frequent student reports of feeling isolated found in high-track classes seem to provide support for the assertion that those at the upper levels experience relationships that lead them to affiliate with the schooling experience.

There is some additional support in our findings for the hypothesis that students from different groups have different types of involvement with their schooling experience as a result of the type of social relationships they experience. High-track classes tended to be more characterized by a greater frequency of active learning activities and more on-task behavior in the classroom as well as a considerably higher level of student involvement as students themselves perceived it than were the low-track groups. However, no differences were observed in the number of opportunities students had to direct classroom activity, to express opinions, or to work cooperatively together. It seems clear that in *all* types of classrooms students were primarily passive participants. Indeed, there is little evidence in the data that the structure of learning activities in any track level was such that students participated in decision making or in classroom or group leadership for any more than a small fraction of class time. However, high-track students appear to have experienced more active involvement than others, even on this small scale.

Bowles and Gintis assert that the values and personality characteristics necessary for the maintenance of an unequal society are produced in students through their social relationships. They suggest that for students from the lower social strata—those seen as most likely to enter the manual-labor force—school and classroom relationships promote acceptance of coercion and obedience to established authority. Willis and others remind us that students' open rejection of school plays a part in this process. On the other hand, for students from the upper social levels—those most expected to enter elite positions—relationships foster independence, internal control, and affiliation with others.

It is likely that the differences in relationships found in our classrooms contribute to the differences in values and dispositions toward institutions suggested by these scholars. Our study does not indicate whether the differences in relationships found among track levels correspond to those found at different occupational levels in the economic hierarchy. What we saw is merely consistent with the proposition that students from different socioeconomic positions experience differences in their classroom relationships and types of involvement in learning activity. Furthermore, these differences have a strong potential for leading students differentially either toward affiliation with and active involvement in social institutions or toward alienation from and a more negative involvement in the institutions they encounter.

The view of schools as meritocratic institutions where, regardless of race or class, those students with the "right stuff" are given a neutral environment where they can rise to the top is called into question by our findings. Everywhere we turn we see the likelihood of in-school barriers to upward mobility for capable poor and minority students. The measures of talent seem clearly to work against them, resulting in their disproportionate placement in groups identified as slow. Once there, their achievement seems to be further inhibited by the type of knowledge they are exposed to and the quality of learning opportunities they are afforded. Further, the social and psychological dimensions of classrooms for those at the bottom of the schooling hierarchy impose more constraints on students. Negative relationships and low levels of student involvement appear not only to restrict their chances of learning but to socialize students in such a way that they are prepared to stay at the bottom levels of institutions, not only as teenagers in schools but in adult life as well.

We know that some bright students who begin with racial and economic handicaps do excel in school. Some of these students manage to struggle to the top despite the constraints they encounter in their school experience. And because they do, we often point to them as examples that confirm the meritocratic nature of schooling. We like to say that because some students use the schools to achieve upward mobility, both educationally and economically, that schools in general are structured to provide students from all backgrounds with an equal chance to do so. But the overcoming of barriers by a small percentage of students certainly is not evidence of the unbiased nurturing of the talents of all students. Our notion of schools as meritocratic institutions seems to be on very shaky ground.

But the notion of meritocracy is somewhat removed from the concept of equality. Meritocracy is based not on equality itself but on the idea of equality of *opportunity*, on fairness. In schools this is translated to mean that every student is given an equal chance to do well. If a student does not, it is due to the lack of ability, initiative, or sustained effort on the student's part not to any school practices that might have gotten in the way. Educational equality itself can mean something quite different. It can mean that all students are provided with the same kinds of experience in schools—a common set of learnings, equally effective instruction, and equally encouraging educational settings. Our data show that in the twenty-five schools we studied students were not treated equally in their attempts to learn English and math.

But notions of equality can go even further than this concept of equal treatment. Educational equality can be interpreted to mean that students are provided with the resources necessary to ensure that they are all likely to *acquire* a specified set of learnings. This might be translated in schools to mean that resources are allocated and instruction designed so that those entering schools least likely to do well are given the best schools have to offer. Certainly we found no evidence of this kind of equality operating in schools. Indeed, we found the opposite to be the case. Those least likely to do well were given the least in the three areas of school experience we studied. Those most likely to do well were given the best.

We are reminded of two conflicting views presented in Robert Frost's "The Death of a Hired Man." Warren says:

> Home is the place where, when you have to go there
> They have to take you in.

In such a home, even a comfortably appointed room with its own television set would not indicate full acceptance and equality of family membership. How similar to the ungracious reception given to low-tracked students! Fortunately, in Frost's poem, Mary counters Warren's begrudging sense of obligation with her own more generous and unmeritocratic view:

> I should have called it
> Something you somehow haven't to deserve.

Can the right to equal education be really seen in any other way?

7

Student Attitudes: The Legitimation of Inequality

How did the students in our twenty-five secondary schools feel about the experiences we have been describing? Were students in the top track especially pleased, or even smug, about the obviously preferential treatment they received? Were those at the bottom outraged at what seems to be so obvious—that they were getting so much less than others? Could they not have known? Could they not have cared? Is it possible that they thought they were getting just about what they deserved?

We have scrutinized the differences in the schooling experiences between those students identified as the most able and those identified as the least. But the answers to the questions posed above are crucial to the issues we have been considering throughout this book. How students felt about what they experienced can give us valuable insight about the most personal effects of the differences in the day-to-day classroom events that we found. How students feel about themselves and their school experience is likely to direct how they conduct themselves in schools and their adult lives.

Finding the answers to these questions is not easy in a study like ours. We collected our data from thousands of students at only one point in time. At that time we did have some hunches about how track levels in our schools might be different from one another, but we could not anticipate the exact nature or extent of the differences we would find. Clearly, then, we could not have asked our students specifically how they felt about phenomena we were not even sure existed. And, of course, by the time we had analyzed our data, these students were scattered in other classes or had gone on to other schools. It was not possible to go back and ask them how they felt about what we found.

A strength of the study, however, was that we had collected a considerable amount of information about how students felt about themselves, their classes, the subjects they were studying, and their schools. We also asked them about their educational plans. By bringing these data together to look at how student attitudes differed among track levels, we could add to our understanding of how students reacted to the effects of different school experiences.

We used our data in three ways in order to better understand if and how track differences were related to student attitudes. First, we compared the student responses on *each* of the attitude measures across track levels. Then we looked at the pattern that the responses to *all* attitude measures formed within each track, and then we compared these patterns across tracks. Third, we looked to see how these patterns were consistent or differed at the junior and senior high school levels. We felt that by considering all three of these analyses we could begin to interpret students' feelings about their differential treatment.

We had to be very careful in our interpretations, however. For, unlike the classroom-process characteristics we have been looking at, this group of attitude measures does not—with one exception—gauge attributes of the *classes* themselves but rather attitudes of the *individuals* in those classes. Our assumption here was that the track level of the class a student is in will be related to his or her attitudes. Nevertheless, we could not assume from our data—gathered at one point in time in only one of the five or six classes a student was likely to be taking—that, even if these associations exist, there is a causal relationship between that particular class and the attitudes reported. While it is likely that student attitudes influence track placement and that track placement affects student attitudes, neither conclusion could be drawn from these data alone. Furthermore, some of the things we asked about—how students felt about themselves, for example—are attitudes that probably develop over a long period of time. While we knew that the students we studied were likely to have been in classes at the same track level in many subjects and had probably been in these kinds of groups throughout most of their prior school experience, our data could not help us be certain about the role of track placement in the development of these long-term attitudes. We lacked the necessary controls on pre-track-enrollment variables (self-concepts, family-background characteristics, attitudes toward school, future plans, etc.) and the longitudinal information about these attributes in students needed to make these conclusions. In spite of these cautions, regarding our analysis of the data, patterns emerged that allowed us to begin to interpret students' feelings about their differential treatment.

What we could determine from our data is that different kinds of attitudes tended to cluster at various track levels. In other words, students with similar kinds of attitudes seemed to end up in the same track level. Were those attitudes different in important ways from those of students in other levels? And, more specifically, did the attitudes exhibited by students in various tracks seem to be those that were likely to restrict or enhance the chances of their school success and their positive relationships with educational and other social institutions? Does a relationship between track placement and student attitudes have implications for our consideration of inequality?

We were very much interested, then, in exploring, to the extent possible, the *nature* of the relationship between school experiences and student attitudes. We wanted to consider what role the differences in classroom experiences might play in either the formation or the reinforcement of different kinds of student attitudes. Especially in light of the Bowles and Gintis notion that it is the different attitudes students acquire or have reinforced in school that enable our society to maintain the existing state of social and economic inequality, this relationship between school treatment and attitudes seemed directly connected to our overriding concern with inequality and schooling practices.[1]

There are at least three possibilities about the nature of this relationship that we chose to consider. First, school experiences might work to reduce the initial differences in attitudes students have about themselves and their place in schools and might challenge class- or family-based expectations about their futures. If this were the case, schooling could be viewed as working toward greater equality. Second, school experiences might serve to increase initial differences in these student attitudes and, thereby, exacerbate the inequalities that exist in the larger society. And, third, it is possible that school experiences have no effect on the way students see themselves and their appropriate places in schools. Initial differences among students in these attitudes may neither increase nor decrease as a result of what happens to them in schools.

This last circumstance could be variously interpreted. But consistent with Bowles and Gintis's view, the absence of evidence that initial differences in student attitudes are lessened with schooling could be viewed as the result of the reinforcement by the school of these differences and as thereby constituting a perpetuation or reinforcement of cultural inequities.

Sorting out what role schools might be playing in producing or reinforcing attitudes in students is not easily done, however. While it is usually assumed that socialization or attitude formation most often occurs as the cummulative result of experience, it may be that certain critical events—such as the labeling and classification that are a part of tracking—may have very powerful effects in quite a short period of time. Further, the *overall* time frame for this process is not entirely clear. Because the type of socialization that Bowles and Gintis suggest occurs in secondary schools, for example, is largely a reinforcement of attitudes students bring with them from home and a continuation of the differential treatment they experienced in elementary schools, an initial point for this process of school influence on attitudes cannot be isolated. Even the kind of sorting experienced as early as first-grade grouping for reading, for example, is likely to be reflective of differences students already possess.[2]

Bowles and Gintis regard educational selection, the school reward system, and differential treatments students receive as features of schooling that reinforce values. While it is possible that solidifying class-linked attitudes in students forms almost at the moment students are classified into tracks or ability groups, Bowles and Gintis and Willis suggest that the accumulated experience of schooling cements initial differences in student attitudes. Therefore, we would expect to see at least no decrease in differences in attitudes with increased years of schooling. If schooling is seen as *contributing* to social and economic inequity in this way, we would expect to find increased differences.

We compared our data on student attitudes in different track levels in an attempt to gain some insight into this relationship. We wanted to see if the differences we found at the senior high level were similar to or considerably stronger than those at the junior high level, suggesting that track placement may indeed play a role in the production of different attitudes in students and that the school may thereby contribute to inequality through the socialization process. Such a finding would lay to rest the persistent idea that the school, as part of the American melting pot, causes differences to decrease.

Student Attitudes

We looked at ten kinds of information about students' attitudes toward themselves, their classes, the subjects they were studying, and their schools.

To learn how students felt about themselves, we used three self-concept scales that were included in the student survey. One was comprised of eight statements that elicited responses regarding students' views of themselves generally:

At times I think I'm no good at all.
There are a lot of things about myself I'd change if I could.
Most people are better liked than I am.
I often feel like giving up when I can't do my schoolwork.
I'm pretty sure of myself.
Kids often pick on me.
I often wish I were someone else.
I get upset easily when I'm scolded.

Another series of statements related to how students saw themselves in relation to their peers:

I'm easy to like.
I'm popular with kids my own age.
Kids usually follow my ideas.
I'm a lot of fun to be with.

The third set of statements had students report how they felt about themselves with regard to academics:

I'm not doing as well as I'd like to in school.
I am a good reader.
I'm proud of my schoolwork.
I'm good at math.
I'm doing the best work that I can.
I am able to do schoolwork at least as well as most other students.

We also gave the students a list of several plans for their educational futures that they might have considered:

Quit school as soon as possible.
Finish high school.
Go to trade or technical school.
Go to junior college.
Go to a four-year college or university.
Go to graduate school after college.
Don't know.

We asked them to select from this list the statement that best answered each of the following phrases:

1. If I could do anything I want, *I would like to* . . .
2. I think *my parents would like me to* . . .
3. Actually, *I will probably* . . .

The average class score on the third item was used as a measure of the future plans of the students in a class.

Several questions were used to examine students' attitudes toward their schooling experience. The first was a single item asking students to grade their schools: "Students are usually given the grades A, B, C, D, and Fail to show how good their work is. If *schools* could be graded in the same way, what grade would you give to this school?" Two student survey items were used to assess students' attitudes toward the subjects they were studying in their classes: students reported how important they believed each school subject to be and how much they liked each subject. In addition to more specific questions about the class they were in, which we considered in earlier chapters, students responded to a set of more general statements which we used as a measure of overall satisfaction with their class:

Students feel good about what happens in class.
I don't like coming to this class.
After class, I usually have a sense of satisfaction.
I feel good about what happens in this class.

Students indicated their general interest in what they were learning in class by responding on a four-point scale to the following question: how interesting or boring for you is what you are learning in this class?

What Students Told Us

We found a fascinating array of attitudes among the students. It was immediately clear that track-level membership corresponded closely with certain kinds of attitudes, but seemed to bear no relationship to other kinds of attitudes.

Those attitudes that were highly related to track level were students' views of themselves and their educational plans for the future, whereas feelings and judgments about the quality of their schools, how satisfying their classes were, how interesting and important math and English were to them, and how well they personally got along with others seemed to bear no relationship to tracks.

High-track students had substantially higher educational aspirations than the other students and considerably more positive academic and general self-concepts. This is not very surprising. After all, aren't these the very students who have been told throughout school that they are smarter, the ones that we openly label "high achievers" and even "gifted"? While it is also not very surprising, it seems especially interesting to note the important differences among track levels in general self-concept. High-track students reported more positive self-perceptions not only in academic areas (e.g., "I'm proud of my schoolwork" and "I'm good at math") but generally as well (e.g., "I'm pretty sure of myself,") which seems unrelated to specific school activities. Students in the low-track classes had the most negative views of themselves both academically and generally and the lowest expectations for their educational futures. Students in the average track once again fell nearly halfway between the high and low groups on these measures. Student satisfaction with their classes, subjects, and schools did not vary systematically with track level.

We can conclude, then, that student attitudes clustered in high- and low-track levels in the following patterns. Students in high-track classes had significantly more positive attitudes about themselves and had higher educational aspirations than did students in low-track classes. However, students in all the track levels did not differ markedly in how much they liked English and mathematics or how important they believed these subjects to be. Neither did they differ significantly in the grades they gave their schools nor in the interest and satisfaction they expressed with the English and math classes they were taking. For the most part the attitudes students expressed on these measures were quite positive. While none of the groups was wildly enthusiastic about its school experiences, each seemed to be telling us that its school and classes were okay. Without oversimplifying things too much, we can conclude that students in low-track classes tended to be saying that school's all right, but I'm I'm not so good. In contrast, students in high-track classes were feeling pretty good about both their schools *and* themselves.

Legitimating Inequality

Having documented these unsurprising results, we can return to Bowles and Gintis and Willis to understand what these student attitudes might mean with respect to educational and social inequality. As you will recall from chapter 6, Bowles and Gintis assert that students' school relationships reproduce the attitudes and consciousness of various levels of workers in society by fragmenting students into groups and then rewarding different capabilities, attitudes, and behaviors. Willis and others claim that students' acceptance or rejection of the schools' treatment of them is a crucial part of this process. These institutional relations tailor "the self-concepts, aspirations, and social class identifications of individuals to the requirements of the social division of labor."[3]

This view of school sorting and socialization processes has two distinct but overlapping components. First, as a result of the social organization (tracking) of both schools and instruction—the structure that results from the sorting of students—all of them learn attitudes that are regarded as necessary for the maintenance of a hierarchical and authoritarian society. Next, as students experience differences in both the contents and the contexts of this schooling structure, different groups of students are socialized toward different positions within the larger society. In other words, *all* students learn respect for the school hierarchy and its authority and view rule following, direction taking, punctuality, and passive participation as appropriate institutional behaviors, even if they do not adopt these behaviors. But in addition to these shared components of socialization,, there are important differences in the attitudes reinforced and engendered in different groups of students.

"Legitimation of inequality" is what Bowles and Gintis call this reinforcement of different attitudes in different groups. Through this legitimation process, students learn to accept the unequal features of the larger society—hierarchical authority structures and unequal pay, for example—as natural. If students at the top of the strata view elite positions as their due, it should not be surprising that students at the bottom come to see limited future roles in society as largely appropriate and acceptable for them. In other words, students are trained to view as legitimate the principles that govern the existing social order (the unequal distribution of power and material goods) and to see themselves as largely responsible for their own places in it.

Bowles and Gintis assert that schools accomplish this differential socialization and the legitimation of its attendant inequalities through the "ostensibly objective and meritocratic selection and reward system of U.S. education."[4] They see this process as occurring through the structure and events of everyday school life, which, as Karabel and Halsey elaborate, "upholds those meritocratic values that justify differential rewards; the separation of the 'successful' from the 'failures' provides daily object lessons in inequality."[5] Others, Willis, for example, suggest that students choose to reject school values altogether, and this "choice" legitimates further unequal treatment. In both views the form and content of schooling practices used to organize instruction—such as curriculum tracking and ability grouping—play a major role in enabling students to internalize failure resulting from the stratification process as an individual rather than a social or structural problem. Through the selection and allocation system within schools and the differential educational treatments students receive, schools either reinforce or modify students' self-concepts and aspirations, so that they view their current and easily predicted social-class roles as appropriate.

As we have seen, the findings show that student attitudes were distributed among track levels in ways that are consistent with the concept of legitimation of inequality. Indeed, we might conjecture, as Bowles and Gintis do, that these students had internalized the legitimacy of the hierarchy and assumed responsibility for their own places in it.

The fact that the students in the high-track group reported higher levels of educational aspirations than low-track students, and, consistent with these plans, more positive academic self-concepts attests to different expectations for their future roles in society among students in the two track levels. This suggests that students at the bottom of the schooling and in many cases the societal hierarchy had adjusted their aspirations accordingly, and yet did not view the school as treating them unjustly. The patterns among the other variables are even more consistent with the concept of legitimation. Students in low-track classes expressed no less satisfaction with their schooling experiences than did high-track students. They graded their schools as highly as students in the other track level. Generally, they said they liked their subjects as well and rated them at about the same level of importance. Low-track students were about as satisfied with the classes they were in and regarded what they were learning to be as interesting as students in the high track. Nevertheless, low-track students had more negative attitudes about themselves generally; they were less likely than others to disagree with the statements that there were a lot of things about themselves they would change, that they were not as well liked as most people, and that at times they thought they were no good at all.

The juxtaposition of these findings points to a pattern of attitudes among low-track students that would be likely to facilitate the legitimation of inequality. Students in low tracks had lower aspirations, felt more negative about themselves academically, and expressed more feelings of general unworthiness than did students in higher classes. Yet, in judging their schools—imbued with hierarchical structures—and their classes—characterized by the more negative social relationships observed in this study—they reported the same levels of satisfaction as other students. We can only speculate, but it may be that low-track students see themselves and their own inadequacies as responsible for their current positions and future roles in the hierarchical structure. After all, how could they be expected to arrive at a view that the hierarchical structure of the school might be responsible for their roles in the face of the unrelenting socialization they experience to the contrary? In fact, they appear to see the schools as no less acceptable than do students at the top, whose schooling experiences and attitudes about themselves and their futures are quite different.

The Culpability of Schools

The differences in attitudes found among track levels are consistent with the legitimation of inequality concept. To what extent do differences in *experiences* cause or reinforce these attitude differences? Again, the ready response of some is to offer characterological, meritocratic, or even "innate intelligence" explanations. We wished to explore the schools' role in *creating* differences as distinct from *reflecting* differences. To this end separate analyses were conducted for the sixty-eight junior high and seventy-one senior high classes over the set of student-attitude measures to determine whether track-level differences were consistent at the two schooling levels and whether we had any evidence that these attitudes were stronger at the senior high level. Additionally, a further analysis was made in an attempt to discover any differences in the extent to which individual classes followed overall track-level patterns at the two schooling levels. What we found was that while the substance (i.e., attitudes toward themselves and their school experiences) of track-level differences at the two levels was almost identical, the extent of the differences was considerably greater at the senior than at the junior high level. Further, by looking at attitudes class by class at the two levels we found that classes at the senior high school level conformed to the predominant track-level patterns slightly more consistently than did classes at the junior high level.

What does this information tell us? First, it is clear that, at both levels, the patterns of student attitudes at different track levels were quite consistent among *classes* at both levels. That this consistency increases at the senior high level strongly suggests not only that low- and high-track classes, on the average, become more distinctly different on this attitude dimension with additional years of schooling but also that the dominant track patterns extend to more individuals as years of schooling increase.

The student-attitude data, when analyzed separately for the two schooling levels, suggest that the differences high- and low-track students experience in their classes may indeed contribute to the production of the differences in their attitudes. While it is likely that these attitude differences are reflective of class and status differences students bring with them from home, that these differences are greater and found more consistently at the senior high school level may, as the scholars we have cited suggest, point to an active role of schools in formulating and reinforcing students' attitudes toward themselves, their futures, and schools. Of course, longitudinal data on individuals are necessary to confirm this apparent increase and sophisticated statistical techniques are required for assessing the schools' contribution to the production of these greater differences. Nevertheless, the data presented here are strongly suggestive that differences in classroom social relationships result in differential socialization of students, having the effect of the legitimation of inequality. Further, this socialization process appears to intensify this legitimation with years of schooling.

Could this be possible? Could schools really work in such unpardonable ways? Doesn't common sense tell us that kids in top groups are simply smarter and know it—and that kids in low-track classes are just not so bright and that they, too, know it? Isn't it logical that the students have the self-concepts they do? And isn't it also logical that these "natural" distinctions, first noticed in the early years, become more pronounced as school content becomes more complex and specialized in the upper grades? Aren't the students simply being realistic about what their educational futures are likely to be?

These are the things common sense tells us about individual differences and how they influence the ways people feel about themselves and what they expect in the future. But two other kinds of thinking need to be brought to bear on our common sense assumptions. First is a careful consideration of *when* these "smart or dumb" decisions are made about children. Usually such decisions are made when children are about five or six years old, during the time they are beginning to learn to read in the first grade. Children who come to school knowing how to read or, once there, learn very quickly are pronounced *bright*. Those for whom reading is still a puzzle at the end of the first grade are judged *slow*. The decisions made at this point usually stick, and the sorting, selecting, and differential treatments begin and continue—reading groups, math groups, and so on—throughout the elementary grades. Certainly, by the time they are in secondary school high-track students do tend to act smart and low-track students do seem pretty dull. But given what we know about what children have experienced, what can we conclude with any certainty from these observations? Not enough, surely, to make us feel very confident about what common sense tells us.

The second line of thinking is indicated by the body of research on tracking and student affective outcomes reviewed in chapter 1. Not only has track position been directly related to self-esteem, with lower-track students scoring lowest on self-esteem measures, but placement in lower tracks has been shown to have a corroding effect on students' self-esteem as well. Other studies have shown that, even with ability level and status origins controlled for, track level can be an important determinant of future educational plans. These findings have been expanded to establish the effects of tracking, not only on educational aspirations, but on goal-oriented behavior too. Controlling for pre-track-enrollment achievement, goals, and encouragement from others, one study found that those in college tracks were more likely than students in other programs to apply for college admission and that they had an enhanced probability of acceptance. Another recent study of track misperceptions supports this work, with the finding that low-track membership has a frustrating effect on students' college plans over and above the effects of aptitude and grades.[6]

This work, taken together, certainly cautions us to question our common sense explanations about why students in various tracks have the attitudes and expectations they do. It appears that the features of schooling and the judgments of school people come together to help produce and maintain the social and economic inequalities we see all around us.

8

Vocational Education

One of the most frequently articulated goals of vocational education has been to increase the economic opportunities of poor and minority youth by providing them with specific, marketable occupational skills. In addition to studying tracking in academic courses, we had an opportunity to look fairly carefully at the vocational programs at our twenty-five schools. As a part of our inquiry into these programs, we sought to ascertain how well they seemed to be reaching this goal. We were especially concerned about this aspect of vocational programs because a number of scholars who have written about this subject have seen them as a means of sorting poor and minority students into programs that *limit* their future opportunities and, in fact, relegate them to low-level occupations and social status.

We know that vocational courses are an integral part of the tracking system at most secondary schools. This is usually a result of a number of interrelated practices. First, at many schools—most frequently at the senior high level—there is a separate sequence of courses that constitute the vocational track. This track is made up of both vocational courses designed to prepare students to go directly from high school into the job market and academic courses required for graduation. For most vocational-track students the required academic courses are the low-track classes we have been examining in the previous chapters. Second, while some vocational courses, especially in senior high schools, are seen as appropriate for all students in that they provide a general introduction to the world of work and careers, most of the students in the highest tracks do not take them. The college-bound students in the high-track classes are usually so occupied with meeting college entrance requirements that they don't have room in their schedules for vocational courses. As a result, these courses are usually taught to fairly homogeneous groups of students seen as low achieving or low ability. At the junior high school level, schools usually provide classes that give students some experience with what are often called the home arts—cooking and sewing—and the manual arts. But again, in many places—at least in our collection of schools—the top-track students take other courses, such as foreign language or music, instead. In these ways, then, vocational education is clearly tied to tracking.

Given the wide range of vocational courses offered in our schools, we suspected that a subtle, and most likely unintended, form of tracking was going on within vocational education as well. We suspected too that, if it existed, this more subtle vocational tracking would be likely to exacerbate the consequences of both academic tracking and the overt tracking of some students into a heavily vocational curriculum. We thought, in fact, that this tracking might indeed serve to stratify students further along race and class lines and then to limit even further some students' opportunities for economic and social success. To gain some insight into how this might happen, we sought to uncover any differences in the scope and substance of vocational programs provided to different groups of students and to consider the implications of these differences for students' opportunities.

In this chapter we will explore the relationship of vocational education to this kind of social stratification. Specifically, we will consider both research that has been done about the benefits of vocational education for students and theory regarding how vocational education may itself serve a stratifying function. Guided by this work, we will then look at the evidence we have regarding vocational education and stratification in our twenty-five schools.

The limited amount of research on the returns of vocational education programs both to industry and to students themselves has not yielded encouraging findings. Berg analyzed the effects of education on performance in the work place in his provocative book, *Education and Jobs: The Great Training Robbery*. He reported that his study indicated that higher levels of educational attainment are not associated with worker productivity. In fact, among the factory workers in the studies Berg considered, those who had completed high school programs were no more productive than those who had dropped out.[1] In another study, Clark and Sloan found that most skilled workers did not acquire their training in vocational programs; they learned the most needed skills either informally or on the job.[2] These and other studies indicate that industry has not gained measurably from vocational training programs. Other work has demonstrated that students who complete vocational programs are not able to use their training to enhance their access to employment. Two studies from the 1960s showed that graduates of vocational programs were no more likely to be employed than were high school dropouts.[3] Further, workers themselves have judged on-the-job training to be more useful than formal vocational training.[4] No differences have been found in the extent to which vocational and nonvocational (general curriculum) high school graduates report being hired at the levels and at the salaries that they had hoped for or in their ability to perform the jobs they found.[5] Finally, graduates of vocational programs do not seem to hold more favorable career positions than graduates of general high school curricula.[6] Grubb and Lazerson, summarizing much of this work, conclude that few students in vocational programs have found work appropriate to their specific training and that they have only rarely been advantaged in terms of income, employment, job mobility, or status as compared to graduates of academic programs. Thus, what research evidence we have strongly suggests that participation in vocational programs has not enchanced the employment opportunities of participants.[7]

Some recent studies of the introduction of vocational programs into schools have discounted the rationales business and school people offer for those programs. Touted as a means of providing the increasingly technical training workers may need for employment in an industrial society, vocational programs were to increase economic opportunity for students. However, many of those who study schools suggest that the introduction of vocational programs was more likely a fearful response to the influx of working-class, poor, and immigrant children into the high school and the threat they posed to its formerly elite status.[8] Rather than change the character of the academic curriculum to meet the needs of a diverse student population (and thereby preserve the common school), the inclusion of vocational programs permitted schools to differentiate their curricula and to sort students. As a result, vocational programs provided a means of encouraging working-class children not to drop out of school while keeping them from receiving an academic education. In these programs lower-class students learned attitudes and skills appropriate to manual-labor positions.

A recent analysis of the vocational experiences provided for black adolescents in schools argues that these programs from their inception have been limited largely to preparing youngsters for jobs traditionally held by blacks. Further, black youth have been advised by their schools to make "realistic" career choices. In effect, they have been counseled not to strive to move into occupations generally held by the white middle class. Even the strong push in the 1930s for well-developed nonracist vocational guidance for blacks did little to alter this pattern. At the same time, middle- and upper-class children have retained almost exclusive access to the more prestigious academic curriculum.[9] These analyses lead to the conclusion that the division of secondary schooling into vocational and academic programs throughout the twentieth century has reinforced the social, racial, and economic stratification of American society. Given this history, it is no surprise that studies of vocational students have found that they come more often from lower socioeconomic groups than do students in academic programs. For example, one major study indicated that vocational students differed from the general student population in that the heads of their households had lower-status occupations, lower incomes, and/or lower levels of education.[10] Whether or not nonwhite students are found in disproportionate percentages in vocational programs is a question that has not been given much attention by researchers.

So, we know two things about vocational education. First, research evidence points to the apparent ineffectiveness of these programs in providing either a substantial proportion of the trained workers needed for American industry or increased occupational opportunities for students. Second, many educational scholars agree that an underlying function of vocational education has been to segregate poor and minority students into occupational training programs in order to preserve the academic curriculum for middle- and upper-class students. In this way the differentiated curriculum has served to reinforce the racial and socioeconomic stratification of society. With this view of the stratifying intent of a curriculum split into vocational and academic programs, both the character and the ineffectiveness of vocational education can be better understood. The content of vocational programs is shaped by what is seen as occupationally appropriate for the poor. The ineffectiveness of these programs may lie both in their limited content and in their inability to provide the attitudes and competencies poor and minority students need in order to overcome race and class obstacles to occupational opportunity and social mobility.

What we do not know is exactly how this happens within schools. As with academic tracking, we are fairly clear about the outcomes of vocational training in public schools, yet we know little of what students experience that contributes to these ends. To better understand this process, we wanted to uncover the relationship between student race and ethnicity and the various kinds of vocational education courses that students took in the schools we studied. Two questions guided our inquiry. First, how do vocational programs differ from school to school in both scope and substance? And second, do any differences found among vocational programs suggest that these programs work in a way that minority students (who are usually poor as well) in particular are pushed toward lower-level occupations? We decided to focus our analysis on three questions: (1) Was there a greater overall emphasis on vocational programs in nonwhite and ethnically or racially mixed secondary schools than in white schools? (2) At racially and ethnically mixed schools were nonwhite students found in disproportionately large percentages in vocational education courses? And (3) was the substance of vocational programs at nonwhite and mixed schools markedly different from that at white schools? Within mixed schools, were there particular types of vocational courses in which disproportionate percentages of white and nonwhite students were enrolled?

To analyze our data in these ways, our schools were divided into subgroups based on the race and ethnicity of the students enrolled in them. Students from the following racial and ethnic groups were classified as nonwhite: black, Asian, Mexican-American, and other. Using these categories, seven of our schools at the senior high level were categorized as "white" schools; four others were categorized as "mixed"; and the two remaining were classified as "nonwhite." Among the junior high schools a similar division of schools was made. Six schools were categorized as "white" schools, four as "mixed," and two as "nonwhite."[11]

Several types of data were included in the analysis of vocational programs at the twenty-five secondary schools. First, from master schedules provided by the schools, the teacher resources allocated to vocational programs were computed by calculating for each school the number of teaching hours in each school day spent in vocational subjects.[12] Second, from the master schedules, published course outlines, student registration forms, and other school documents, the content and formats of vocational education courses were determined. Formats included the length of class time—regular class period or extended time period—and location—on- or off-campus. From the curriculum materials submitted by teachers of vocational courses, lists of the instructional topics and skills taught were used to further define the content of the courses offered. From these sources, vocational education courses were categorized into seven basic content types: general industrial arts; home economics; business; preparation for skilled trades; military preparation; agriculture; and general career, consumer education, or supervised work experience. Third, the race/ethnicity data we collected about students were used to identify the distribution of students from various ethnic and racial groups in these various types of vocational education programs. With these data on the amount of teacher resources allocated to each school's vocational program, the content and format of the vocational courses, and the race or ethnicity of the students taking these courses, schools could then be compared on each dimension in an attempt to answer our questions about the relationship of vocational education and educational equality.

Allocation of Teachers to Vocational Education Programs

Vocational education programs in our thirteen senior high schools used more teaching resources than any other subject area. With an average of 22 percent of the total numbers of high school teachers in the sample, vocational education programs ranked slightly above English, which had an average of 20 percent of the teachers, and substantially above all other subjects. Math and social studies had the third largest share, with 13 percent of the total high school teachers each. At the junior high school level, vocational educational programs were the fourth largest in this regard (along with science) at our twelve schools. Programs in English (22 percent), math (18 percent), and social studies (14 percent) occupied greater percentages of teacher resources at the junior highs than did vocational education, with 12 percent of the total.

Considerable variation existed among the senior high schools, however. At seven of the schools, vocational programs occupied the largest percentage of teachers of any of the subject areas, ranging from 21 to 42 percent. Among the six schools where vocational education programs did not rank first, the percentages of teaching resources ranged from 13 to 21 percent. At four of these schools, vocational education programs ranked second. Only at two of the schools, where the subject area shared teaching resources fairly equally, did vocational education programs rank below second in percentage of total teaching resources. Clearly, vocational programs were very extensive at the senior high school level. At four of the schools, more than one-quarter of the total instructional program was in this area.

Although the range was not as great as at the senior high school level, the percentage of teacher resources in vocational education also varied among the junior high schools, which included one school with only 4 percent of teacher resources devoted to vocational subjects, four schools with 7 percent, six schools with 8 to 15 percent, and one with 22 percent. We found no relationship between the extensiveness of vocational programs at junior and senior high schools in the same community.

When we considered the allocation of teacher resources separately for schools differing in the racial and ethnic composition of their student populations, we did not find that the variation in resources at either the junior or senior level was associated with student race or ethnicity.[13] On the average, similar percentages of teacher resources were allocated to vocational programs at white and at nonwhite or mixed schools. We can conclude, then, that there was no greater overall emphasis—in terms of teaching resources—on vocational education programs in nonwhite or racially mixed schools than in white schools in our sample. And because teacher resources provide a good estimate of the proportion of the school's total instructional emphasis in a particular area, it seems clear that, on the average, white schools and those with a substantial nonwhite population gave about equal emphasis to vocational education.

Racial Composition of Vocational Education Programs at Multiracial and Multiethnic Schools

Among the mixed junior high schools we did not consistently find disproportionate percentages of nonwhite students in vocational classes. Similarly, the three mixed senior high schools about which we had student race/ethnicity information did not follow a consistent pattern of class composition.[14] Generally, it seems that the sample of multiracial/ethnic vocational classes we studied is too small and the schools too diverse to permit us to generalize about the assignment of students from various racial and ethnic groups to vocational education programs.

Vocational Education Content and Format and Student Race

Both the content and the format of vocational education programs at the two groups of schools—white and mixed or nonwhite—differed markedly at the senior high schools and somewhat at the junior high level. Further, at the senior high school level, the enrollment of various racial and ethnic groups in different types of vocational education programs followed distinct patterns.

As we have noted, vocational courses were offered in seven areas: (1) general industrial arts; (2) home economics; (3) business; (4) skill or trade preparation; (5) military preparation; (6) agriculture; and (7) general career, consumer education, or supervised work experience. Although somewhat varied, the content of nearly all these courses was almost exclusively technical or vocational in nature. Very few teachers of these courses appeared to have used vocational topics as an avenue to general education in any broader sense: the acquisition of academic skills, personal development, or social understanding. One or two teachers did list such course objectives as "analyze own goals and values" and "self-knowledge," but these more general goals were limited almost exclusively to "people-oriented" vocational courses, such as child care and home economics. For example, a teacher of a family living course at a black urban high school said, "Our most important objective is to help the student understand the significance and meaning of the capacity to love." And at a junior high school in a rural Mexican-American community, "awareness of the need for adjusting to change" and "acceptance of others' individual differences" were listed by a family living teacher as course objectives. Other than these examples, the attempt to provide general educational content in vocational courses appears to have been virtually nonexistent in the classes and school programs we studied.

In addition to the content differences, we found differences in the structural format of various vocational courses. Some courses were contained within the regular school schedule and occupied only one class period each day. Other courses extended over a longer period of time and were conducted as either on-campus laboratory or shop classes or partially or entirely off-campus. Interestingly, neither the content of vocational education courses nor the format was consistent among schools. Some of the variations appear to be associated with the geographical location of schools—agriculture at rural schools, for example. Most differences, however, seem to be related to the racial and ethnic makeup of a school's student population.

Table 8.1 displays some of the characteristics of the vocational education courses offered at our junior high schools. Several types of information are included in this table: (1) the number of different courses offered by the schools in each of the seven content categories, (2) the formats of the courses offered, (3) the racial category of schools offering the courses, and (4) the racial composition of courses of various types within the mixed schools.[15]

From the information included in table 8.1 we can see that junior high vocational education programs were more similar than they were different. Courses of similar content and format were offered at most of the schools. Eleven of the twelve junior high schools offered classes in home economics to their students, and ten schools offered classes in general industrial arts. White and nonwhite students across the sample seem to have had fairly equal access to these courses.

Three types of courses were not consistently offered at this level. Business courses (typing) were offered at five of the schools, consumer or general vocational education at three, and trade preparation at only one. Despite the overall similarity in offerings across schools, what differences there were in junior high school programs seem to be related to the racial composition of the student body. The percentages in table 8.2 show that while home economics and general industrial arts courses

TABLE 8.1

Characteristics of Vocational Programs at Twelve Junior High Schools and Race/Ethnicity of Students

| | Regular School Class | | Extended Time/Off-Campus | |
| | White Schools N of Courses | Nonwhite & Mixed Schools N of Courses | White Schools N of Courses | Nonwhite & Mixed Schools N of Courses |
Content Type				
Business	I (1 school)	I[a], 2[b], I[c] (4 schools)		
Trade Preparation				6[b] (1 school)
Military				
Agriculture				
Home Economics	6 (6 schools)	2[a], 4[b], 2[c] (5 schools)		
General Industrial Arts	11 (6 schools)	I[a], 2[b], 3[c] (3 schools)		
Consumer/Career/Misc.	I (1 school)	I[c] (1 school)	I (1 school)	

Above the format columns: *Format* spanning all four; *Regular School Class* spanning first two; *Extended Time/Off-Campus* spanning last two.

[a] Mixed school, class enrollment predominantly white
[b] Enrollment predominantly nonwhite
[c] Mixed school, race/ethnicity of enrolled students not known

Table 8.2

Distribution of Vocational Course Types, in Twelve Junior High Schools by Race/Ethnicity of Schools

Type of Course	White Schools	Nonwhite/Mixed Schools
Business	5%	16%
Trade	—	24%
Military	—	—
Agriculture	—	—
Home Economics	37%	32%
Industrial Arts	47%	24%
Consumer/Career/Misc.	11%	4%
	100%	100%

dominated the curriculum at the white schools, courses preparing students for specific occupations—offering both business and manual skills—constituted a substantial portion of the course offerings at nonwhite and mixed schools.

The program at one of the schools is illustrative of these differences. A mixed school in which 50 percent of its student population was Mexican-American was the only school to offer courses preparing students for specific trades. These courses occupied two hours per session and took students off the campus. The specific content included home and community services, operation of photocopy machines, horticulture, general mechanical repair, building maintenance, and general construction trades. Nonwhite students made up the bulk of the student enrollment. In sum, while similar vocational programs were available to white and nonwhite junior high school students, what program differences existed appear to have been related to the race/ethnicity of students, with courses offering specific skill training more often found at schools with a substantial nonwhite population.

Greater program differences were found at the senior high school level. Characteristics of the high school programs are shown in table 8.3. Not only were high school vocational programs quite varied, but the differences among them are clearly associated with the racial and ethnic makeup of the schools' student populations. Further, within schools of mixed racial or ethnic composition, the enrollment of white and nonwhite students in various types of vocational education courses followed distinct patterns. The following findings are illustrative of these differences.

Students at white and nonwhite or mixed schools had about the same number of vocational course offerings available to them—an average of 13 different course titles at white schools and 13.5 at nonwhite and mixed schools. Nevertheless, at the two sets of schools the substance of these courses differed considerably. Table 8.4 shows the percentages of vocational courses of various content types at the two sets of schools. The most obvious differences are in the percentages devoted to business, trade preparation, and general industrial arts courses. Students at white schools had considerably more extensive business and industrial arts programs avilable to them and considerably more restricted programs in trade preparation than did students attending nonwhite or mixed schools. Students at the latter group of schools had greater

TABLE 8.3

Characteristics of Vocational Programs at Thirteen Senior High Schools and Race/Ethnicity of Students

	Format			
	Regular School Class		Extended Time/Off-Campus	
Content Type	White Schools N of Courses	Nonwhite & Mixed Schools N of Courses	White Schools N of Courses	Nonwhite & Mixed Schools N of Courses
Business	32 (7 schools)	6[a], 8[b], 2[c] (6 schools)	4 (3 schools)	2[a], 6[b] (4 schools)
Trade Preparation	8 (5 schools)	1[a], 4[b] (2 schools)	3 (1 school)	20[b], 1[c] (5 schools)
Military	1 (1 school)	2[b], 2[c] (4 schools)		
Agriculture	4 (2 schools)	2[a] (1 school)		1[b] (1 school)
Home Economics	13 (7 schools)	4[a], 10[b], 2[c] (6 schools)		
General Industrial Arts	22 (6 schools)	6[b], 3[c] (5 schools)		
Consumer/Career/Misc.	3 (3 schools)	2[b], 1[c] (3 schools)	2 (2 schools)	1[c] (2 schools)

[a] Mixed school, course enrollment predominantly white
[b] Enrollment predominantly nonwhite
[c] Mixed school, race/ethnicity of enrolled students not known

TABLE 8.4

Distribution of Vocational Course Types at Thirteen Senior High Schools by Race/Ethnicity

Type of Course	White Schools	Nonwhite/Mixed Schools
Business	39%	27%
Trade	12%	31%
Military	−1%	5%
Agriculture	4%	3%
Home Economics	13%	19%
Industrial Arts	25%	10%
Consumer/Career/Misc.	6%	5%
	100%	100%

access to programs in military training and home economics than did students at the white schools.

The formats of the courses offered at the two groups of schools differed as well. At the white schools, 10 percent of the courses were scheduled for extended time periods and/or were conducted all or in part off-campus. At the nonwhite and mixed schools 37 percent of the courses were of this type.

Not only did the white schools have considerably more business courses available than did nonwhite and mixed schools, but within the mixed schools greater percentages of white than nonwhite students tended to be enrolled in the business courses offered. Of the thirteen business courses sampled at mixed schools, eight (62 percent) had a disproportionately high white enrollment, three (23 percent) had a disproportionately high nonwhite enrollment, and in two (15 percent) information about the race/ethnicity of the students enrolled was not available.

Within the business category there also appears to have been a difference in the type of courses made available to white and nonwhite students. Courses oriented toward management and finance were offered predominantly at white schools. Across the schools, both white and nonwhite students had access to courses in clerical skills such as typing, shorthand, bookkeeping, and office procedures. Courses in retailing were available at both types of schools as well. However, only students attending white schools were offered the following kinds of courses: the role of business, banking, taxation, business careers, the stock market, business machines, data processing, and business law.

Five all-white schools and five mixed or nonwhite schools offered courses preparing students for specific trades or with employable manual skills. Nevertheless, both the number and content of these courses varied considerably at the two types of schools. Eleven such courses were available at white schools, twenty-six at mixed or nonwhite schools. Both types of schools offered specific courses in drafting, machine shop, auto repair, and hospital or health occupations. Students at white schools had courses in marine technology, aviation, and power mechanics available as well. Students at nonwhite or mixed schools were offered the following: cosmetology, building construction, home and community services (institutional cooking and sewing), vocational child care, mill and cabinet shop, needle trades, upholstery, printing, commercial art, commercial photography, and housekeeping and food services. None of the white schools offered these courses to students.

The format of the trade preparation courses differed as well. Of the thirty-seven different courses offered, twenty-four extended beyond the regular class time period and/or were conducted off-campus. Of these twenty-four extended programs, twenty-one (88 percent) were at mixed or nonwhite schools, and twenty (83 percent) were attended all or mostly by nonwhite students. Three (13 percent) were attended by whites, and in one course (4 percent) the racial and ethnic composition of the class was unavailable. The three classes of this type attended by whites were the only ones in any of our schools that were conducted at the local community college.

Trade preparation courses differed, then, in the number, content, and formats of programs available to and attended by white and non-white students. Nonwhite students were more likely to be enrolled in courses in low-level skills, which were extended in length and often conducted in an off-campus setting.

Differences can also be seen in the opportunities students from different racial or ethnic groups had for preparation for military careers. Of the five such courses offered, four (80 percent) were at nonwhite or mixed schools. The single course at a white school was distinct from the others (which were standard ROTC programs) in that it was classified as a science rather than as a vocational education course and included science topics as well as military preparation as the focus of instruction.

Three schools, all in rural locations, offered agriculture classes. Two of the schools were white, and one mixed. At the white schools, agriculture classes were held on-campus and fit the regular class format. At the mixed school one of the two courses was of this type and enrolled mostly white students; the other was an extended off-campus program and enrolled mostly Mexican-American students.

General industrial arts courses were available at six of the seven all-white schools and at five of the six nonwhite or mixed schools. These courses were of a general education type, providing instruction in working with various kinds of materials rather than occupational preparation. All of them fit into the regular class period format. However, there was a discrepancy between the two types of schools in that while a total of twenty-two course offerings of this type were available across the sample of white schools, only nine such courses were offered at the nonwhite or mixed schools.

Including vocational education courses of all content types at the high schools, thirty-nine were of the extended-time or off-campus format. Of these, only nine were offered in the white schools: four (44 percent) in the business area, three (33 percent) in trades (community college courses), and two (22 percent) in supervised work experience. In contrast, at the nonwhite or mixed schools, thirty courses of this format were offered: seven (23 percent) in business, twenty-one (70 percent) in trades, one (less than 1 percent) in agriculture, and one in supervised work experience. Of the thirty-nine programs across the schools, twenty-six (67 percent) were attended either all or predominantly by nonwhite students and eleven (28 percent) entirely by white students. The racial/ethnic makeup of the remaining two classes was unavailable.

These observations of program differences clearly suggest that white and nonwhite high school students had very different vocational education opportunities available to them. Additionally, at schools of mixed racial or ethnic composition at this level, whites and nonwhites tend to have been enrolled in different types of courses.

Our study of vocational programs, then, yielded three major findings regarding the relationship of social stratification and vocational education programs. First, there was no evidence that, in the twenty-five schools studied, those with substantial nonwhite populations emphasized vocational education *as a subject area* more than did schools with all-white populations. While there was variation in emphasis among the schools, especially at the senior high level, the differences did not appear to be related to the race or ethnicity of the students enrolled. Second, no conclusive evidence emerged that disproportionate percentages of nonwhite students at the schools with mixed populations were enrolled in vocational education classes per se. While it was the case that at one junior high and two senior highs more than two-thirds of the students enrolled in sampled vocational education classes were nonwhite, at the three other mixed schools no disproportionate enrollment of nonwhites was found.

From these analyses it appears that white and nonwhite students participated in vocational education in fairly equivalent ways. Nonwhite and mixed schools were not more vocational in nature than were white schools. Nonwhite students in mixed schools did not appear to be consistently enrolled in disproportionate numbers in vocational programs. But it is not enough merely to consider the overall vocational emphasis in a school's instructional program or the percentage of white and nonwhite students enrolled in vocational courses. It is clear from the other differences we found that *substantive* differences both between and within school vocational programs resulted in marked differences in the vocational educational experiences of white and nonwhite secondary students.

It is important to note here that because socioeconomic status information on individual students was not collected as a part of A Study of Schooling, we could not consider the relationship between students' economic positions and vocational education directly. If we had had this information, it probably would have provided additional insight into the problem addressed here. It may be that, in vocational education, socioeconomic status is more highly associated with differences in the types of programs offered and attended than are race and ethnicity. This certainly has been the case in the study of many other educational factors. It probably was the case, as Evans and Galloway found,[16] that the students in vocational programs at our schools were generally of lower socioeconomic status than those who did not take vocational courses. The differences we found, then, were probably reflective of differences between the experiences of poorer white and poorer nonwhite students.

Two major implications can be derived from what we found in our data. First, the results of our inquiry point to the importance of looking beyond simple measures of school resources or student enrollment in programs when considering questions of educational equity. For, as the findings throughout this book indicate, it is likely that the differential socialization of children from various racial and economic backgrounds results from the *programmatic* differences they experience in schools. Within subject areas, if access to certain kinds of knowledge or organizational arrangements is restricted for some students and enhanced for others, schools cannot be said to be providing equal education or even equal opportunity. Just as we found with academic tracking, this was the case with the vocational programs in our schools. Differences in the experiences of white and nonwhites, likely to have important consequences for their social and economic futures, were found only in the actual *substance* of programs—their curricular content and organizational arrangements. The most straightforward and quantifiable features of these programs—the proportion of teaching resources allocated to vocational programs at schools and the proportion of students from different groups enrolled in vocational subjects at mixed schools—masked these substantive differences. Had these been the only factors we considered, very different and misleading conclusions would have been reached.

The second implication of what we found flows from the *direction* of the substantive differences in the vocational education experiences of whites and nonwhites. The kinds of differences that emerged indicate that nonwhites more than whites were being directed in their vocational training toward futures in lower-class social and economic positions. Programs enrolling predominantly or all nonwhite students were more likely to center around specific training for low-level occupations than were courses enrolling mostly whites. These differences were found as early as junior high, with courses in clerical skills and manual labor offered almost exlusively in nonwhite and mixed schools. Junior high vocational courses in white schools were nearly all of a more general type—homemaking and general industrial arts. Skills taught in these courses are those regarded as useful to all, regardless of occupational status. Knowledge of foods and their preparation and general woodworking skills, for example, have no social-class divisions and are considered as appropriate for the future attorney or teacher as for the future mechanic or domestic worker. This is not true of such skills as building maintenance or commercial sewing, which are tied to specific low-level occupations.

This content distinction was even more clear at the senior high school level. Business courses available to nonwhites were those that taught clerical or retail sales skills. White students, on the other hand, were offered programs emphasizing the managerial and financial aspects of the business world as well—courses in taxation and the stock market, for example.

Even more blatant than the differences in vocational business courses were the content differences in programs dealing with manual skills. Programs in this area at schools with white populations were comprised largely of general industrial arts classes, with only limited programs offered in preparation for specific manual occupations. Few courses of the general industrial arts type had a predominantly nonwhite enrollment at mixed schools, and very few such courses were offered at nonwhite schools. Courses serving nonwhite student groups were more likely to consist of training for specific low-level occupations.

Two occupational training programs offered to whites but not to nonwhites in the sample were marine technology and aviation, vocations of relatively high status. Thus, the *content* of vocational courses offered to nonwhites consisted largely of specific preparation for low-level occupations.

Furthermore, the differences found in the *format* of vocational courses most likely to be attended by whites and nonwhites were such that they would be likely to augment the effects of the content differences. Programs at white schools tended to be held on-campus (or on a college campus) and to fit into the regular school schedule. It seems likely that students taking courses of this type would perceive their classes to be "regular" classes and themselves to be part of the regular school program. In contrast, courses taken by nonwhites often tended to be less closely linked to the regular school program: many extended beyond the regular class period and were held at off-campus locations. This format was found as early as junior high in one of the mixed schools we studied. It seems very likely that students who spend extended periods of time in vocational training courses and who leave the campus for on-the-job experience would feel considerably distanced from the nonvocational program at their schools. It may be that nonwhites were led in these ways to believe that schools and the more "regular" program of courses offered were not appropriate for them. Since courses of this format were offered as early as junior high school, perhaps to students as young as twelve years, very early decisions about the relevance of academics and schooling to future opportunities may be taking place for some. These decisions may greatly affect the social and economic positions the students eventually attain.

Clearly, then, programmatic differences in the vocational education experiences of whites and nonwhites in our schools point to a stratification of students and a differentiation of programs, with serious social and economic consequences. Nonwhite students were enrolled earlier and more extensively in programs training specifically for low-status occupations.[17] Moreover, these programs more often took nonwhites off the school campus for extended periods of time, a format likely to distance them from academics and the regular context of schooling.

These differences in themselves imply that inequities exist in the educational experiences of many of the nonwhites taking vocational education. If the questionable returns to individual participants in vocational training programs are considered, these inequities are greatly compounded. The end result of many such programs in public schools may be that large numbers of nonwhite students are channeled early into education and training for specific low-level occupations rather than encouraged to continue in more academic programs. These students may be eased out of the school setting through on-the-job training during the school day. They may be likely to leave school early believing they have been trained in marketable skills, only to find that they cannot translate these skills into occupational advantage.

The findings of Wilms and Hansell concerning postsecondary programs are relevant here, too.[18] In postsecondary vocational programs, while initial selection for high- or low-status programs does not appear to reflect differences in socioeconomic status or race (although Wilms and Hansell did find a low, but significant, positive association between being black and enrolling in low-status programs), the gatekeeping function we have seen in secondary programs may be fulfilled through student dropouts at the postsecondary level. Among those students who drop out of programs, thereby forgoing the small possibility of translating training into enhanced success in the labor market, were disproportionate percentages of poorer and black students. We may be seeing here largely a difference in form rather than in substantive result between secondary and postsecondary vocational programs. This hunch is further supported by the Wilms and Hansell findings of the low likelihood of a positive return to students in programs training for higher-status jobs. While nonwhite students might have been as likely as whites to enroll in such programs, few of them, whether graduates or dropouts, could find jobs related to their training. So while they were not singled out for exclusion initially, black students seem unable to use postsecondary vocational programs as an avenue for entry into higher-status occupations. Thus the public provision of vocational education at both the secondary and postsecondary levels may represent no real increase in opportunity for black students.

It is unlikely that vocational training programs provide either the type or the scope of education necessary to overcome race and class obstacles to employment. It has been suggested by several scholars that while schooling is related to employment opportunity, specific skills learned are not the critical elements. Lester Thurow indicates that for employers the function of education is not to impart skills but to "certify" that an individual is trainable. Trainable individuals are those who have been successful at school and thus display motivation, general literacy, and an industrial type of discipline.[19] This attitude toward prospective employees is certainly reflected in a recent commentary in the *Los Angeles Times* by Cornell C. Maier, chairman and chief executive officer of Kaiser Aluminum and Chemical Corporation. Maier wrote:

Thousands of jobs in California are going unfilled because of a shortage of qualified applicants. These are not highly technical or specialized jobs, but entry-level positions that require basic competency in reading, writing and computation. . . .

Business is willing to train employees to meet the increasingly complex demands of the marketplace, but can do so only if those employees are ready to be trained and promoted.[20]

Randall Collins suggests that since the same characteristics—those largely related to inherited social status—are required for occupational success and school attainment, educational success can substitute for occupational screening by employers.[21] Herbert Gintis theorizes that educational qualifications are, for the most part, a reflection of the personality characteristics that employers look for when hiring.[22] This relates to the opportunities of nonwhite vocational students in the following way. It is unlikely that employers view graduates of vocational programs, and certainly not early leavers, as having been successful at school. Students from vocational programs, in fact, may be seen as school failures, unable to succeed in the more academic programs. As a result, employers are likely to prefer nonvocational students, who appear to be more certified as trainable. For nonwhite vocational students, these difficulties may be even more pronounced. Because of the historic barriers faced by nonwhites in obtaining any but the lowest-level positions, employers may require greater assurance of their possession of the desired cultural and personality characteristics. Vocational education program attendance does not appear to supply this assurance.

One tangential, but crucial, consideration in the whole issue of the schools' culpability in limiting the future opportunities of poor and minority students is the extent to which students choose to enroll in the vocational courses they take. Further, if these choices do exist, to what degree do they seem to be genuine choices, based on realistic alternatives and thorough, accurate information? As we saw in chapter 2, only three of the thirteen high schools we studied said that students and/or their parents were among the *primary* decision makers in a student's curriculum-track placement. At none of the twelve junior highs studied were students or their parents reported to have a primary decision-making role. Almost invariably the schools indicated that counselors and teachers had the greatest control over how students were assigned to curricula. Usually, too, test scores were cited as very influential in the selection process.

We know that at many schools students are asked to indicate whether they prefer placement in a curriculum leading to college entrance, one emphasizing vocational preparation, or a more general course (not leading to higher-status colleges). These choices, however, are not made free of influence. They are informed choices—informed by the school guidance process and by the other indicators schools use to determine what appropriate placements are likely to be, such as test scores and the recommendations of teachers and counselors. It is possible, given these circumstances, that even if student choice *had* been reported to be a major factor in placements, student decisions would not differ greatly from those made about them by their schools.

Another important factor in the school's role in limiting opportunity is the flexibility students have in switching from one program to another or in taking a variety of types of courses, both academic and vocational. In our twenty-five schools most students were locked into their curricular placements. The general rule at most schools was that nearly all students remained in their assigned curricula from year to year.

Clearly vocational education along with academic tracking plays a part in restricting the access minority students have to future opportunities. But, as with academic tracking, any significant change in the processes and effects of vocational education must follow a careful examination of the assumptions we make about it. This is seldom done, especially in the policymaking realm. As late as April 1983, the Presidential Commission on Education in its report *A Nation at Risk* suggested as a solution to the declining quality of education that both academic and vocational tracks be improved and toughened and that the general (middle) curriculum be viewed as the "culprit."[23] Caution must be exercised in following this course, for without a thorough and deep look at the equity issues, it could be interpreted as a mandate for stepped-up social stratification via the schools. Expanded vocational emphasis is likely to continue to sort students along racial and economic lines. In view of our findings, school people and policymakers should seriously reconsider the appropriateness of vocational training in secondary schools.

The relationship of tracking, vocational education, and equality is certainly a complex one, not so much born out of an overt elite conspiracy as emerging as part of a culture saturated with a hierarchical structure of political, economic, and social opportunity. It is likely that these programs do not serve the democratic ends most Americans want their schools to achieve.

9

Some Constitutional Questions

How can it be legal for schools to treat some students so much better than others? Isn't it likely that there are some violations of fundamental rights embedded in the processes we have been looking at? Considering what we know about how tracking affects the kind of education secondary students get, it is difficult not to question the legality of the process. Tracking can be easily thought of as a barrier to educational equality because it so clearly limits the access some students have to certain school experiences. Viewed in this way, tracking is a likely target for a court challenge on constitutional grounds. Nevertheless, constitutional issues are sticky ones. As we shall see, regardless of how clear the injustices of tracking appear to be, the question of its legality is as unclear today as was that of many racially discriminatory practices prior to the 1950s.

Citing the equal protection clause of the Fourteenth Amendment, the Supreme Court in 1954 struck down the "separate but equal" concept of educational equity. In doing so, the Court made two rulings with far-reaching consequences for the conduct of schooling in the United States. First, the separation of students by race was determined to be *inherently* unequal. Second, the Court required that education be made available to all on equal terms.[1] The impact of these rulings, especially in view of the changes in our thinking about what constitutes equal educational opportunity and the vigor with which the judicial system has attempted to translate these concepts into practice, has been felt in nearly all areas of public education. It is likely that aspects of educational practice, not yet challenged on these grounds in the legal system, will be subject to scrutiny by the courts in the future. It is also likely that many of these challenges will involve the distribution of educational resources and opportunities to various groups of students *within schools* rather than focusing only on between-school inequities. In view of these legal realities impinging on schooling, taken together with what we know about tracking, this kind of sorting of students will probably be subject to further legal action in the future.

In this chapter we will look at what we know about the processes and effects of tracking in light of the constitutional guarantees that make it a likely target for those who are challenging barriers to equal educational opportunity. Commentary on the law found in law review journals and the texts of actual court cases are helpful in this examination as they provide concepts likely to influence both the character of legal challenges to tracking and the direction of the courts' responses to such challenges. Legal commentary helps to unravel these often intricate points of law. Cases in which tracking has already been considered by the courts give us some indication of what might be legal precedents. Other cases that might be considered analogous—those dealing with related issues—can help us speculate about new legal approaches that might be adopted in a challenge to tracking.

Because public schools are governmental agencies, tracking is a governmental action. More specifically, tracking is a governmental action that classifies and separates students and thereby determines the amount, the quality, and even the value of the government service (education) that students receive. The classifications made are both durable and stigmatizing. Further, they do not appear to be essential to the process of providing educational services. In fact, for some students they may interfere with the educational process. For all these reasons, the federal courts may be very much interested in public school tracking.

Before considering the legal issues in detail, however, it is worthwhile to review more carefully those characteristics of tracking that are likely to be the focus of any legal action. As we have seen, the most fundamental characteristic of all tracking systems is that they classify and separate students for different educational treatments. We know that the extent and type of separation may be different in different schools and among children at different ages. We know that tracking may be as limited as within-class groupings, where it is largely the pace rather than the content of instruction that is varied and where children meet for relatively short periods of time (reading groups, for example). This type is most common in the early elementary grades. On the other hand, tracking may comprise an almost complete separation of students, so that they are provided with distinctly different learnings on the basis of assumptions about their educational and occupational potential. This type occurs at many secondary schools. Nevertheless, *all* tracking systems create classifications that determine both the quantity and the type of education students receive. This classification process affects children's access to education.

We have also noted a set of widely held beliefs that characterize tracking and influence how it is practiced. One is the belief that students differ greatly in their academic potential and aptitude for schooling—differ so much, in fact, that distinct educational treatments are necessary to help students learn. Further, student differences are considered to be so great and so difficult to manage that the segregation of various kinds of students into separate instructional groups is required to administer these different treatments effectively—in other words, to do the teaching. Another assumption is that although people in schools often say that learning deficiencies can be remediated and that students with educationally impoverished backgrounds can "catch up" through special temporary compensatory programs, in practice this catching up is considered the exception rather than the rule. In fact, the aptitude characteristics on which students are classified (even when measured by achievement tests) are seen by almost everyone as quite stable, perhaps even unchangeable. While not everyone holds that academic abilities are inherent and immutable, it is generally believed that this kind of aptitude is not likely to be changed very much by educational experiences. A third belief is that the classification and sorting of students by their learning potential can be accomplished accurately and fairly easily. We saw in chapter 1 how little evidence supports these assumptions and in chapter 2 the historical events that have encouraged and sustained them.

Despite their questionable grounding, these three beliefs result in a number of tracking practices that influence the strength and duration of the impact of classifications on the opportunities of students.

First, following from the view that the wide differences among students makes it necessary not only to group them homogeneously but to teach them differently, students in various tracks have substantially different experiences in schools. We have seen clearly that this was the case in the Study of Schooling secondary schools.

One such difference stems from the fact that the separation of students based on school procedures for estimating academic potential leads to marked differences in the composition of classes. Minority children and those from the lowest socioeconomic groups have been consistently found in disproportionate numbers in classes at the lowest track levels and children from upper socioeconomic levels have been found to be consistently overrepresented in higher tracks. In view of the studies that have linked class composition with academic achievement, these differences are likely to affect differences in the education of students at different track levels.[2] Additionally, many teachers say that low-track teaching assignments are less preferable to others. As a result, low classes are often taught by the least experienced teachers in schools.[3] Both teachers' dislike of their assignment to low-track groups and their relative inexperience are likely to affect the education of students in such groups.

Further, we have seen in our twenty-five schools that both the content and the methods of instruction vary markedly in classes at different levels. Students in high groups are more likely than others to have access to knowledge most valued in society. Further, there is evidence that students in low groups spend less time in learning activities and are less likely to experience instructional strategies associated with academic achievement. All these factors indicate that the education received by students classified and placed at different track levels is different.

If these differences served to enhance the learning of different groupings of students, they could from a legal viewpoint be considered fairly neutral. Yet we know that tracking and presumably the differential treatment that accompanies it have not led to gains in student achievement.[4] In addition, it has had negative effects on the achievement of students in average and lower groups with the most adverse effects on those students at the bottom levels.[5] Thus, it seems possible that the educational differences resulting both from the separation of students itself and from the educational treatments students subsequently receive may be of concern under the concept, established in *Brown*, that education must be available for all on equal terms.

Second, probably because student aptitude, used as the primary basis for tracking classifications, is seen as quite stable, placements are only infrequently reevaluated. As a result, student classifications tend to be permanent and tracks inflexible. Students graduated from high school "general" or "vocational" programs are quite often those who were classified as slow in primary grades and grouped accordingly. In this way, the classification process has long-term effects on the learning opportunities of students.

Moreover, these classifications and placements are more than simply long-lasting. For while ability classifications are seen as characteristics of students themselves, they are not usually viewed as neutral attributes. To be labeled "slow" and placed in a "basic" class, for example, does not merely result in an educational treatment that is different from that given to students labeled "bright" and placed in an honors class. If this were so, ability classifications would be analogous to the identification of blood type, for example, which has consequences for various medical treatments. This, however, is not the case. The classifications "slow," "basic," "remedial," differ greatly in prestige from those of "fast," "bright," or "honors," both in schools and in society in general. A student classified and placed in low tracks, whatever the particular terminology employed, is identified as "dumb," a stigmatizing label with effects that are extremely difficult, if not impossible, to overcome.

Furthermore, a stigmatizing low-track label not only may adversely affect a student's self-perceptions but is also likely to lower the expectations for his or her learning held by peers, teachers, and school counselors. These lower expectations may result in a self-fulfilling prophecy, with students achieving only what is expected of them. As is well known, many of the teacher expectation studies have shown different outcomes for similar students resulting from teacher behaviors modified by their different expectations for them.[6] The stigmatizing effects of track levels and the concomitant harm, especially to misclassified students, are also issues that may be of interest to the courts.

Third, despite these long-lasting and potentially harmful effects of tracking decisions on students, the classification process is rarely well defined or consistently carried out. As we have seen, many districts, in fact, have no formal policy regarding the criteria for ability-grouping placements; in other districts, policy exists but is not carefully followed. Decisions are often left to individual administrators, counselors, and teachers. Parents and students are often not informed as to placement criteria, or the differences in educational treatments offered to different groups, or even the restrictions on students' access to further educational or occupational opportunities that may result from various placements. We have seen too that in some districts and schools parents are not routinely informed that their children are being classified and tracked at all.

We know that student placements are based largely on the results of standardized tests of achievement or aptitude that may not always be appropriate for these decisions. In some schools, either the content or the norm group of a test may render it an ineffective measure for some groups of students—those with language or cultural differences, for example. In other situations, test administration is inappropriately conducted. Furthermore, test results are sometimes used to make decisions about placements in program relatively unrelated to the content; reading tests, for example, are often used to determine placement in a variety of subjects. Test scores are not the only widely used criteria for classification, however. Many decisions are based on teachers' and counselors' observations of past academic performance, student behavior in the classroom, student dress and speech styles, and other subjective information. The lack of defined policy and the cavalier use of test results and subjective judgments are characteristic of tracking classification processes in many school districts. And because these classifications so often come to be seen as unchanging and virtually unchangeable characteristics of the students thus categorized as "slow," "average," "honors," and so on, classification processes, which are often haphazard, have serious and long-term effects on the educational opportunities of students. Under such circumstances, the misclassification of students is a matter of substantial consequence.

Several characteristics and effects of tracking, then, may be susceptible to legal action in relation to the provision of equal educational opportunity. In sum, these are: the separation of students resulting in disproportionate placements of poor and minority students in low groups; the reduced educational quality in low groups; the limited access low groups have to higher education or some occupations; the relative permanence of ability classifications and inflexibility of grouping systems; the stigmatization of low-track students; and the misclassification of students resulting from inappropriate or haphazard classification processes.

Turning to the question of the legality of tracking itself or of the characteristic practices associated with it, two precepts from the Fourteenth Amendment must be considered:

. . . nor shall any state deprive any person of life, liberty, or property without due process of law, nor deny to any person within its jurisdiction the equal protection of the laws.[7]

The principles of *due process* and *equal protection* may both be applicable to a legal challenge to tracking. Due process challenges governmental actions on procedural grounds, requiring that fair and just procedures be followed before denying an individual access to any important governmental benefit or constitutionally protected right (life, liberty, or property). Additionally, federal cases have established the right of procedural due process before an individual may be stigmatized by public officials. In the most frequently cited case, *Wisconsin v. Constantineau,* the Supreme Court ruled that a due process hearing was required before an individual could be labeled a "drunkard," a label determined by the Court to be stigmatizing.[8] This case has been used as precedent for the requirement of due process safeguards in situations where a stigma was likely to result from a government-affixed label.

Procedural due process applies to access to education directly following the ruling in Goss v. *Lopez* that education is a "property" right and that denial of this right is subject to due process.[9] While the *Goss* decision entitled a child to due process before a change of status that results in exclusion from school for any reason, it may be applicable to tracking as well, although this has not been tested in the courts. The classification process that is an essential feature of tracking effects a change of status in the children involved and excludes them from particular types of educational experiences. This limited access affects not only the quality and quantity of education children receive but also their future educational and occupational opportunities. Because of these parallels, it seems likely that procedural due process requirements could be extended by the courts to include tracking decisions.

Due process procedural protection in education has been further developed in cases involving the labeling of handicapped children and their exclusion from regular school programs. Established due process procedures resulting from these cases include the provision of a notice and a hearing for any mentally retarded child being assigned to special classes.[10] The *Mills* case extended these safeguards to all "exceptional" children being considered for any type of special school placement.[11] Fundamental to these procedures are the following safeguards: (1) the appointment of an independent hearing officer, (2) the presumption that the best placement is in a regular class, and (3) shifting the burden of proof from the child involved to the school. This third safeguard places the school in the position of having to show that the classification of exceptional children and their placement in special programs are reasonably related to providing these children with a better educational opportunity than is available in the regular school setting.

The basic purpose of the due process requirement stemming from these cases is to prevent harm from accruing to students misclassified and misplaced in special programs. Both the stigma resulting from erroneous labeling and the reduced educational opportunity resulting from misplacement are harms that have been seen by the courts as warranting constitutional protections. A procedural due process hearing provides parents and out-of-school professionals with the opportunity to question or challenge the appropriateness of a classification for a particular child.

While classification and placement in a low track do not constitute total exclusion from regular school programs or confer the same stigma as labels of "retarded" or "learning disabled," the difference seems to be in degree rather than in kind. Both classifications result in a stigmatizing label and reduced educational opportunity and are generally permanently affixed to a child. Therefore, it seems that not only the basic due process rights established in *Goss* but the specific procedures and safeguards established in the *PARC* and *Mills* cases as well could be extended to track classifications and placements.

Procedural due process requirements, however, do not challenge the legality of the classifications themselves; they only set requirements for fair application. For a substantive challenge to ability classifications, one that challenges the government's right to make such discriminations among students at all—however fairly they might be made—plaintiffs must usually look to the second cited principle of the Fourteenth Amendment, that of equal protection. The equal protection provision prohibits certain kinds of discriminatory practices—denial of voting privileges because of race or sex, for example.

Yet, while the basis for making a substantive challenge to the practice of tracking itself is clearly the equal protection clause, the application of equal protection guarantees to school practices has certainly not been well defined. Questions of equality in relationship to public school practices are clouded by such issues as what standards should be applied to assess adequacy in schools and whether equality means equal access, equal treatment, or equal outcomes for students. And, further, equal protection questions regarding education are confused by considerations of what standards or criteria the courts should apply when evaluating state actions in this area.[12]

Generally, the equal protection clause has been interpreted to mean that any action by the government cannot discriminate against persons in similar circumstances unless the different treatment can be shown to be justifiable—in other words that it is necessary to achieve a valid governmental goal.[13] Two tests, or standards of judicial review, have traditionally been applied, each under a particular set of circumstances, in cases challenging practices under the equal protection provision. The more common and less stringent test is that of "minimum rationality." Using this test, the Court requires only that the classifications or discriminations made have some *rational* relationship to a legitimate governmental goal. When this test is applied, the Court assumes that the state action is constitutional. The burden is on the plaintiff to show that a classification is arbitrary or unreasonable in relationship to government purposes. Not surprisingly, the absence of *any* reasonable relationship has been quite difficult to prove by plaintiffs. The second and much more stringent test applied to equal protection cases is a more recent one, emerging clearly in the decisions of the Warren Court—that of strict scrutiny or strict review. If government action can be shown to infringe on a "fundamental interest" or create a "suspect classification," this test may be invoked. The important differences between this test and that of "minimum rationality" is that when the strict scrutiny test is applied the burden of proof shifts to the defendant—the government agency under challenge. The government must prove that its action in classifying and discriminating among individuals not only is rationally related to a government goal but is *essential* to the achievement of a *compelling purpose* of government. Under this strict review procedure, defendants have only rarely been able to prove that discriminatory action is essential to a compelling interest of the state. To establish the need for a strict scrutiny test, clearly the most advantageous position for a plaintiff, the plaintiff must argue that a fundamental interest has been infringed upon or that a suspect classification has been created by governmental action. These two criteria have not been clearly defined in education cases.

Whether or not education in itself is a fundamental interest subject to constitutional protection is a matter of some controversy. Several arguments have been put forth in the legal literature and in the language of cases for the recognition of education as a fundamental interest. Most notably in *Serrano* v. *Priest* the court advanced that education is critical in gaining access to other basic personal rights, including securing employment, participating fully in the political process, and exercising completely the rights of free speech and association.[14] Additionally, the court concluded that education merits treatment as a fundamental interest because it is universal and compulsory, because it occupies ten years or more of a child's life, and because it shapes individual character and intellect. In sum, in the *Serrano* decision, the court concluded, "We are convinced that the distinctive and priceless function of education in our society warrants, indeed, compels our treatment of it as a 'fundamental interest.'"[15] However, a more recent Supreme Court decision, in *San Antonio Independent School District* v. *Rodriguez*, reversed the trend toward according education fundamental interest status for judicial review.[16] The Court concluded, "Education, of course, is not among the rights afforded explicit protection under our Federal Constitution. Nor do we find any basis for saying it is implicitly so protected."[17]

However, in *Rodriguez*, the fundamental interest avenue was not completely blocked. The Court conceded that education may be considered a fundamental interest if "the system fails to provide each child with the opportunity to acquire the basic minimal skills necessary for the enjoyment of the rights of speech and of full participation in the political process."[18]

Following the position taken in *Rodriguez*, the Supreme Court recently reaffirmed that public education is not a right granted to individuals by the Constitution.[19] But in *Plyler* v. *Doe*, the Court struck down the denial of public education to the children of illegal aliens in Texas partly because education is more than "some governmental 'benefit' indistinguishable from other forms of social welfare legislation. Both the importance of education in maintaining our basic institutions, and the lasting impact of its deprivation on the life of the child, mark the distinction."[20] In the decision the Court discussed at some length the impact on an individual of denial of a basic education. Important to our argument is that the Court determined that because of the magnitude of these consequences a stricter standard of review than the "minimum rationality" test was appropriate in this case. "In light of these countervailing costs, the discrimination contained in §21.031 the [Texas statute under consideration] can hardly be considered rational unless it furthers some substantial goals of the state."[21]

Thus it appears that, for now at least, challenges citing violation of the equal protection clause in regard to school practices will not receive the strict scrutiny standard stemming from the consideration of education itself as a fundamental interest of the state. Yet the ruling in *Rodriguez* paved the way for viewing a minimal level of education as a "fundamental interest," and it appears that in *Plyler* the Court chose to take that course, clearly leaving the door open for cases involving access to education to be subject to careful and special judicial review.

When plaintiffs in cases challenging school practices under the equal protection provision have demonstrated that suspect classifications have resulted from governmental action, the Court has invoked the strict scrutiny standard of review. Although the term has never been neatly defined, it can be inferred from equal protection cases that a "suspect" classification of people is one based on congenital and immutable characteristics that are inherently impossible to escape and that the group involved is a discrete and insular minority with no control over its status.[22] Traditionally, suspect classifications have been those based on race, national ancestry, or citizenship status. The Court utilizes strict scrutiny in cases involving suspect classifications because these groups have been viewed as requiring special protection. Racial segregation is the governmental action that has most commonly been shown to create suspect classifications in schools. As a result, in segregation suits school districts have been required to prove that a compelling government interest has been served by segregative acts under the strict scrutiny standard of review. It is clear that they have been unable to do so.

Whether or not a plaintiff could find relief under the equal protection clause claiming that low-track classification and placement were discriminatory governmental actions affecting his or her access to education is unclear.

Under a minimum rationality standard of review, it seems highly unlikely that such a challenge would be successful. The Court would assume the constitutionality of the tracking system, and the defendant school district would simply have to show a rational relationship between grouping and educative purposes. This relationship has been fairly well established in case law during the past century. In 1877 an Illinois court decided: "Under the power to prescribe necessary rules and regulations for the management and government of the school, [the board] may, undoubtedly, require classification of the pupils with respect to proficiency or degrees of advancement in the same branches."[23] In fact, there is no case on record in which academic ability alone has been held as an unconstitutional criterion for classifying students for educational purposes. Tracking has been seen as a technique legitimately used by educators, an aspect of school people's special expertise. The courts have therefore been unwilling to challenge academic classifications.

If, however, the plaintiffs could establish that low-track classification denied access to the level of education necessary to acquire the basic minimal skills recognized in *Rodriguez* as a fundamental interest or constituted a denial of education with consequences of the magnitude of those found in *Plyler*, the strict scrutiny standard of review might be applied by the courts. In that event, the defendant school district would then bear the burden of proof and would be required to show that such classifications were not merely rationally related to a governmental purpose—education—but were essential to achieving a compelling state interest. Given the lack of evidence that tracking enhances either achievement or affective educational outcomes and the evidence that tracking is likely to be detrimental to students in the lower groups, it is unlikely that the school district could show that a compelling government interest was being served. However, the extent of harm implied by denial of access to education for the provision of basic minimal skills would be difficult to establish. It seems likely that such a challenge would need to assert that functional illiteracy resulted from low-track placement. This would probably require proof that similar children in other classifications did acquire these basic minimal skills or evidence that the same students in other situations (with subsequent tutoring, for example) had their academic deficiencies remediated. While there are no precedents for a case such as this, some parallels may be seen in the education malpractice suit of *Peter Doe* v. *San Francisco Unified School District*.[24]

The only successful court challenges to tracking thus far have been in cases where these practices have resulted in racially identifiable groups. In these cases the classification process was seen as creating suspect classifications, and cases were then subject to a strict scrutiny standard of review.

Hobson v. *Hansen* is the best known and probably still the most important ruling on tracking.[25] The *Hobson* decision was based on the disproportionate classification and placement of both poor and minority children in low-track classes. In *Hobson*, Judge Skelly Wright found the track system of the Washington, D.C., schools to be constitutionally invalid in that it violated the equal protection clause of the Fourteenth Amendment. Because the system was found to restrict access to what the court called a "critical personal right" and created suspect classifications of poor and minority children, the school district was required to prove that the track system was providing maximum educational opportunity for children of widely ranging ability levels—that is, it was serving a compelling governmental interest. The court ruled, "The track system amounts to an unlawful discrimination against those students whose educational opportunities are being limited on the erroneous assumption that they are capable of no more."[26] Further, "Even in concept the track system is undemocratic and discriminatory. Its creator [School Superintendent Hansen] admits it is designed to prepare some children for white-collar, and other children for blue-collar, jobs. . . . Moreover, any system of ability grouping which, through failure to include and implement the concept of compensatory education for the disadvantaged child or otherwise fails in fact to bring the great majority of children into the mainstream of public education denies the children excluded equal opportunity and thus encounters the constitutional bar."[27]

The *Hobson* decision was based on the following findings: (1) the inappropriateness of the aptitude tests used to assign black and disadvantaged children to groups, based as they were on a white, middle-class norm group; (2) the reduced curricula and the absence of adequate remedial and compensatory education in the lower track; (3) the rigidity of the track system, which made movement out of the bottom track almost impossible; and (4) the stigma placed on a child assigned to the lowest track. This decision, however, was limited to the Washington, D.C., school track system, and the judge declined to contradict the assumption that tracking in general can be related to the purposes of public education. Further, the decision in the appeals case of *Hobson—Smuck*

v. *Hobson*—narrowed the original order to abolish the Washington tracking system.[28] Instead of abolishing the system entirely, the *Smuck* ruling abolished only the system as it existed at the time of *Hobson*. Thus the district was permitted to reinstate a system of ability grouping as long as the misuses cited in *Hobson* were avoided.[29]

Since the *Hobson* case other litigation has dealt with ability classifications and grouping of students. The cases most directly linked to tracking in general are those in which it was implicated in the resegregation of students on the basis of race soon after schools were ordered to desegregate. In *Moses v. Washington Parrish School Board*,[30] one of several similar cases in the Fifth Circuit Court, the court held that tracking violated black students' Fourteenth Amendment rights for the following reason:

Homogeneous grouping is educationally detrimental to students assigned to the lower sections and blacks comprise a disproportionate number of the students in the lower sections. This is especially true where, as[here], black students who until recently were educated in admittedly inferior schools are now competing with white students educated in superior schools for positions in the top sections.[31]

In a more recent case in the Fifth Circuit, *McNeal v. Tate County School District*, the court ruled that a desegregated school district could not employ a tracking system that resulted in racially identifiable classrooms until it had operated a unitary system long enough to ensure that the harmful effects of prior segregation had been overcome.[32] The court summarized earlier findings of related cases:

Ability grouping, like any other non-racial method of student assignment, is not constitutionally forbidden. Certainly educators are in a better position than courts to appreciate the educational advantages or disadvantages of such a system in a particular school or district. School districts ought to be, and are, free to use such grouping whenever it does not have a racially discriminatory effect. If it does cause segregation, whether in classrooms or in schools, ability grouping may nevertheless be permitted in an otherwise unitary system if the school district can demonstrate that its assignment method is not based on the present results of past segregation or will remedy such results through better educational opportunities.[33]

The Fifth Circuit has been consistent in its treatment of tracking. For example, in *United States v. Gadsden County School District* the court followed the language of *McNeal* in ruling on ability grouping.[34] It upheld the lower court ruling prohibiting the use of tracking because the district failed to show that the assignment method was not based on the "present results of past segregation" or that the grouping system would provide better educational opportunities and thus remedy the prior harm of segregation.[35] Interestingly, the judgment of a lack of proof of better educational opportunity in the *Gadsden* case was based on the lack of mobility of low-track students. "The evidence before the court fails to disclose that, during these past years when such grouping has been employed, any meaningful number of students moved upward in these group sections, either during the year or from year to year."[36] What is significant here is the consideration of *educational* (track mobility) as well as racial effects in the decision of the court.

Thus it is clear that tracking challenges have been successful only where racially identifiable classes have resulted and in school districts with a history of prior de jure racial segregation. In these cases, with the exception of Hobson and to a much lesser extent *Gadsden*, the focus of the court has been on the issue with legal precedent—racial separation—and not on issues that deal with equity in educational access, treatment, and outcomes for all students.

Two other cases not directly related to the classification and placement of normal children in ability groups are also relevant here. Both concern the disproportionate placement of minority children and set new requirements on districts' classification procedures. In *Larry P.* v. *Riles*[37] and *Larry P.* v. *Riles*[38] (also knows as *Larry P. II*), the court ruled that black students could no longer be placed in classes for the educable mentally retarded on the basis of IQ tests that resulted in racial imbalance in these classes. The ruling stemmed from the failure of the defendant school district (San Francisco) to show a rational relationship between the use of IQ tests and a student's academic potential. This injunction against the use of standardized IQ tests with black children was extended to the entire state of California in the 1979 decision. Similar findings resulted from *Lora* v. *Board of Education of the City of New York* in which black and Hispanic students claimed that, because they were being placed in disproportionate percentages in special schools for emotionally disturbed children, their rights were being violated.[39] The court found the placement procedure, which included testing and subjective criteria, to be a violation of students' rights to equal protection and due process. These two cases are significant for two reasons. First, they both concerned racial imbalance within *types* of school programs in school districts withiout a history of maintaining dual school systems. Furthermore, the rulings in these cases assessed the harm to be a result not of prior segregation but rather of procedures now in use. And second, both cases were precedent setting in procedure in that they focused directly on the educational processes involved as well as on the segregative aspects of the classification systems in question.

These two important departures from previous cases have implications for future education cases in general and possibly for tracking cases as well. School districts employing tracking systems that result in racially identifiable classes, whether or not they use procedures that are ostensibly racially neurtral and whether or not they have a history of segregative actions, are likely to be challenged under the principles established in these cases. And, as the research has made clear, studies of most multiracial schools and districts have found that tracking does result in the placement of disproportionate numbers of minority students in low tracks. It is possible, then, that districts, or even states (following from the *Larry P.* decision), may be prohibited from classifying students in any way that results in racial imbalance among school programs.

These two cases also open the door for a careful court scrutiny of educational effects of different programs. In *Larry P.* it was found that classification and placement in special programs for the retarded have lifelong effects on the future educational and vocational opportunities of students. In *Lora*, after examining the classes in which minority students were placed in regard to class size, extracurricular activities, special programs, and support systems, among other aspects, the court ruled that these placements constituted a denial of equal educational opportunity. While the courts in these cases scrutinized program processes and effects in conjunction with their segregative effects, the rulings certainly lead the way to examination of educational processes in programs as barriers to educational equity. This of course has implications for the legality of the differentiated educational experiences in *all* tracking systems.

No cases involving tracking except *Hobson* have claimed that suspect classifications other than racial ones have been created by this kind of grouping. However, it is possible that future cases may elaborate on *Hobson*'s use of the poor as a suspect class, without the confounding issue of race. Since it has been clearly established that poor children are disproportionately placed in low tracks, this might be the basis of a claim of equal protection violation in future cases.

Another possibility is that intelligence classifications themselves might be viewed as suspect. Certain aspects of these classifications are similar to other classifications that are now considered suspect. Intelligence is considered immutable and beyond an individual's control. Negative stigma is attached to those labeled of low intelligence, and some forms of discrimination result.[40] While no court has yet considered intelligence classifications themselves as requiring the special judicial protection resulting from a strict scrutiny standard, such an argument is possible in relation to tracking. And if the claim were made in conjunction with the assertion that these classifications were used to restrict access to education as a fundamental interest—access to basic minimal skills, perhaps—the chances for a successful outcome would be greatly enhanced. It is clear, however, that for a tracking case to successfully plead a denial of equal protection without the existence of racially identifiable groups, the courts would have to make a considerable shift in their current posture toward tracking and intelligence classifications.

A further requirement for a successful challenge to governmental practice under the equal protection clause is that of invidious discrimination—that is, a discriminatory intent on the part of government. Until quite recently, the existence of objective evidence of discriminatory *effects* was sufficient to meet this requirement. This was especially true in suits brought against school boards or agencies with a history of de jure segregation. Since the 1976 ruling in *Washington* v. *Davis*, a case involving a challenge to testing for public employment, a discriminatory effect alone, such as the creation of racially disproportionate groups, has been insufficient to establish intent.[41] What does constitute proof of discriminatory purpose at this point is unclear as the courts have both accepted and rejected various types of evidence since the *Davis* decision.

The judge in the *Larry II* case noted, "The simplest method for ascertaining administrative or legislative intent is to move in the direction of an 'objective' test based on the foreseeable effects of a challenged decision."[42] While this method is inconsistent with the *Davis* decision, it has been found acceptable in cases where there was evidence of prior de jure segregation. Most courts have moved only slightly beyond a purely objective effects standard by creating "a *presumption* that school boards and others charged with discriminatory intent *intend* the natural and foreseeable consequences of their actions" (italics added).[43] The presumption of intent was used in the *Lora* case, for example.

In recent cases, however, the Supreme Court has required a stricter standard of proof of discriminatory intent. A general presumption of intent based on objective evidence of effects alone cannot be construed as proof of intent. Other factors, such as the historical background of decisions, the events leading up to decisions, any departures from normal procedures in the decision-making process, and statements by those involved, must be taken into account as well.[44]

What is important here is the recognition that objective evidence of the discriminatory effects of tracking will not in itself satisfy the requirement for proof of a discriminatory purpose. In cases using racial groups as suspect classifications being denied equal protection as a result of tracking practices, proof of discriminatory intent may be especially difficult when the school districts involved have no history of de jure segregation. If, however, ability classifications were to be considered suspect by the courts, the grouping of students according to these classifications for the provision of different kinds of schooling—given what we know about the resulting stigmatizing of low groups and the limiting of their educational experiences—would probably be evidence enough of invidious discrimination.

No court has yet ruled that the practice of tracking in itself constitutes a violation of equal educational opportunity. Nor have the processes involved in classification and placement been seen as requiring procedural due process protections. Yet it is clear from the research on tracking that the practice constitutes a governmental action that restricts students' immediate access to certain types of education and to both educational and occupational opportunities in the future. Further, a stigma results from placement in low groups that is likely to have negative long-term consequences, including lowered self-esteem and aspirations of students and lowered teacher expectations for them that can result in a self-fulfilling prophecy. Despite these potential harms, placement procedures often include inappropriate measures and ill-defined subjective criteria. All these effects have been found to be constitutional violations in other contexts (with racial minorities and handicapped students), so it may be that they can be applied in cases involving children not determined to be a class deserving special protection of the court. Family lineage, wealth and education of parents, cultural differences—to select and discriminate according to these factors was abhorrent to the founders and followers of American democratic institutions long before the current classes of race and handicap were generally acknowledged. How appropriate if the next battle against the harms and pretentions of social-class superiority were to show from its inception its relevance to the suburban white middle class as well as to identified minorities.

But whether the characteristics of tracking could stand the constitutional test is less salient than the fact of the courts' extreme reluctance to become involved in the details of school operation. In his parting words in the *Hobson* decision, Judge Wright commented: "It is regrettable, of course, that in deciding this case this court must act in an area so alien to its expertise."[45] This reluctance, however, is based on more than a wish not to infringe on educators' areas of special competence. Important too is the court's awareness of how difficult it would be to frame a remedy to harms ensuing from day-to-day schooling practices. Beyond the development of suitable remedies, the degree of court intervention in the administration of schools that could be required to ensure that such remedies were carried out is undoubtedly repugnant to most justices—witness the complications in the Boston and Los Angeles school desegregation cases, for example.

These difficulties are real and the court's reluctance to face them directly is understandable. Yet the fundamental issues—students' rights to equal protection of the laws and due process being violated by the processes and effects of tracking—cannot be ignored. It seems imperative that the issue be confronted in the spirit of the mandate in *Brown:*

Where a state has undertaken to provide a benefit to the people, such as public education, the benefits must be provided on equal terms to all the people unless the state can demonstrate a compelling reason for doing otherwise.[46]

10

The Search for Equity

This book began with the proposition that a serious gap exists between what school people—and parents as well—hope and intend will be accomplished by tracking secondary school students and what actually happens as a result of tracking. The school board member cited in chapter 1 who defended tracking so vehemently did so because he sincerely believed that tracking was in the best interests of the students in his school district. But as we know from the research about it, tracking is *not* in the best interests of most students. It does not appear to be related to either increasing academic achievement or promoting positive attitudes and behaviors. Poor and minority students seem to have suffered most from tracking—and these are the very students on whom so many educational hopes are pinned. If schooling is intended to provide access to economic, political, and social opportunity for those who are so often denied such access, school tracking appears to interfere seriously with this goal. Yet, despite what we know about the effects of tracking, the practice persists.

The essential question that remains is *why*. Why do we continue a practice that clearly runs counter to what we say we want? I suggested at the outset that one reason school people continue to track is that the practice is an integral part of the culture of secondary schools: the collection of organizational arrangements, behaviors, relationships, and beliefs that define how things are at a school. In other words, tracking is one of those relatively unquestioned practices that belongs to the "natural" order of schools. I also suggested that the widespread belief that tracking is in the best interests of students rests on at least four unexamined assumptions that underpin that school culture: (1) students learn better in groups of those who are academically similar, (2) slower students develop more positive attitudes about themselves and school when they are not in day-to-day classroom contact with those who are much brighter, (3) track placements are part of a meritocratic system with assignments "earned" by students and accorded through fair and accurate means, and (4) teaching is easier when students are grouped homogeneously, and teaching is better when there are no slower students to lower the common denominator. We looked at these assumptions in light of the research evidence about them and found them to be unwarranted. Now we can look at them again in light of the tracking we found in our twenty-five schools. The data about our 297 classrooms help us to understand why these assumptions are unwarranted and why their practical result—tracking—has effects that are opposite to what is intended.

Why don't students achieve more in homogeneous groups? The answers are obvious for those in low-track classes and certainly understandable for those in middle groups. First, we have seen that students in different groups were exposed to dramatically different qualities of knowledge. Decisions were made about the appropriateness of various topics and skills for students in different tracks which served to limit sharply what some students would learn. The lower the track, the greater the limits—quite different from any compensatory, or even democratic, intent. As a result, high-track students got Shakespeare; low-track students got reading kits. High-track students got mathematical concepts; low-track students got computational exercises. Why?

Very likely, these course-content choices were made in the same well-intended spirit as most tracking decisions. But what is determined to be best for students is often grounded not only in what appears to be the students' current levels of achievement—where they are now—but also in some assumptions about their educability—where they are capable of going. These decisions are undoubtedly based not only on teachers' and school administrators' biases, resulting from the assumptions we have discussed, but also on biases built into the supposedly fair sorting devices themselves—objective testing, previous grades, observation of social behavior in the classroom, and so on.[1] Judgments about what students will have a chance to learn follow judgments about what students *can* learn. The crucial criteria underlying the judgments go unexplored. Does a certain type of school-valued performance (score or grade) or behavior (responsiveness to a particular teaching modality, such as lectures) indicate greater educability in students?

Further, once some decision is made about the educability of a group of students, how do we determine that the curricular offerings we provide are appropriate? We decide, for example, that groups of students who exhibit certain kinds of academic and social behavior (usually those less valued by schools and less consistent with school processes) are less educable. Then we go on to decide that a reduced academic content is appropriate for these students. These decisions are not usually a result of critical reflection on a variety of alternatives, but rather most often result from unquestioned and almost automatic responses. They are decisions based upon what are considered appropriate courses for students given existing school practices and cultures. Rarely is the possibility of changing existing structures and practices considered on the ground that significant numbers of students are not challenged with high-status learning.

Added to the unmistakable differences in the information students at our schools had available to them were the differences in their classroom learning opportunities. Both in the time students had to learn and in the quality of the instruction they received, we found differences among track levels. High-track students had more time to learn and more exposure to what seem to be effective teaching behaviors than did other groups. These critical features of the classroom were not equally available to all students.

The learning opportunities teachers provide in classrooms are greatly influenced by the students they interact with. Thus, groups of students who, according to the dictates of conventional educational wisdom, seem to behave as if they were less able and eager to learn are very likely to affect a teacher's willingness or even ability to provide the best possible learning opoportunities. It does not take a giant leap in logic to conclude that students who are exposed to less quantity and quality of curricular content and classroom instruction will not have their academic achievement enhanced. This is exactly what happens when low and average students are grouped together for instruction. It becomes painfully obvious why low-track students' learning is not best promoted by tracking.

Further, it seems equally apparent that negative academic results come about for these students *because* of tracking. Classroom differences that inhibit the learning of those in low and average groups are a *result* of placing these similar students together for instruction. These differences are institutionally created and perpetuated by tracking.

What about those at the top? Given that they seem to have the best of what schools have to offer, wouldn't it follow that their learning is enhanced by tracking? Even though the research on academic outcomes and tracking is inconsistent in regard to high-track students, it does not appear that they do consistently better in homogeneous groups. At least, only a small portion of the studies have found this to be true. The brightest and highest achieving students appear to do well regardless of the configuration of the groups they learn with.[2]

How can this be possible? Aren't the best students held back if teachers are obliged to teach to the "lowest common denominator"? Aren't poorly motivated students a distraction for the achievers? If the kinds of classroom experiences we studied are at least in part responsible for how well students do and if the effect of having average and low students in class is a diminished quality of classroom experience, how *could* the best students do well in these environments? Some of the data we collected lead us to speculate about these issues. Seventy-three of the English and math classes we studied were heterogeneous groups, classes that teachers and administrators at the schools identified as being composed of students of all achievement levels. What we found in these seventy-three classes leads us to hypotheses about why *everyone* usually seems to do at least as well (and low and average students usually better) when placed in mixed groups.

In the area of curricular content, it is important to remember that in both math and English classes the topics of instruction were similar in high and average classes. Low classes were those that were markedly different in the information students had access to. This similarity between the average and high classes in English also extended to the cognitive levels of the tasks students were assigned. In math classes few differences were detected in the level of cognitive processes required of students: recall, comprehension, and application predominated at every level. In the areas of learning time and quality of instruction, average-track classes could be placed about halfway between the high and low tracks. With this information in mind, we can investigate what the curricular content and learning opportunities in heterogeneous groups tended to be like. Using discriminant analysis, a statistical procedure that can classify groups according to their scores on a variety of measures, we could look at the heterogeneous classes on selected characteristics and combinations of characteristics.[3] We found that 35 percent of the heterogeneous classes were identified as being more like high-track classes in these aspects than any other level. An additional 36 percent were found to be more like average classes. Because of the similarity in the knowledge to which high and average classes were exposed, we found that about 70 percent of the heterogeneous English and math classes we studied were exposed to the highest level of curricular content.

Why is this significant? First, it leads us to question the assumption that the presence of low and average students in classes has the effect of diminishing the quality of classroom experiences. To the contrary, it appears that the presence of a number of the brightest students in class may raise the quality of both the content presented and the kinds of learning opportunities available to students of all types. At best this challenges one of the assumptions used to organize the structure of schooling. At worst it suggests that tracking can be described only in terms of its negative attributes: it exists to deny opportunity, to create further differences.

This speculation relates specifically to the widely held notion that teaching in heterogeneous classes is geared to the lowest common denominator, that instruction in such classes is aimed at a level just below the average of students in class. On the basis of this belief, heterogeneous classes should have been classified predominantly as being most like the average group, but with a substantial portion of them classified as being like the low track. We would expect that very few if any heterogeneous groups would have characteristics most like classes in the high track. The findings, in fact, pointed in the opposite direction. They did not support the commonly held assumptions about what heterogeneous classes are like, but rather indicated that heterogeneous classes are considerably more advantaged in terms of classroom content and processes than many average- and nearly all low-track classes. Considering these circumstances, we begin to gain some insight into why even those students who get placed in high tracks do well in heterogeneous groups: it is at least as accurate, and probably much more so, to suggest that classes in practice are geared to the *highest* level of students, not the lowest.

A second assumption on which tracking is said to be based is that slower students develop more positive attitudes about themselves and their schools when they don't have to face daily a classroom populated by those who are judged to be brighter. We know from the research considered in chapter 1 that tracking is associated with lower self-concepts, school deviance, and dropping out of school altogether. And remember, many of the studies cited there controlled for the kinds of characteristics that might be the cause of this result—socioeconomic status and measured aptitude, for example. Track level, it seems, has an effect over and above these more obvious influences. We certainly saw lower self-concepts and lower educational aspirations in our low-track students, findings consistent with this other work.

What in our data might help us begin to understand these results? Important questions regarding the effects of the substantially different social milieus that characterized the different track levels must be raised. Does the perception of teachers as more concerned and supportive and of peers as nonthreatening allies in the classroom lead to better feelings about oneself as a student or as a person? Would this type of atmosphere encourage a student to stay in school and, while there, to take a more positive stance toward the schooling enterprise? On the other hand, what about a classroom where teachers are perceived as more punitive and in fact do devote a considerably larger portion of their time to issues of behavior and control, where peers are viewed as more unfriendly and excluding, and where arguing and disruption are more characteristic of student exchanges? We believe that we would be likely to find strong relationships among the characteristics of punishment, control, unfriendliness, exclusion, argument, and disruption, and how students feel about themselves, how they behave in school, and how long they actually remain in school.

Again, we can look to our heterogeneous classes for clues to what the low-track student experiences. In our sample of heterogeneous classes, the relationships between teachers and students were most like those in high-track classes in 46 percent of the classes, most like average classes in 37 percent. This means that only 17 percent of the heterogeneous groups had teacher-student relationships that were, like those in low-track classes, considerably more negative than in the other two track levels.

In the area of students' relationships and interactions with their peers, much the same pattern was found. In 37 percent of the heterogeneous classes as a whole, the students related to one another more like students in high-track classes than like students in average or low classes. In English classes, however, there was a considerable similarity between the relationship in high and average classes. An additional 35 percent of the heterogeneous English classes had student relationships much like those in the average English classes. In all, then, 56 percent of the heterogeneous classes were among the group of classes with the most positive and supportive relationship.

These comparisons are important because they tell us that in at least 83 percent of the classes where slower students were mixed with others they had markedly more positive relationships with their teachers; in at least 56 percent of the classes they had substantially more positive relationships with their peers. This leads us to consider how classroom-climate differences might play a part in students' self-perceptions and school-related behaviors. It certainly helps explain why heterogeneity has a positive rather than a negative effect on students who would otherwise be in low-track classes.

The third assumption, that tracking is part of a meritocratic schooling system and that student placements are both deserved and fair, has been discussed as a central theme of this book. Our data about what happens to students in low-track classes make it difficult to see the results of this system as fair. Those students who seem to need the most appear to be getting the fewest schooling experiences that are likely to promote their learning in all the areas we see as important—academic, social, personal, and even vocational. In fact, in all four aspects of schooling, the students who are the least advantaged experience a diminished quality of schooling.

In America we find the notion of sorting students in public schools on the basis of class-linked criteria (e.g. family wealth, social status) abhorrent. We pride ourselves on the use of objective measures of aptitude and potential. But as we saw in chapter 1, these measures are not so objective or class-free as we would like to think. Our selection process may in part be very much class related, with the screening devices that appear to be objective having much the same results as if we sorted directly on background characteristics. Of course, our system is not so closed as this makes it seem. Students of every race and class can be found at every track level at schools. And there is an additional minority that receives little or no attention from civil libertarians as victims of "meritocratic" tracking. Even a child of white, middle- or upper-middle-class, college-educated parents from an advantaged neighborhood can be at a very early age set on a path that leads to less education. At the age of fifteen or twelve or even younger, children who are slower, or perceived to be slower, to mature or to develop academic or social skills may be consigned to classes that will *increase* the gap between them and other students who start out with a greater appearance of capability. Yes, poor and minority students are not equally represented in the various levels. They do not, it seems, have an equal chance to be placed in top groups. However, given the slowness of social and educational change on behalf of the poor and minorities, all students might be better served if we remember that even in the most advantaged schools there are tracks where the "lowest" students are placed and stay.

What we have been considering here is the degree to which fairness and meritocratic means and ends are manifest in school tracking. What we have seen is the apparent unfairness in the school experience itself. But what about the long-term consequences of track placements? How is track placement likely to influence the life course of students? To explore these latent consequences of tracking and the issue of meritocracy, it is useful to revisit the ideas of Bowles and Gintis and others whose work has touched on the question of schools as meritocratic sorters. This group of social scientists has suggested that the function of schooling is not to provide a meritocratic avenue to success in adult life. To the contrary, they view schools as serving primarily to reproduce the current inequities of our social, political, and economic systems. The fact that some children of advantaged families may be held down adds irony, but not justice, to that view.

Scholars who discuss the role of schools as agents of cultural reproduction do not view the inequities in the educational experiences of students and the differences in students' attitudinal and achievement outcomes as the products of inadequate educational technology. Nor do they see these differences as resulting from the inefficient functioning of schools, as many other school critics do. These popular technological explanations of within-school differences and inequities assume that the school is a neutral institution—not reflecting the interests of any one group in society but simply inadequate to meet the needs of the variety of students it encounters. These explanations are rooted in the widespread belief that schools are meritocratic and that through them individuals, regardless of their social, economic, or ethnic background, are able to realize their potential and achieve economic and social mobility. When this mobility fails to occur, especially for identifiable groups of children such as the poor and minorities, explanations of the types cited above are often given. Less generous traditionalists, however, often look to the individual students or to groups of students themselves for explanations of differences in schooling experiences and educational failure—to lack of individual motivation, cultural deficiencies, or genetic handicaps, for example.

Those who have taken a cultural-reproduction perspective on schools view them as societal structures that reflect the values of the larger society and operate in ways consistent with the maintenance of the existing social order. These theorists, then, examine the form and content of the schooling experience in a nontraditional way.

British sociologist Michael Young's discussion of the unequal distribution of power in society as a consequence of the uneven distribution of cultural knowledge among social, economic, and other groups has direct implications for the distribution of knowledge among groups in school.[4] Young posits that some groups have access to more power in society because of the different kinds of knowledge made available to them and not to others. This unequal distribution of power is maintained by those already in power be their control of the ways in which institutions transmit knowledge. High-status knowledge, as defined by these powerful groups, is distributed disproportionately to those from privileged backgrounds.

Michael Apple (1978), an American curriculum theorist, builds on the work of Young by defining high-status knowledge and its relationship to the maintenance of power.[5] Using an economic metaphor, Apple proposes that high-status knowledge is linked to the reproduction of economic inequality in that it is made a scarce commodity whose distribution is limited. This scarcity and limited distribution are the sources of its importance in the security of power in society. Schools function in this process to legitimate and distribute to select groups these cultural resources that are related to unequal economic forms. Apple defines high-status knowledge in corporate societies as the technical knowledge necessary to keep these economies operating at a high level. Because the generation and preservation of this technical knowledge largely take place in the universities, high-status knowledge in secondary schools is that which provides access to the university. Thus, highly academic knowledge becomes the scarce commodity with limited distribution in schools that provides access to future power in society.

Bourdieu and Passeron add that this high-status knowledge is one of the mechanisms used to place and retain students in different social and economic groupings.[6] The high-status knowledge, biased in favor of the middle class, serves to assign students from lower-class backgrounds to lower-status positions. Whether this high-status university-access knowledge is viewed as a limited commodity or as already under the "ownership" of the middle and upper classes, the result is the same: the existing society is reproduced. The dilemma here is inescapable. Schools have a dual role. First, they are obliged to follow, reflect, and reproduce the nature of the society in which they exist. But, second, they are also responsible for changing society as it exists in favor of what "ought" to be. In the battle between the force to conform to norms and the abstract desire to change the norms, it is clear which tendency prevails.

Bowles and Gintis assert that schools socialize students to meet the demands of the occupations they will be expected to assume within the existing class structure.[7] Like the other reproduction theorists, they contend that the educational system operates in this manner not as a result of the conscious intentions of teachers and school administrators but rather because the social organizations of schools are so similar to those of the work place. In this view, social relationships and interactions in schools are structured to fragment students into stratified groups where different capabilities, attitudes, and behaviors are rewarded. Thus the educational system turns lower-class children into workers who will be subordinate to external control and alienated from the institution, but willing to conform to the needs of the work place. Paul Willis and Robert Everhart have elaborated this view to show how differential treatment and student resistance interact in this process.[8]

In Basil Bernstein's view, schools become differentiated as they attempt to fulfill the needs of society by imparting specific knowledge and skills to students.[9] This can be a divisive influence when children are separated into groups, often reflective of social class, to aid the development of specific skills in selected students. While a student's level of involvement in school is initially determined by the family's understanding and acceptance of the school's means and ends, social relationships and interactions in the school modify and enhance this initial determination. It is likely that in a differentiated (tracked) school, a lower-class student with initial low involvement, placed in a homogeneous group, will become increasingly uninvolved and alienated from the school. This results, according to Bernstein, because the nature of the particular teacher-pupil authority relationships and an emphasis on reward and punishments lead to greater or lesser achievement depending on the student's placement.

An essential element in the cultural-reproduction perspective is that the differential treatments groups of students receive result in both cognitive and noncognitive outcomes. The production in students of the "appropriate" attitudes (appropriate to their track or social stratum) results from the process discussed in chapter 7, the process Bowles and Gintis call the legitimation of inequality. Most of the reproduction theorists discuss this legitimation process and suggest that students come to accept the unequal features of the larger society—hierarchical authority structures and unequal pay, for example—as natural. And, further, even those at the bottom come to see their own limited future roles in these structures as largely appropriate and acceptable.

Bowles and Gintis assert that schools accomplish this legitimation through the illusion of a meritocratic education system.[10] Karabel and Halsey see the structure and events of everyday school life as upholding meritocratic values and justifying differential rewards.[11] In this same vein, Apple suggests that the form and content of schooling practices used to organize procedures such as tracking play a major role in encouraging students to internalize failure resulting from the stratification process as an individual rather than a social problem.[12] Bordieu and Passeron assert that this process is facilitated by the fact that those in the lower social strata value the culture of the dominant groups and, as a result, tend to devalue their own. Because the schools focus on the dominant culture and cultural styles, students are easily persuaded that the school's authority is legitimate. In this way, schools can, with little or no coercion, "convince the disinherited that they owe their scholastic and social destiny to their lack of gifts or merits."[13]

The unequal distribution of those instructional topics and skills considered prerequisite to university attendance that we have seen in the 297 classes studied here support this view. Students in high-track classes, whom we know to be predominantly white children from the middle and upper socioeconomic levels, were those students presented with this high-status knowledge. Our findings also show that students at the top were being provided with the largest quantity of time in which to learn and that they were more exposed than other groups to instructional practices that are highly associated with student achievement. These data clearly support the theorists' assertions of an unequal distribution of knowledge in a direction that favors the already privileged. Track levels in schools, reflective of social and economic groupings in society, were provided with differential access to school knowledge in such a way that the children of more powerful societal groups had greater access to the kind of knowledge that may, in turn, permit them greater access to social and economic power.

The findings of this study clearly support the assertions concerning the kinds of differences in social relationships that exist in different kinds of classes and provide empirical evidence for some of the effects of these differences posited by Bowles and Gintis, by Willis, and by Bernstein. The data support the notion that relationships in classes where poor and minority students are most likely to be found—low-track classes—are characterized by alienation, distance, and authority to a greater extent than were high-track classes. The greater proportion of time teachers spent on discipline and student behavior, students' perceptions of their teachers as more punitive and less concerned about them, the more negative feelings and behaviors students reported they exhibited toward one another, and the more negative student attitudes expressed toward classroom experiences found in low-track classes certainly support this view. At the same time, the less time spent on behavior by teachers, students' perceptions of teachers as less punitive and more concerned about them, the lower levels of student hostility toward peers and apathy toward the classroom situation, and the less frequent student reports of feeling isolated found in high-track classes all seem to provide support for the assertion that those at the upper levels experience relationships that lead them to affiliation with the schooling experience.

Our findings, then, show that student attitudes are distributed among track levels in ways that are consistent with the cultural-reproduction view. Classes in the high-track groups consistently had students with the highest aspirations and the most positive views of themselves, both generally and in relation to academics. As might be expected from other studies, students in low-track classes reported the lowest levels of aspiration and the most negative feelings about themselves both academically and generally. Important differences in the degree of students' satisfaction with their schools, subjects, and classes were *not* found among track levels. This similarity among tracks could be a result of many factors. However, it is important, in view of the legitimation of inequality thesis, to note that low-track students did not express lower levels of satisfaction despite the evidence that they are at the bottom of an unequal hierarchical schooling structure. We cannot assert that this lack of dissatisfaction is due to a perception on the part of these students that schools are neutral and meritocratic or to a belief that their own deficiencies are responsible for their positions. But we do not find evidence *contrary* to this view either. In fact, these findings seem to be what would be expected given the cultural-reproduction hypothesis. They do not support the "common sense" claim that low-track students achieve less because they are hostile to the school itself.

In all three areas of classroom process examined—curricular content, instructional practice, and social relationships and interactions—the differences found among track levels are illustrative of this theoretical position. The data on student attitudes provide further support. While no set of data is ever likely to *conform* so general and comprehensive a perspective on the function of schooling, the classroom processes and student attitudes investigated in this study were found to operate in a way consistent with the cultural-reproduction theory.

It is not essential to accept this view to conclude that the differences in educational outcomes and in the day-to-day schooling experiences of different social groups may have the effect of maintaining inequities that clearly correspond to the inequities in the larger society. Certainly the conduct of schooling benefits those at the upper societal levels and burdens those at the bottom. This may be clearly seen even in schools where the burdens have been superficially obscured by some special advantages or financing given to low or remedial classes. This view of inequity has been supported almost universally in studies of schooling outcomes and is further supported by A Study of Schooling data.

The clearly established link between educational inequities and inequities in the larger social structure has important implications for educational reform and has been widely considered in educational theory and research. As is well known, one of the guiding ideologies of American education has been that with the expansion of schooling would come greater opportunities for economic and social mobility for members of all groups, resulting in a social structure based more on merit than on race or social status. This view, however, has not been borne out in the research that has considered the effects of bringing schooling to an ever-widening range of the population. After decades of reform in this direction, class and race still emerge as major influences, not only on the level of school attainment, but on adult social and economic status as well. Yet many still believe that school reform toward the provision of more equitable education for all groups is a viable first step in the larger movement toward a more egalitarian society. Educational innovations such as open schools and multicultural curricula have been based in part on the notion that if schools can be reconstructed so that students learn to value human diversity and reject exploitation, broad social changes through the subsequent reform of other institutions by these individuals can result. It is apparent, however, from research over the past two decades that these kinds of reforms have been exceedingly difficult, if not impossible, to implement fully in public schools. In fact, it is possible—likely, according to some—that schools and society exist in symbiosis to preserve the norms that limit change.

The more radical critics of schooling—and most of the cultural-reproduction theorists are among this group—are pessimistic about the possibility of educational reform. They believe that without major shifts in the distribution of economic and political power school reform toward equity is impossible since the elite groups who now control schools would never permit these reforms to occur. We can conclude that the cultural-reproduction theorists are correct in their description of the problem. Whether their pessimism is justified remains to be seen.

Whether school reform can stimulate broad social reconstruction or can only result from such reconstruction, it is clear that if equity is to be attained, educational reform should comprise only one aspect of broader ideological and structural shifts in American society. Ideally, the equalization of the benefits of education for all groups should be a reflection of a movement toward a more equitable social system—one in which racial and ethnic diversity are valued and the access of all groups to political, economic, and social power is ensured. However, as the history of the struggle for equality shows, these far-reaching changes are neither easily attained nor close at hand.

Given the unlikelihood of educational reform in the context of broad social reconstruction and the apparent impotence of school reform to trigger major economic and political changes, it seems important that school reformers focus their efforts toward more limited ends. If school change does not appear to result in a society that is fair and equitable, perhaps educational reform should concentrate on making schools themselves fair and equitable places for students to be.

This focus on creating more equitable schools seems to imply reforms toward two separate but related goals. First, schools must relinquish their role as agents in reproducing inequities in the larger society. Schools should cease to sort and select students for future roles in society. Second, schools must concentrate on equalizing the day-to-day educational experiences for all students. This implies altering the structures and contents of schools that seem to accord greater benefits to some groups of students than to others.

The focus on more equitable schooling as an end in itself is not new. Many reforms have been suggested, ranging from Illich's deschooling proposals to Jenck's notion that schools should simply concentrate on improving the quality of life for the children and adults who are in them.[14] But the crucial issue here is that when specific schooling practices are found to provide unequal benefits to some groups of students and impose unequal burdens on others, then these practices must be stopped. While the question of the long-term effects of these reforms on equity in a more global sense is certainly of the utmost importance, the staggering complexity of this larger issue should not be allowed to paralyze attempts at specific reforms. School people must not fall into the trap of thinking that early preparation for an unjust world requires early exposure to injustice.

The findings of this study point toward school reform directed at eliminating features of schooling that produce inequities in the daily experiences of students in school and also help create and maintain inequities in the larger society. These findings point to one structural element of schools—tracking—as responsible for a large measure of day-to-day schooling inequities. It follows that secondary schools should be reorganized so that students are no longer separated into homogeneous ability or achievement groups. Furthermore, whatever type of reorganization replaces tracking should not result in the separation of racial and socioeconomic groups or in the creation of classroom groups that promote inequities in students' classroom experiences.

What organizational pattern that would promote more equitable schooling can replace tracking? While definitive answers did not come out of this study, some likely directions emerged. Our findings seemed to support the hypothesis that heterogeneous grouping, reflecting not only the full range of student achievement and aptitudes but also the socioeconomic and ethnic diversity of schools would provide more equitable educational experiences than does a system of tracking.

It seems likely, in fact, that the reorganization of schools so that the predominant pattern becomes the use of heterogeneous groups could equalize students' educational experiences in several ways. First, if students were given a common curriculum, ideally comprised largely of the high-status knowledge now primarily reserved for students in high tracks, the closing off of students' access to future opportunities would be considerably postponed and perhaps lessened. All students would be at least exposed to those concepts and skills that permit access to higher education. And if some students do not grasp the concepts as quickly or comprehensively as others, they will have been given a beginning, a chance. While one would hope that the medium of instruction would be varied to accommodate a variety of learning styles in the classroom and further equalize students' opportunities to learn, differences in students' acquisition of this knowledge would nevertheless be likely. But such differences would not be predetermined by the structure of the school. Nor would there be institutionalized expectations regarding who among the students are most likely to achieve. With tracking, the knowledge a student acquires is largely influenced by the group in which he or she is placed. Relying on assumptions about the value of homogeneous ability and achievement grouping, schools use testing and other sorting mechanisms to separate students according to their differences in these areas. The belief is that these identified differences are predictive not only of the amount of knowledge a student is likely to acquire but also of what kind of knowledge is most suited to his or her needs. Schools then institutionalize and magnify these differences by identifying them with labels and imparting different kinds of knowledge and treatments to students in various tracks. With heterogeneity—widely mixed groups— on the other hand, these limiting distinctions among students would be minimized. This new organizational pattern would additionally provide an environment more responsive to changes in students' motivations, interests, and aspirations: all factors that may influence the kind and amount of knowledge a student acquires. Such changes, not incidentally, are a prominent goal stated by existing school organizations. Exposure to a common curriculum and a teaching-learning environment more receptive to changes in students should postpone the sorting and selection process now being accomplished by tracking until after the completion of secondary education. This would both remove the burden of selection from the secondary schools and give students additional time to exercise choice about their future plans. This change may also have the result that all students at the conclusion of their secondary education will have had more exposure to high-status knowledge, more time spent in learning activity, more exposure to effective instructional practice, and more positive social relationships in classrooms than many students—especially the poor and minorities—seem now to experience with tracking.

But as we have noted, school practitioners generally have held the belief that the instructional task is simplified when the range of student differences in class groupings is narrowed. It is important to address this view in the context of a proposal to reorganize secondary schools toward heterogeneity, since in school rhetoric, at least, it appears to be a major barrier to this change.

A fundamental question embedded in this view is to what extent the range of student differences in classrooms is really narrowed by tracking. It is clear that homogeneously grouped students share some characteristics—most probably measured aptitude or achievement and socioeconomic status. Yet even within the limited range of these two characteristics considerable variation exists among students, certainly in learning styles and learning needs as well as in a whole host of other areas—motivation, interests, and creativity, to name just a few. So even when working with homogeneous groups, teachers must deal with considerable student diversity.

Another consideration arising from this rationale of easing the teaching task is the relative nature of what seems easy. Perhaps what appears to be instructionally easy is largely a reflection of what teachers are accustomed to, the traditional way of conducting instruction. Moreover, some traditional instructional methods—lecturing, for example—may be easier with homogeneous groups, especially with those labeled as high achievers. But considering the complexity of the teaching task in a classroom of thirty or more students, these traditional ways may not, in fact, be the easiest way to maximize learning for all students. And while it is clear that change is always difficult, with the use of less traditional instructional strategies teachers might perceive that heterogeneous groups are just as easy to teach as homogeneous ones or can achieve maximum learning outcomes just as easily. Finally, as another in a long list of ironies associated with tracking—it is in the *highest* track groups that the greatest diversity may be found among students. These students certainly have the potential to benefit enormously by teaching strategies designed to tap widely differing experiences, interests, and skills.

Are there reasonable and feasible alternative instructional strategies that are suitable for heterogeneous groups of students? I think so. But new assumptions about teaching and learning are required for their use— as well as the giving up of the old assumptions. We must, first of all, be willing to consider that something else might work better. Having done that, we can begin to consider alternatives.

One educationally sound and manageable alternative to homogeneous grouping and traditional teaching methods is a whole group of strategies developed from a model of cooperative learning. Researchers at Johns Hopkins University and the University of Minnesota have been intensively involved in devising and testing teaching strategies that employ student cooperation as the essential ingredient. Cooperative learning approaches are based in part on the assumption that students are likely to learn best when they are actively working with others in small *heterogeneous* groups, in which the substantial instructional potential of student-to-student interaction is exploited. David and Roger Johnson point out, for example, that while we tend to make much use of interaction between teacher and students and between curriculum materials and students in traditional instruction, we tend to ignore the instructional potential of student-to-student interaction.[15]

The way students interact with one another is to a large extent a result of how teachers structure learning goals—that is, how the classroom tasks are organized and how rewards for learning are allocated.

First, if classroom tasks are organized—as they usually are in secondary schools—so that the whole class or groups of students within the class are working individually on the same tasks and competing with each other for rewards—by getting the highest score, the most answers right, and so on—then tasks are structured so that students work alone in a contest with others to see who is superior and who is inferior. This structure discourages student interactions about learning. We can say that students in this situation are *negatively interdependent* in that each student's success is dependent upon the failure of others. This happens whenever a class or a group within a class works as individuals, when they are rewarded as individuals, and when those rewards are assigned by comparing one student with another—for example, grading on a strict curve or simply making a class distribution of scores and then assigning grades or rewards according to how the scores fall in the distribution. This negative interdependence influences the way students interact. They often treat one another as rivals and are unwilling to share information or resources. These conditions also make initial differences in skill level or learning rates very important in determining which students get rewards. So to ensure a "fair" competition in this kind of classroom structure, teachers often group similar-seeming students together.

A second way that teachers structure learning is to have everyone in the class or in a subgroup within a class work independently on a task and then to allocate rewards on the basis of some fixed standard or set of criteria. This is most familiar in the form of establishing a certain percent right for a grade on a test or a specific time requirement for successful completion of a task. In this situation each student's learning is independent of the others. Although they are not struggling against one another, students essentially face the learning task alone. Often in this structure students see rewards as scarce and as a result are unlikely to help others learn.

These two ways of structuring learning in classrooms, individually or competitively, are by far the most common methods teachers use. Even on the rare occasions when students work together in small groups, they are almost always judged, graded, and rewarded as individuals; therefore, one of these two structures is operating. In both structures, initial individual differences usually become the most salient factor in determining who gets rewards. Those who start out knowing most or who learn fastest have a definite advantage in either structure. Under these two task structures, most teachers find it very difficult to provide instruction that allows for different learning rates and styles. For this reason teachers are right in saying that working with diverse groups of learners is not easy. Individualistic and competitive structures work best in situations where separating learners into those who learn easily and quickly and those who don't takes place. For unless groups are fairly homogeneous, these methods do not seem very manageable. And, it is important to note, in neither of these arrangements are students given any incentive to interact with one another about learning; in the competitive structure it is clearly a disadvantage for them to do so.

A variation of the individualistic modality—often reserved for the lowest or remedial track—involves what is euphemistically called "individualized" learning. Frequently this means that the student works in isolation and relates to nothing but the materials themselves. Additional elements of the classroom climate detract from positive student-student interactions. Notions that sharing information and helping one another constitute cheating or that purposeful interactions too closely resemble lack of order further inhibit group activities, especially among the lower tracks. Finally, as we have seen, we have the very firm patterns that are established in the students themselves. Some fully expect to learn quickly and easily; lacking that, they expect to already know most of the content or skills being taught. And they expect the rewards. Others expect to learn little, lose in the competition, and get few rewards.

But there is another way of structuring classroom learning tasks that has three advantages over competitive and individualistic methods: (1) a built-in incentive for students to interact with one another as learning resources; (2) a means of accommodating learner differences in the learning process; and (3) a way of greatly minimizing or eliminating the effects of initial differences in students' skill levels or learning rates in the assigning of rewards for learning.

These advantages come about when the teacher provides a cooperative learning structure in the classroom. Cooperative learning occurs when teachers have students work together in small groups on a task toward a *group goal*—a single product (a set of answers, a project, a report, a piece or collection of creative writing, etc.) or achieving as high a *group average* as possible on a test—and then reward the entire group on the basis of the quality or quantity of its product according to a set standard of success. In other words, the essential elements of a cooperative learning structure are a group goal and criterion-referenced evaluation system, and a system of rewarding group members on the basis of group performance.

That the use of cooperative learning structures has proved to be very effective in achieving a number of cognitive and affective outcomes for students has been well documented. Included among these outcomes are increased academic achievement, more positive attitudes toward instructional activities, and enhanced intergroup and interpersonal relationships.[16] It appears likely, then, that cooperative learning strategies are an appropriate place to begin to develop the substance of a instructional mode designed to counter the limited, uninspired classroom instructional practices and homogeneous groupings that are almost ubiquitous in American schooling.

The most salient issue coming out of the rationale that homogeneous grouping is necessary because it is instructionally easier concerns the justifiability of the rationale itself. In view of the disparities in noncognitive student outcomes touched upon here and well established in the literature and the inequities in the daily classroom experiences of students that are associated with tracking, is simplifying the teaching task reason enough to continue the practice? It seems unlikely that many would say that it is. Besides, if we seriously consider the resources that go into maintaining tracking now, and if we view the increased efforts associated with using new methodologies as connected more with the newness and change required than with the methods themselves, then we may more readily consider this rationale.

Until a major social reorganization occurs that results in cultural, political, and economic equity for all groups or until a major reconstruction of schooling takes place in which the educational process encourages individuals to refuse to tolerate an unequal social system, more limited reforms should be attempted to help equalize the effects of schooling. A reorganization of secondary school grouping patterns appears to be one such necessary reform. Whether or not such reorganization has the long-term effect of discouraging societal inequities, it seems clear that the replacement of tracking with heterogeneous groups would result in more equity in the daily experiences of students.

Equity. That has been the central issue of this book. There is every indication that the achievement of equity need not require averaging the quality of education students receive so that top students receive less and low tracks receive more to create a large, homogeneous middle. There is every reason to believe that there are essential, intrinsic qualities in the values and processes that promote equity, and that these qualities (fairness, the common welfare, cooperation, among others) will result in the highest levels of achievement.

Some Questions Left Unanswered

As with most research, important issues arise from the findings of our study that cannot be addressed with the data but merit some attention in the discussion of tracking and inequity.

First is the question of intentionality. While the purpose of our inquiry was not to confirm the existence of a powerful and oppressive force that works to ensure school failure and maintain social inequity, the findings are certainly consistent with this view. It would be easy, if simplistic, to attribute our findings to deliberate efforts on the part of school people to limit the educational experiences of some students and augment those of others. Yet even cultural-reproduction theorists—Apple, for example—maintain that inequities stem from the cultural context and systemic properties of schools rather than from the intentions of the adults within them.

Additional data from A Study of Schooling tends to support this view as well. When English teachers were asked which of four schooling functions should be most emphasized at their schools, more than 85 percent chose either the intellectual or personal development of students over the social and vocational functions.[17] If we view the social and vocational functions of schooling as having an instrumental focus— serving the economic and social purposes of the larger society—and the intellectual and personal functions as having a more intrinsic focus— acquisition of the culture and the development of individual thinking and expression—we can speculate that teachers may behave in ways that conflict with what they believe schools should do. The differential socialization—serving largely the social and economic needs of society— that is likely to result from the different classroom processes and teacher behaviors observed in this study appears to be contrary to the intrinsic functions of schooling which these same teachers say are the most important.

It is possible, of course, that the behavior of adults in schools is determined more by the institutional structure than by their own intensions, or that the interaction that occurs between student characteristics and school characteristics produces classroom environments that result in unintended behaviors on the part of both students and teachers leading to the differences observed here. At any rate, the blame for the inequities perpetrated on different racial and socioeconomic groups in schools should not be placed too quickly. It is clearly a subject for further inquiry.

A second important issue that arises from the findings of this study, when they are viewed in the context of the research on tracking and schooling outcomes, concerns the causal link between the inequities in school experiences observed here and the differences in student outcomes reported in other studies. Again, it would be easy to assume, for example, that the more hostile and negative classroom relationships experienced by the low-track students in this study explain the lower levels of self-esteem and higher levels of school deviance and dropping out found in other studies. But this connection has not yet been established. Furthermore, neither the data nor the methodology of this study can establish this link. Given the juxtaposition of these sets of findings, however, we can hypothesize about the relationship between differential classroom processes and student outcomes. Given the likelihood of this connection, this issue certainly warrants further inquiry as well.

11

The Tracking Wars

Much has changed over the past twenty years, but much remains the same. Academic standards and test-based accountability, ideas only germinating in 1985, now dominate American schooling. Market mechanisms for improving schools—choice and competition, relief from regulations, a focus on bottom-line outcomes, and straightforward privatization—that were pretty marginal in 1985 now sit at the center of the school reform stage. Equity remains a prominent value, but its framing has shifted dramatically. Desegregation has been supplanted for the most part by a high-stakes, "no excuses" agenda composed of reforms that push all schools, however segregated by race or social class, to have all students meet challenging academic standards, with "no child left behind."

These new directions in American schooling seem profoundly incompatible with practices that sort students into classrooms where they experience strikingly different and unequal resources, opportunities, and expectations. Nevertheless, tracking remains firmly entrenched in American schools. That tracking persists is not the result of inattention; neither is it for a lack of effective alternatives.

In the years since *Keeping Track* was published, tracking has reached educators', researchers', and the public's attention on several levels. More than ever before, Americans know that tracking exists; that students' assignments to various classes are not random, unstructured happenings; that this nearly ubiquitous schooling practice has been designed and implemented to achieve some purposeful end; and that tracking cannot be ignored in thoughtful examinations of schooling. Tracking is now more often understood as an active intervention in the lives of children—a willful practice chosen by policymakers and educators. Following close behind this increased awareness has been intense scrutiny to determine whether tracking actually accomplishes the educative purposes it purports to accomplish, and whether it is consistent with the democratic goals of schooling.

The answers to these questions have troubled many progressive policymakers, educators, and public commentators on educational quality and equity. Concerned that tracking violates a social justice standard that assures individuals and groups equitable access to educational resources and opportunities, many have argued that tracking is inconsistent with the American dream of schooling that provides every child an equal chance to succeed.[1] Reformers around the nation moved to detrack schools. These progressives were joined by an unlikely set of allies: widely read conservative academics such as Diane Ravitch and Mortimer Adler, who argued that tracking's differentiated curriculum is antithetical to schooling's goal of ensuring that all students learn the traditional Western canon.[2]

At the same time, however, tracking's defenders have charged that the research jury is still out, that any problems with tracking can be fixed without dismantling it, and that, if policymakers and schools move toward detracking too fast and unadvisedly, they place educational excellence at risk. Some claim that inequalities associated with tracking are gone, and that today's grouping is free of the problems of earlier times. The characterization of this debate as "the tracking wars" is not my own, but I can hardly disagree with it; it aptly describes the intensity of the responses and interactions among the critics and advocates of tracking and detracking.[3]

This chapter explores the tracking wars. Here, I describe the push by those seeking to end tracking and the push back by those determined to keep it. I also address, with research evidence, issues that have been debated on the overlapping battlegrounds of research, school practice, and reform. In chapter 12, I turn to the experiences of the schools that have sought to reduce or eliminate tracking. Although the detracking movement has not supplanted tracking as the norm, many schools did detrack, and many continue to do so. The experiences of these schools demonstrate the potential that detracking has to remove huge obstacles standing in the way of success for students (particularly students of color from low-income families) across the country. They also offer sobering lessons about Americans' profound ambivalence about what they want from their schools.

The Push to End Tracking

By the end of the 1980s, concerns about tracking had entered the popular discourse and influenced public policy goals. Harsh judgments about tracking's effects were reported in the popular media, including such articles as "Is Your Child Being Tracked for Failure?" (*Better Homes and Gardens*), "The Label That Sticks" (*U.S. News and World Report*), and "Tracked to Fail" (*Psychology Today*).[4] Leading policy groups made recommendations for eliminating or at least curtailing tracking practices, and many school reformers took action.

The National Governors' Association, for example, proposed eliminating tracking as a strategy for meeting the ambitious national education goals they had set in 1989. The governors saw tracking as a major impediment to their goal of educating all students to demonstrate mastery of challenging subject matter, so that the United States would be first in the world in science and mathematics achievement on tests taken at the completion of grades four, eight, and twelve.[5] The NAACP Legal Defense Fund, the ACLU, and the Children's Defense Fund all raised tracking as a second-generation segregation issue. And the U.S. Department of Education's Civil Rights Division targeted tracking as critical in determining racially mixed schools' compliance with Title VI regulations. Educator groups also adopted antitracking policy positions. At its national convention in 1990, the National Education Association recommended (albeit cautiously) that schools abandon conventional tracking practices. Several of the major subject matter organization of teachers—the National Council for the Social Studies, the National Council of Teachers of English, the National Council of Mathematics Educators—all went on record as saying that tracking posed serious barriers to high-quality and equitable teaching and learning. Some state education agencies, including those in California and Massachusetts, declared that tracking should be eliminated, at least prior to senior high school.[6] These policy proclamations reflected some actions already being undertaken around the country, and they triggered others. Many have been remarkably successful. In 1987, for example, the Southern Regional Education Board, led by Gene Bottoms, joined with a group of state partners to launch *High Schools That Work (HSTW)*. *HSTW* sought to diminish tracking by eliminating the general track and combining challenging academic courses and modern vocational studies. The guiding idea was that curriculum that seems beyond the reach of many students *in its abstract form* may be attainable if taught in a more concrete context in which students could connect and apply classroom abstractions to out-of-the-classroom contexts. Notably, *High Schools That Work* was not simply a reform aimed at benefiting students who are poorly served by the current structure of the high school curriculum—charity for the disadvantaged. Another potentially huge advantage of this approach concerns the large number of college preparatory kids who are pretty good at mastering abstractions for a test and then quickly forgetting them. These students might come to understand the meaning of what they've learned and perhaps even be able to remember and apply it later on. *HSTW* tried to improve the high school curriculum for everyone, including the highest achievers.

In 1990, the Carnegie Corporation, acting on the recommendations in the Council for Adolescent Development's widely distributed report, *Turning Points*, identified detracking as central to reforming middle grades education. Creating heterogeneous classrooms (read, detracking) was one of seven key recommendations meant to create school environments that are caring, healthy, and democratic as well as academic. Throughout the 1990s, Carnegie made major investments in states and schools as they restructured their junior high schools and middle schools, including moving away from tracking to small, heterogeneous teams as the schools' central organizing feature. *Turning Points* prompted hundreds of middle schools to change the way students were grouped for instruction, both between and within classrooms. Most created inclusive, mixed-ability teams of students who were taught by an interdisciplinary team of teachers.[7]

The Coalition of Essential Schools (CES), a major high school reform network, declared in 1992 that high schools must abandon tracking for both academic and social reasons. The *CES* director, Ted Sizer, argued, "If we want citizens who take an active and thoughtful part in

our democracy, they must get trained for this in school—working together on equally challenging problems, and using every possible talent
toward their solutions."[8] Detracking should proceed, *CES* argued,
through structural changes, such as breaking large schools into smaller
heterogeneous "houses" and teaming teachers; organizing curriculum
around themes or projects; and practicing more personalized relationships between adults and children.

Even the College Board, long thought to be concerned only with
the college preparation of high-track high school students, criticized
tracking for posing barriers to minorities' access to college. In 1989, the
College Board launched its *Equity 2000* project aimed at replacing
lower-level math classes with college preparatory math in two hundred
racially diverse high schools in partner districts. Teachers received assistance in working with mixed-ability classes, creating backup classes,
and increasing parental support. Students were supported with Satur-
day and summer academies on college campuses for entire families.[9]

At the same time these policy initiatives were beginning, courts
began to take a more intense look at tracking. In Rockford, Illinois; San
Jose, California; New Castle County (Wilmington), Delaware; Woodland Hills, Pennsylvania; and Augusta, Arkansas, plaintiffs in school
desegregation cases charged that the districts' tracking undermined
desegregation because it resegregated minority and white students
within schools. In 1994, the federal magistrate and judge in Rockford
found, based in large part on analyses of its tracking practices, that the
district engaged in racial discrimination. The same year, the federal
judge in Arkansas ordered that the district cease its use of ability grouping by class.

In 1992, Woodland Hills schools, and in 1994, San Jose schools,
accepted consent decrees and the continued jurisdiction of their federal courts, partly because of evidence that the tracking system in each
district was segregating students and restricting African American and
Latino students' access to the schools' best educational opportunities.
In contrast, the plaintiffs were unsuccessful in the Wilmington, Delaware, desegregation case, where the judge virtually ignored the tracking evidence, and no detracking order was ever issued.[10] In 1995, the
four Delaware county school systems involved were released from further court supervision with their tracking systems intact.

Other detracking efforts were very much homegrown. For example, an innovative San Diego high school English teacher, Mary Catherine Swanson, noticed that when her mostly white school became more diverse owing to an attendance boundary change, the school's tracking system relegated most of the newcomers to low-track classes. Outraged, Swanson created AVID (Advancement via Individual Determination), a scheme that placed supposedly unqualified students into college-track classes and provided them with a support course in which they learned study skills and received academic tutoring. AVID has now expanded to schools across the nation.

Around the country, educators like Swanson began to detrack their schools on their own. Many were inspired by the stories of detracking schools featured in Anne Wheelock's book *Crossing the Tracks: How "Untracking" Can Save America's Schools.*[11] These could hardly be called ideological moves in response to an organized equity agenda; rather, they were in the main teachers and principals who wanted nothing more than to bring high-quality curricula and learning conditions to all students. Given the evidence, as well as the pronouncements from high-status policy and educational authority, the educators' own lived schooling experience, and their willingness to tackle a significant challenge, it simply made good educational sense to give detracking a try.

In fact, responses to the new awareness of tracking were often deeply personal. In my own experience speaking about *Keeping Track* to researchers, educators, and policymakers, nearly everyone recognized him- or herself in the tracking scheme. Conversations often began with uncharacteristically personal reflections and revelations: "My daughter was in the honors class, but she moved to her new school and . . ."; "I never knew I wasn't taking college prep classes . . ."; "my child already knows how to read, but he's stuck in a class where kids don't know the alphabet . . ."; "I was the only Latina taking calculus,"and so on.

Often, discussions of tracking also produced instant tension. After all, the data were saying some very unappealing things about American schools and the willingness of Americans to participate in the unequal treatment of children. These data could not be dismissed out of hand, since they were consistent with what most people could observe or experience in one form or another. To suddenly hold tracking as problematic in public discussions or in print could and did open a Pandora's box of challenges and controversies. On the one hand, many equity-minded reformers were quick to embrace the data, not only because tracking per se was an obstacle to equal treatment, but because it might bolster their broader, preexisting equity agenda. On the other hand, detractors were incensed that what they had long considered the best, perhaps only, way to ensure (and protect) pockets of academic excellence in otherwise less-than-excellent schools was now being cast in so glaring and negative a light. Educators were often frustrated as they recognized inequality but felt there was no reasonable alternative.

I was optimistic, or at least hopeful, that the data from the twenty-five schools discussed in *Keeping Track,* which showed more positive conditions in heterogeneous classes, could assuage fears and point everyone in a helpful direction, even though these data were not conclusive. After all, not one of the heterogeneous classes in the *Keeping Track* schools was formed because of a detracking policy. It was hard to know how they might differ from classes that reform-minded schools might create. However, the data made me comfortable about repeating to educators and parents what I'd recommended in the book: Schools should get out of the business of sorting and find alternatives that provide all students with challenging learning opportunities. I also shared with these groups what I knew from the research about the extraordinary promise of cooperative, small-group learning. It wasn't much, but many educators seemed encouraged to try. In chapter 12, I return to the potential of detracking, putting the successes of some of these reforms within a larger, national context. First, however, I examine questions at the heart of *Keeping Track,* considering changes and consistencies in how students have been grouped over the past twenty years.

The Push Back

Objections to detracking were immediate and loud, often undermining the potential for reasoned dialogue about legitimate concerns that detracking would compromise the education received by the most academically able students. Such concerns could not be addressed in environments in which detracking was instantly assumed to be an assault on opportunities for high achievers. It wasn't so much that anybody questioned the findings of inequality (at least at first); rather, the implications of heterogeneity were so totally unacceptable that thought-ful discussion was often derailed with caricatures and scenarios of doom. The loudest and most highly organized objections came from educators who specialized in "gifted and talented" education. Separate programs were the cornerstone of their practice and theory, and they feared, probably correctly, that calls for detracking placed those programs at risk. Supported by powerful parent advocacy groups, the gifted-education community soon came out swinging.

The arguments ran the gamut, asserting that gifted students were as far from the norm and as "needy" of separate learning environments as low-IQ students; ridiculing the idea of mixed-ability classrooms by comparing them to a varsity football team that accepts everyone who wants to play, regardless of skills; warning that detracking would place "our nation's most precious resource" (gifted students) at risk; and suggesting that average and below-average students feel better if they are not confronted each day by the intellectual superiority of their gifted peers. These arguments were bolstered by "research reviews" purporting to show that students, particularly gifted students, should be kept in separate, homogeneous classes.[12] Most shrewdly, opponents of detracking quickly defined tracking out of existence. As long as there was a theoretical possibility that a student's track might change, they contended, assignment to low or high classes was simply an educational determination more properly called ability grouping. Conceding that the narrower, rigid tracking may well be bad, they distanced those critiques from "ability-grouped classes." High-ability groups, they con-cluded, are not discriminatory, even though minority students may be underrepresented in them. "Flexible grouping," particularly as applied to elementary classrooms, became the key definitional defense.

Notably, these new arguments and research reviews were not, as a rule, published in mainstream research or peer-reviewed journals. Rather, they appeared in professional journals for teachers and admin-istrators, such as *Education Leadership*, in specialized publications for professionals, advocates, and parents of gifted students, and in the popular media. Although these reviews were mostly produced in the early 1990s, they continue circulating in the advocacy literature today.[13] In 2001, for example, the Hoover Institution printed a regurgitation of the alleged evidence and arguments in these earlier reviews in an edited collection of essays by conservative reform advocates and researchers.[14]

Another set of objections emerged in the school desegregation cases. In most of these cases, the defending school districts' experts lauded the district's tracking practices. For example, Christine Rossell, a political scientist and defense expert in the San Jose, Rockford, New Castle County, and Woodland Hills cases, argued that racial bias played no role in tracking and that racially identifiable classes were a consequence of racially neutral meritocratic assignments based on students' achievement.

Most recently, resistance to detracking policy and court orders has come from some conservative education policy analysts and advocates who argue that detracking is part of a liberal school reform agenda seeking to impose governmental regulations on schools. Conflating majoritarian preferences and local control, they minimize policy and legal rationales for protecting some groups of students from the misapplication of those preferences. They argue that any necessary redress is available to all through the ballot box (electing a new school board, for example) or through the educational marketplace, where parents can choose their children's schools.[15] The central theme in this argument is that schools should be held accountable only for outcomes and that regulations—even those intended to ensure equity—are illegitimate impositions on community preferences. Such supposed regulation hamstrings local efforts to accomplish the real business of schools: increasing student achievement. Prominent among this group is Tom Loveless, whose paper for the Fordham Foundation, "The Tracking and Ability Grouping Debate" (1998), and book *The Tracking Wars* (1999) argue that research fails to support the indictment of tracking, so local communities should be free to decide whether or not to detrack their schools. After broadly mischaracterizing detracking as a necessarily draconian (abrupt and total) imposition upon a school, Loveless writes,

No evidence indicates that abruptly and universally abolishing tracking would help anyone. It may even harm the students it is intended to benefit. Proclamations that tracking is undemocratic, inequitable, or educationally unsound cannot be reconciled with the non-effects found by research. Polls indicate that parents, teachers, and students support tracking. That part of democracy that premises governmental action on the preferences of the governed stands in favor of tracking's use. Moreover, the intervention advocated by Jeannie Oakes, attempting to dictate schools' operations and procedures from courtrooms and legislative arenas, is rapidly going the way of the dinosaur. Results are now assuming a dominant role in public policy. In this spirit, states and districts should establish clear expectations for achievement, judge schools by whether they attain them, and leave decisions about tracking and ability grouping to teachers, parents, and principals. Some schools will track, others will untrack.[16]

Battlegrounds and Evidence

From my perspective, the tracking wars have taken place on three overlapping battlegrounds. The first is the battleground of research. Tracking's defenders charge repeatedly that the research on tracking is inconclusive and that detracking advocates either misread or, worse, deliberately distort the evidence. Their claim is that we don't really have solid evidence that tracking creates unequal opportunity, or that it discriminates against low-income students or students of color, or that it affects students' outcomes negatively. The second is the battleground of school practice. Here, tracking's defenders assert that tracking has changed so fundamentally in the past twenty years that whatever problems might have characterized it previously are no longer present. (A related argument is that, given these changes, findings from earlier research on tracking are no longer relevant.) A third battleground is that of the direction of reform. Here, tracking advocates have adopted a "mend it but don't end it" stance, asserting that, because detracking would bring more harm than good, whatever flaws actually remain can be fixed within the context of tracking. For example, if low-track classes are found lacking, they can be improved. If placement practices work against low-income and minority students, they can be made fairer. In fact, a very recent concession is that, ironically, the detracking movement itself has made tracking more equitable.

The Research Battleground: Scientific Uncertainty or Solid Evidence?

In sum, defenders of tracking dismiss the claim that solid evidence shows tracking's serious constraints on educational opportunities, its unfairness to any particular group of students, or its negative effects on students' schooling outcomes.

Some of the most visible tracking advocates have attacked reformers' motives as well as researchers' findings. The professor of gifted education John Feldhusen charged in 1991 that "some school reformers have arrogated unto themselves a political-social agenda" and that "research is cited and twisted." James Kulik, the author of a widely circulated and widely critiqued research review favoring ability grouping, wrote, "Our children will be the losers if reviewers continue to twist research findings to fit their personal and political philosophies." Other critics are less overtly combative and affect evenhandedness, preferring to charge opponents of tracking with obtuseness and poor scholarship rather than with purposefully endangering children and democracy. Loveless, for example, argues that the research is simply too inconclusive to warrant any recommendations for change. Asserting this point repeatedly in *The Tracking Wars*, he claims that "the best evidence and the most informed, fair-minded experts were so evenly divided [when the move toward detracking began]" that the "empirical research has failed to resolve the most important questions about tracking." He continues, "Information is sparse on the curriculum and instruction employed by different tracks" and claims, "the suspicion that schools unfairly assign poor or minority students to low-track classes has been refuted." He writes further that "few, if any, of the questions about tracking's effects are settled, and research is ambiguous on the policy direction schools should pursue."[17]

I do not believe the research is ambiguous. Backers of tracking have produced no credible challenge either to the core findings of *Keeping Track* or to the increasing body of evidence from other research: tracking students is a common practice; tracking supports and creates systems of unequal education; tracking is not necessary (or even helpful) for achieving the nation's educational goals. Certainly, the research on tracking, like that in any area of social science investigation, has not been perfectly consistent in its findings.[18] Neither has the serious research community been unanimous in its agreement about what the findings mean or what they imply for practice. However, the weight of evidence makes clear that tracking has created unequal schooling, and that in turn has had a disproportionate limiting effect on the schooling of African Americans, Latinos, and low-income students. And virtually all researchers agree that practices that label some students "low achievers" and give them dumbed-down schooling—whether called ability grouping, tracking, or something else—do neither the students nor the nation any good. In the following section, I offer the conclusions I've reached on three important questions: Does tracking create unequal opportunity? Does tracking discriminate? Does tracking matter for students' outcomes?

Soon after the publication of *Keeping Track*, I began to examine whether the findings in the twenty-five schools would hold up across a broader range of schools and classrooms. Whether tracking creates unequal opportunity and whether those inequalities were most detrimental to low-income students and students of color lay at the heart of the analyses in *Keeping Track*. Those findings have been replicated over and over throughout the ensuing years. Extensive research has also added to our knowledge of the discriminatory effects of tracking and its detrimental effects on our system's most vulnerable groups of students.

In a nutshell, more recent research confirms the critique offered in *Keeping Track*. The central rationale for tracking is that differences in curriculum and teaching are essential to address the differences in students' abilities and that addressing these differences benefits both high- and low-tracked students. However, no serious reader of the tracking research disputes that tracking brings with it very different expectations for achievement, access to subject matter and critical learning opportunities, instructional strategies, and resources (including teachers). These disparate expectations, access, and resources have a predictable effect on student learning: low-track students fall further behind. Similarly, there is broad agreement that the differences among various tracks are typically not reasonable accommodations to student differences.

This evidence of disparities in opportunity, on its own, should spark serious educational and policy concern. But the disparities per se are compounded. The advantages and disadvantages associated with tracking are not distributed fairly (if such fair allocation of opportunities were even possible), and they result in racial inequalities. African Americans and Latinos bear a disproportionate burden of disadvantage because of their overrepresentation in lower classes. Again, this compounded and unfair assignment of disparities should redouble concern to the level of outrage. But there's more.

In practice, placing students into tracks is accomplished by a variety of mechanisms that have enormous potential for discrimination. More recent research reveals that these mechanisms include subjective assessments of ability, parental influence, irrelevant or narrow evaluations, counseling and advice, and so forth. Further, even when Latino and African American students meet the school's or district's own stated criteria for admission into higher-level classes, it is no guarantee that they will be placed in those classes: yes, those students who overcome the disparate impact of unequal opportunities and evaluations are still, often, placed in lower-level classes. Finally, the following sections demonstrate that fixing the practices that tracking engenders or requires (improving testing and counseling; resisting parental pressure for favored positions; etc.) cannot make tracking an educative or equitable school practice.

DOES TRACKING CREATE UNEQUAL OPPORTUNITY?   Working with a team of research colleagues at RAND and with the support of the National Science Foundation, I examined the relationship of race, social class, and tracking to students' opportunities to learn science and mathematics in a national sample of six thousand classrooms in twelve hundred schools. Survey data from school principals and from mathematics and science teachers allowed us to examine differences between schools and within schools.[19] The results, which we ended up calling *Multiplying Inequalities,* were striking. Differences in opportunities to learn science and mathematics resulted from the combined effects of disparities between tracks within schools and differences among schools' tracking practices. Consistent with the data reported in *Keeping Track,* high-track classes consistently offered richer learning opportunities and more resources, including more highly qualified teachers, than low-track classes.

At the grossest level, we found that senior high school tracking shapes the number and type of academic courses students take. Low-track students are seldom required to take as many math and science classes as high-track students, and they rarely do. Additionally, those not preparing for college take advanced classes only rarely. In every aspect of what makes for a quality education, kids in lower-track classes typically get less than those in higher tracks and gifted programs.

At all levels of schooling, low-track math and science courses offered less demanding topics and skills, while high-track classes typically included more complex material and more thinking and problem-solving tasks. Teachers of low-ability classes also placed considerably less emphasis than teachers of high-track classes on more general learning goals, such as having students become interested in science and mathematics, acquire basic concepts and principles, and develop an inquiry approach to science and a problem-solving orientation to mathematics. The ability to meet such goals does not depend on students' prior achievement or skill levels. Researchers and educators increasingly see reaching these goals as possible for all but seriously impaired students, and policymakers increasingly describe them as essential for all students. Nevertheless, those teaching low-tracked classes typically reported these goals as less important for their students. Additional research is consistent with these findings of clear track-related differences in students' access to knowledge.[20]

Multiplying Inequalities reaffirmed that low-track teachers of mathematics and science consistently spend more time on routines, seatwork, and worksheet activities. They introduce technology, such as computers, in conjunction with low-level tasks, such as computation. Iris Weiss replicated these analyses in 1994 and concluded, "Instructional activities follow similar patterns: low-ability science classes spend more time reading from textbooks and completing worksheets than high-ability classes, and they spend less time than high-ability classes participating in hands-on activities or being asked to write about their reasoning about solving a math problem."[21]

Teacher quality also differed among tracks. Although some schools rotate the teaching of low- and high-ability classes, one outcome of tracking is that classes at different track levels are not equally desirable to teachers. Teachers may jockey among themselves for high-track assignments, or principals may use assignments as rewards and sanctions. Such political processes work to the detriment of low tracks because they usually end up with the least well-prepared teachers. In *Multiplying Inequalities,* for example, we found teachers of low-ability science and mathematics classes typically had less experience, were less likely to be certified in math or science, held fewer degrees in these subjects, had less training in the use of computers, and less often reported themselves to be "master teachers" than their upper-track colleagues. These troublesome assignments are most evident in schools with large minority and low-income populations because these schools have fewer well-qualified teachers to begin with. In such schools, low-track students are frequently taught math and science by teachers who are not certified to teach those subjects, if they are certified at all. Here, too, our findings are consistent with other national studies.[22]

Specific differences in the content and pedagogy of classes at different track levels are summarized in the following table:

TABLE 11.1

Grouping-Related Differences in Learning Opportunities

High-Group Advantages	Low-Group Disadvantages
Curriculum emphasizing concepts, inquiry, and problem solving	Curriculum emphasizing low-level facts and skills
Stress on students developing as autonomous thinkers	Stress on teaching students to follow rules and procedures
More time spent on instruction	More time spent on discipline or socializing
More active and interactive learning activities	More worksheets and seat-work
Computers used as learning tools	Computers used as tutors or electronic worksheets
More qualified and experienced teachers	More uncertified and inexperienced teachers
Extra enrichment activities and resources	Few enrichment opportunities
More engaging and friendly classroom atmosphere	More alienating and hostile classroom atmosphere
Hard work a likely classroom norm	"Not working" a likely classroom norm
Extra enrichment activities and resources	Few enrichment opportunities

Source: Oakes et al., *Multiplying Inequalities.*

Students of all abilities benefit from these sorts of high-group advantages. Further, there is not so much as a hint in the research literature that supports the construction of meritocratic school norms in which "high-ability" students are more deserving of these advantages than other students.

DOES TRACKING CREATE RACIAL DISPARITIES IN EDUCATIONAL OPPORTUNITY?   What the above discussion confirms is that American schools do not serve high-track and low-track students equally. Likewise, no one disputes that low-income African American and Latino students are enrolled disproportionately in low-track classes. *Multiplying Inequalities* revealed that the racial disparities associated with tracking are national patterns that appear in three contexts. First, many schools that serve predominantly poor and minority populations offer a lower percentage of high-track classes when compared to affluent schools serving white and Asian students. Second, in racially mixed schools minorities are typically underrepresented in high-ability classes. In senior highs, low-income, African American, and Latino students are underrepresented in college preparatory programs, and they are more frequently enrolled in those vocational programs that train for the lowest-level occupations. A third context of racial disparity related to tracking is in classes that are purportedly at the same track level but turn out to be quite different in the quality of their resources and opportunities at schools serving more- and less-advantaged students. For example, a class called Algebra 2 at a school serving poor students is likely to be less rigorous and be taught by a less-qualified teacher than a class with the same title at a school serving advantaged students. These racial patterns have been documented repeatedly by researchers over the past two decades.[23]

IS TRACKING DISCRIMINATORY?   Are the racial patterns fair? We certainly can argue that they are not fair, given that the differences in the quality of what students experience constrain rather than expand the opportunities of students in low-track classes and that African Americans and Latinos suffer these constraints more often than other students. But many critics argue that disproportionate placements are based on race-neutral data and informed judgments that tailor course offerings and course placements to students' achievement levels. Further, what if it is the students themselves who choose their own classes?

Christine Rossell, who has not studied tracking in research outside of her role as an expert witness, has defended the racially skewed track placements in San Jose, Rockford, Wilmington, and Woodland Hills. Her testimony represented the school districts' view that the racially identifiable classes created by tracking followed the meritocratic assignment of students based on students' achievement levels. In fact, she argued that more racial minorities were placed in high-track classes than actually merited such placement.[24] The segregation within schools that comes with tracking, she argued, is a legitimate consequence of the lower achievement of African American and Latino students, as compared to whites and Asians.

Throughout the 1990s, my colleagues and I examined whether

Rossell and other tracking defenders are correct in denying racial bias in track placements. Researchers tend to agree that students' socio-economic status is associated with track placements, with more advantaged students more likely to be placed in higher tracks than less advantaged students,[25] but the question of racial bias has been much more contentious.

My conclusion is that race in itself does indeed influence track placements, Latinos and African Americans being more likely than whites and Asian students to be placed in low-track classes. Although the lower average of achievement of Latinos and African Americans certainly "explains" (in a statistical sense) much of the disproportionate assignment of these students to lower-track classes, we also find significant and disturbing evidence of racial bias.

I found evidence of how race affects track placements in a second RAND study of tracking—*Educational Matchmaking*.[26] My colleagues and I looked closely at the placement practices in three high schools located in neighboring communities. The schools were preparing students for the same or similar postsecondary opportunities and local labor market; they had similar state resources and were bound by the same state policies. Coolidge High had a very diverse student body, since it was the only high school in its diverse community. Washington High's affluent community location made its student body almost entirely middle- and upper-middle class, white, and Asian. McKinley High's student body mirrored its low-income, African American, and Latino community.

We spent lots of time observing, studying school documents, talking with educators and students, and analyzing students' transcripts and test scores. What we found shed new light on the dynamics of tracking and racial stratification. All three schools offered a wide array of academic courses, from remedial to Advanced Placement. Each school also offered a range of vocational courses; some gave credit for work experience or school service programs, and others offered highly technical and occupationally specific training. Notably, following national patterns, the predominantly white and wealthy school had far more high-track courses, and the high-track classes at this school were far richer in curriculum and instructional resources than the high-track classes at the other two schools.

Each school sought to be fair and accurate as it matched students with courses. They took into account achievement test scores, course-taking histories, grades, teachers' recommendations, and students' aspirations. Nevertheless, our transcript analyses revealed familiar patterns of racial differences. Although most students took *some* vocational education, low-income African American and Latino students took more than others—particularly more occupationally oriented vocational courses. African American and Latino students also took low-track academic courses more often than white and Asian students. At Coolidge and Washington, for example, nearly 75 percent of the Asian students took college-track math, compared with about 33 percent of the whites, only 25 percent of the African Americans, and fewer than 10 percent of the Latinos. Differences in English were not as dramatic, but, at Coolidge, both Asians and whites participated at much higher rates than African Americans and Latinos. At McKinley, African Americans and Latinos took college-track math at about the same rates, but the African Americans were about 15 percent more likely to be in college-track English.

Certainly, these patterns reflected very real differences in minority and white students' previous learning opportunities and their effects on academic preparation. Yet these associations with students' prior achievement do not demonstrate that the schools in our study made fair and racially neutral assignments. In fact, students' race or ethnicity was often important in *determining* the probability of participating in college preparatory math and English, over and above their measured achievement. For example, at diverse Coolidge High Asian students scoring at the 80th percentile nationally in math were more than twice as likely to be in college preparatory math as were Latinos at the 80th percentile. Asian students scoring at the 50th percentile were ten times more likely to be enrolled in college preparatory math *than comparably scoring* Latinos, and four times more likely than African Americans *with the same scores*. At affluent Washington, Asians scoring at the 80th percentile were enrolled in college preparatory at more than twice the rate of Latinos. Whites, too, were advantaged in college preparatory placement over their comparably achieving Latino peers. In the only departure from the pattern of white and Asian advantage, high-scoring African Americans at Coolidge took college preparatory math at slightly higher rates than white students.

Further, because the competition for slots in high-track classes was greater at schools with affluent and white students, minority students had a much better chance of being in the college track if they attended all-minority McKinley. Some students with achievement scores that qualified them for the high track at McKinley would not have qualified at more diverse Coolidge.[27] Latino students with math achievement in the 80th percentile nationally had an 84 percent probability of participating in college preparatory math at McKinley, but less than a 40 percent probability of being in college track at Coolidge. Thus, minority and low-income students found themselves *either* in schools with fewer and less challenging high-level classes or in schools where their own competitive position might not gain them access to resource- and opportunity-rich high-track classes.

In the 1990s, my UCLA research group began a series of studies that, for more than a decade, examined tracking and detracking in four medium-sized, diverse cities where tracking had become part of their desegregation lawsuits: San Jose, Rockford, Wilmington, and Woodland Hills. Notably, each of the cities had maintained majority white populations, even as their federal school desegregation cases proceeded. In San Jose, Rockford, and Wilmington, the plaintiffs' litigation teams had asked me to examine district, school, teacher, and student records and report to the court about whether tracking segregated students by race, whether the schools' tracking practices were discriminatory, and whether tracking deprived students of color of equal educational opportunities. In Woodland Hills, I was asked by the judge—with the superintendent's agreement—to study the impact of the district's desegregation effort. I discuss that evidence in chapter 12.

In San Jose, Rockford, and Wilmington, we conducted qualitative analyses of documents such as curriculum guides, course catalogs, course descriptions, district compliance reports, school plans, assessments by court-appointed monitors, and depositions taken of school district employees in the course of the litigation discovery process. We also did extensive statistical analyses of several years of computerized student enrollment and achievement data. These analyses allowed us to answer a comprehensive set of questions: What were the tracking systems like in these districts? Was tracking an integral structure with other practices (testing, counseling, etc.) that combined to create racially imbalanced classrooms? Could any racial pattern be explained or justified by reasonable educational considerations? What were the consequences for students' educational opportunities? What were the effects on students' achievement and other schooling outcomes? Would it be feasible to dismantle tracking in these districts? Did the districts have the support and capacity necessary to create high-quality, heterogeneously grouped classrooms?

As in my earlier studies, patterns of unequal opportunity and racial stratification were clear. Lower-track classes in all three systems provided far fewer learning opportunities than high-track classes. Teachers expected less of these students and gave them less exposure to curriculum and instruction in essential knowledge and skills. Patterns of racial stratification were also clear. This meant that tracked systems provided African American and Latino students with disproportionately less access to a whole range of resources and opportunities, including highly qualified teachers, classroom environments conducive to learning, opportunities to earn extra "grade points" that would bolster their grade point averages, and courses that would qualify them for college entrance and, in turn, to high-status adult careers.

Moreover, the statistical analyses of students' transcripts and test scores yielded disturbing findings about the accuracy and fairness of track placements. Classes designated for students at a particular level actually enrolled students who spanned a broad range of measured achievement. In other words, the tracked classes produced considerable *racial* homogeneity, but little "ability" homogeneity as determined by the districts' stated criteria.

In all three school systems, African American and Latino students were more likely than their white and Asian peers *with the same test scores* to be placed in low-track classes. For example, in San Jose, white and Asian students with average scores on standardized tests were more than twice as likely to be in "accelerated" classes as Latinos with the same scores. Further, while only 56 percent of very high-scoring Latinos were in accelerated classes, 93 percent of whites and 97 percent of Asians *with comparable test scores* were enrolled in these classes. The table below shows the patterns in Rockford, Illinois. Here, we find discrimination *at both high and low levels of achievement*. Even very high scoring minority students were less likely than their majority peers to be in high-track classes.[28]

Consider the results in Decile 10 above—the very highest-scoring students. Only 63 percent of the 92 minority students in this top decile

TABLE 11.2

Placement of Majority and Minority High School Students with Comparable
Achievement in Regular and Advanced Classes—1998–99, Rockford, Illinois

Math/Reading Achievement— (NCEs)*	Majority Students	Minority Students
Decile 1	775 Percent Advanced: 3%	962 Percent Advanced: 2%
Decile 2	973 Percent Advanced: 6%	1056 Percent Advanced: 4%
Decile 3	1,199 Percent Advanced: 10%	959 Percent Advanced: 6%
Decile 4	1,371 Percent Advanced: 16%	895 Percent Advanced: 13%
Decile 5	1,482 Percent Advanced: 21%	689 Percent Advanced: 19%
Decile 6	1787 Percent Advanced: 34%	583 Percent Advanced: 23%
Decile 7	1,810 Percent Advanced: 46%	444 Percent Advanced: 43%
Decile 8	1,925 Percent Advanced: 58%	305 Percent Advanced: 45%
Decile 9	2,350 Percent Advanced: 72%	207 Percent Advanced: 59%
Decile 10	1,853 Percent Advanced: 85%	92 Percent Advanced: 63%

*NCE: Normal Curve Equivalent

were in advanced classes, compared to 85 percent of the 1,853 majority
students. In Decile 6, a majority student had roughly a 33 percent
greater likelihood of being in an advanced class than a comparably
scoring minority student. And so on, up and down the range of achievement. It was not surprising, given these findings, that both San Jose and
Rockford undertook detracking as part of their desegregation remedies. As noted above, however, similar findings in Wilmington, Delaware, were insufficient to prompt court intervention.

Why, given these findings, is there contentiousness over whether
or not tracking includes racial bias? In part, the debate continues because the impact of discriminatory placements is often masked when

researchers analyze large-scale survey data that aggregate data across school systems. Such analyses obscure differences in track assignments resulting from the student composition of schools as well as the nature of their tracking systems. Moreover, the measures in these surveys are usually too gross to detect differential placement practices within schools. In other words, students are tracked in particular schools with unique student body compositions, and that is where they experience disadvantage and unequal access. This is plain enough to see when one looks at a school or school district. However, when aggregating across school systems, distinct contextual differences are blurred, making racial bias in placements.

Virtually all senior high schools—low-income, high minority, and white and wealthy suburban—are going to have high-track classes. Because tracking tends to be highly normative, relatively high-scoring students, not necessarily students with high scores, will be in the top track. Aggregate across districts, states, or the nation, then average the scores, and you might find (as is the case) that some students of color with poorer scores than whites and Asians are admitted to high tracks. Consequently, when data about two such communities are aggregated, we may find a pattern of track placement that appears to give a slight advantage to black students (after controlling for ability) of being assigned to academic tracks. This aggregation can hide considerable discrimination and underrepresentation of minority students in wealthier, racially diverse communities.[29]

Analyses of the relationship among race, ability, and placements within particular schools and school systems yield a very different understanding. As illustrated in the *Matchmaking* study and the studies of the three desegregating school systems and in similar studies by other researchers, differences in average levels of achievement mask clear evidence of discriminatory placements, with whites and Asians being considerably (and statistically significantly) more likely to be placed in academic classes than comparably achieving African American and Latino students. Substantial discrimination against even high-scoring minorities skewed the racial composition of classes beyond what would have been the case had track placements been made by an unfailingly strict adherence to achievement as the criterion.[30] Notably, researchers who have reconsidered the relationship between race and track placement in large databases, using multilevel methods that control for these between school differences, have sometimes been able to untangle these school and track placement effects. They, too, find that the supposed "black advantage" found in high-track placement nationally does not exist once the model accounts for the racial composition of the school that a student attends.[31]

DOES TRACKING AFFECT STUDENTS' SCHOOLING OUTCOMES?

The best new evidence from the past twenty years adds to *Keeping Track*'s claim that tracking fails to foster the outcomes schools value—academic excellence and educational equity. Tracking is particularly inconsistent with today's national goals of having all students meet high academic standards and leaving no child behind. There is little disagreement that grouping affects students' schooling outcomes with exactly the opposite effect. Nobody today makes evidence-based claims that students in low-track classes benefit from tracking.[32] Incontrovertibly, tracking widens the inequality among students in what they learn in school; students in high-track classes learn more than students in low-track classes. In today's rhetoric, tracking systematically leaves children not in the high track behind. The widening gap is associated with obvious and measurable advantages that allow high-track students to reach their "potential" and disadvantages that depress the achievement of low-track students.

However, the research on the relationship between tracking and students' schooling outcomes is complicated. Researchers' answer to the question of whether tracking affects outcomes depends on their definition of tracking, the outcomes they are interested in, the specific formulation of their research questions, and their research methods. Since achievement test scores are the most frequently studied outcome, let's begin there: the research on tracking and ability grouping consistently finds that the achievement gap between students in high- and low-classes groups grows over time.[33]

My colleagues and I found this differential effect of tracking on students' measured achievement in the *Matchmaking* studies of three comprehensive high schools as well as in our studies of tracking in San Jose, Rockford, Wilmington, and Woodland Hills. In all of these schools, high-track placement led to achievement gains, and low-track placement had negative effects. Students in lower-level courses consistently demonstrated lesser gains in achievement than their comparably scoring peers in high-level courses. These results were consistent across achievement levels: whether students began with relatively high or relatively low achievement, those placed in lower-level courses showed smaller gains (or greater losses) over time than similarly situated students placed in higher-level courses.

In San Jose, for example, "average" students—those with prior math achievement between 50 and 59 Normal Curve Equivalents (NCEs) on the district's standardized test—placed in low-track courses lost an average of 2 NCEs after one year and sustained those losses over three years. By contrast, students with the same "average" scores who were placed in a regular track had gained 3.5 NCEs after three years. Most striking, the students in this same group of "average" scores who took an accelerated course experienced the greatest gains of all— gaining 6.5 NCEs after one year, and a total of 9.6 NCEs after three years. The results were similar regardless of students' prior achievement levels. That is, whether students began with relatively high or relatively low achievement, those who were placed in lower-level courses showed lesser gains over time than similarly situated students placed in higher-level courses.

Our analysis in Wilmington, Delaware, produced comparable results. For example, students with eighth-grade preplacement math achievement scores between 20 and 29 NCEs in 1991 who were placed in a non–college preparatory math course as ninth graders in 1992 had an average 1993 math score three points lower than students with the same low scores who were placed in a college preparatory ninth grade math course. Higher achieving students were comparably impacted; among those who scored 70–79 in 1991, those who were placed in low-tracked math classes fell behind their high-tracked counterparts by eight points. At no level of achievement did students placed in low-track classes outscore those placed in higher tracks. The tracking effects of English classes in Wilmington were much the same.

In Woodland Hills, Pennsylvania, Kevin Welner and I used regression modeling to examine the impact of a single year of high- vs. low-track placement in seventh-grade English classes. We controlled for the prior year's standardized test score as well as for the students' race, junior high school, sex, free/reduced lunch status, and whether the student participated in the district's gifted program. Each of these factors had an impact on the students' later test scores, but the seventh-grade track placement of the student had a substantial impact even after controlling for these other factors. Students placed in the low-track English class in seventh grade scored almost five points lower than their (statistically) identical counterparts who were placed in the high-track seventh-grade class.[34]

We are not the only researchers to note that achievement benefits from high-track placement accrue to students at all levels of prior achievement.[35] These tracking effects appear to result, at least in part, from differences in learning opportunities, rather than homogeneity (which, after all, exists as much in the low- as in the high-track classes).[36] Even staunch advocates of ability grouping concede that research counters the claim that high-ability students benefit simply from separate classes.[37] Separate classes for high-achieving students benefit participants *only* when schools provide those students with an enriched curriculum that differs from that provided to lower-group students. What seems to make a difference for high achievers, then, is not the grouping itself, but the special resources, opportunities, and support that usually exist in high-level classes.[38] But the most significant finding is that track-level differences in teaching and learning cannot typically be defended as educationally appropriate adaptations to individual differences in learning aptitudes or prior achievement. After all, in the four desegregating cities and in the *Matchmaking* study, the beneficial high-track classes were actually quite heterogeneous. And students at all achievement levels benefited academically from being in the high track.

The most significant "tailoring" of curriculum and instruction was to skew the distribution of high-quality opportunities and expectations toward the high-track and away from the low-track classes. Considerable research demonstrates that ability-grouped classes negatively affect low-group students in comparison to their low-ability counterparts in nongrouped classes.[39] Some studies also show that high-ability students often learn less in these classes,[40] at the same time that others show that high-achieving students do equally well in both grouped and nongrouped schools, particularly when the curriculum and instruction are similar.[41]

In addition to tracking's effects on students' measured achievement, tracking influences students' school attainment and life chances. Track placements are quite stable, partly because early assignments shape students' later school experiences. By high school, track location has a far-reaching influence—with college-track students (relative to their otherwise comparable non-college-track peers) enjoying better prospects for high school completion; college attendance, grades, and graduation; and, indirectly, high-status occupations.[42] Moreover, students in low-ability classes have far lower aspirations and take fewer (subsequent) college preparatory classes than do students in higher groups, even when the students are similar in their socioeconomic status, middle school grades, achievement test scores, and post–high school plans.[43] These results are explained, in part, by the fact that college preparatory students receive more information and assistance in developing four-year high school plans and long-term educational and career plans than general education students.[44] The cumulative effects on college matriculation of taking rigorous middle and high school math and science courses are particularly strong for low-income students. Low-income students who take algebra and geometry are almost three times as likely to attend college as those who do not.[45]

The Practice Battleground: Problem Solved or Still Keeping Track?

The second battleground in the tracking wars is the dispute over whether or not American schools still track, and whether the types of grouping that remain are fundamentally different from tracking. Early on in the tracking wars, advocates for separate "gifted" programs adopted a very narrow definition of tracking and argued that ability grouping and tracking are distinctly different practices. Their position has been that tracking may be problematic but ability grouping is not. Others now argue that tracking has changed fundamentally in the past twenty years and that problems associated with past tracking are largely absent from today's schools.

Notwithstanding these assertions, the evidence is clear: American schools continue to track—that is, to construct homogeneous groups and classes. A 1995 analysis of nationally representative data found that tracking is pervasive in secondary schools. Only 14.4 percent of eighth-grade public school students were enrolled in math classes that their teachers characterized as heterogeneous, 15.5 percent in English classes, and 20 percent in social studies and science classes. The rest were in classes described as homogeneous groups at either below average, average, or above average. Similarly, responses from surveyed teachers indicate that only 10.8 percent of tenth-grade public school students were enrolled in mixed-ability math classes, 14.7 percent in mixed-ability English, 17.7 percent in mixed-ability social studies, and 11.6 percent in mixed-ability science.[46]

Other advocates like Tom Loveless articulate the position that, although tracking remains commonplace, it has been stripped of its most problematic features:

The charge of unfairness more accurately depicts tracking's past than its present. In the past, tracking was rigid and deterministic. Schools assigned students to vocational, general, or academic tracks, thereby pre-determining students' entire high school experience—from start to finish and for all subjects. Today, schools rarely assign students to a regimen of college or vocational courses across subject areas. Instead, assignment to math tracks is based on math proficiency, English tracks on reading proficiency, etc. Moreover, most schools assign students to tracked classes based on student choice, once prerequisites have been met. And transcript studies show that most students may independently move up or down in each subject's hierarchy of courses, depending on their performance.[47]

The historical contrast, however, is a classic straw man argument. Little insight is gained by comparing tracking today to its worst excesses in the past; after all, twenty or thirty years ago the sort of tracking that Loveless now disdains could have been defended with favorable comparisons to Jim Crow segregation. We must move beyond the false dichotomy (old tracking and improved tracking) that tracking advocates offer. In fact, nobody disputes that tracking has changed over the past generation. Not long after Sputnik, in fact, most high schools did replace their overarching academic, general, and vocational programs with structures that allowed students to participate in classes at different levels in different subjects.

Evidence about today's tracking does not support Loveless's rosy picture. Despite the changes, tracking maintains the deep structures of inequality that characterized it in the past. The features that are now common, such as personal choice, independent movement, narrowed curricular differences, college preparation in lower-level courses, and frequent negotiations, have resulted in small changes and some improvements. But they have not unlocked the tracking system that still constrains academic and social mobility, in part because schools provide the easiest access to these options to white students whose parents are not poor. Thus, the introduction of options into a more flexible tracking system is at least as likely to increase the education and opportunity gap as to narrow it.

Indeed, most of the research documenting harmful effects of tracking—virtually all of the research cited in this chapter—focused on the newer forms of tracking that Loveless describes. Most of the *Keeping Track* data, in fact, were collected in schools that no longer used rigid three-track academic, general, and vocational systems. As described in chapter 2, only five of the thirteen high schools and none of the middle schools and junior highs had distinct academic and vocational programs. There is no sensible reason for asserting that the research on tracking is not relevant to today's practices.

Certain changes that have been introduced into tracking even appear to perpetuate inequality. Looking specifically at the inclusion of choice into the track placement process, for example, we find that choice doesn't necessarily make the placement process fairer. Students who have limited knowledge about college requirements and career opportunities often require greater intervention on the part of the school to learn about the academic choices available to them and the consequences of taking various courses. Low-income, minority, and immigrant students have the least information about course taking and postsecondary admission requirements, and they often have little access to school counselors and good information on these topics. Research in Indiana, for example, found that in most cases families are not involved in the purported choices students make on their course preference forms. Moreover, most students are unaware of the consequences of their choices. The Indiana data show that large numbers of students (even as late as grade twelve) erroneously believed that the nonqualifying courses in which they were enrolled would actually meet college entrance requirements.[48]

In our *Matchmaking* study, faculty members at the three high schools viewed their schools' course placement process as open and fair to all students. They justified the disproportionate enrollment of whites and Asians in high-track classes as resulting from a fair competition for the available slots and from student self-selection. Several faculty members at these schools brushed aside the disproportionate representation of Latinos in low-track classes—even when Latino low-track students had test scores equivalent to high-track white and Asian students—attributing these disparities to differences in students' choices.

Even when acknowledging that these choices were culturally related, teachers cordoned off school responsibility, focusing instead on racial differences in educational values or family support. Moreover, choice did not operate equally for students from different racial groups. At all three schools, wealthy parents more often took advantage of waiver policies that permitted students to move into higher tracks. Other students were permitted to opt for "easier" academic courses. The schools seemed to accept these choices and only rarely pressed low-income and minority students to stretch beyond their own or others' low expectations.[49]

In another analysis of the impact of introducing choice into course placements, for example, Yonezawa, Wells, and Serna found that the results mimicked old, rigid tracking systems. Educators' attempts at detracking by providing students and parents with greater "freedom of choice" in track placement often resulted in little movement of low- and middle-track students into high-track classes. Even in high schools undergoing tracking reform, low- and middle-track students—most of whom were African American and Latino—resisted entering high-track classes. The relationship between these students' places in the tracking hierarchy and their evolving identities and ideologies strongly inhibited their choices. Hidden institutional barriers within schools, the students' already tracked aspirations, and the desire of students to select classes where they believed they would be respected by peers and teachers all led them to "choose" to remain in lower-track classes.[50] Thus, while many policymakers and educators may view choice as a neutral process for student course enrollment, the empirical evidence suggests that choice operates like other stratifying processes.

This conclusion is buttressed by Samuel Lucas's comprehensive analysis of the impact of the changes in tracking over the past few decades, which yields the sobering conclusion that the inequalities in tracking may be as great or greater in their current forms. He suggests that subtler, more covert systems of in-school stratification have simply replaced the more overt, formal structures. He concludes that the newer arrangements, such as subject-by-subject tracking and placements by choice, provide students with no greater opportunity or mobility than the older ones. Lucas's careful analyses reveal that the culture of inequality and stratification through schooling is uncannily robust.[51]

Why is this so? Despite their many differences, today's practices continue to organize schools and students so that those who seem to be similar can be taught together, separately from other students. Current practices also embody such familiar dynamics of schooling such as giving students different knowledge and learning opportunities thought to be appropriate for different ability levels. Changes in tracking include enhancements and refinements, including the proliferation of new, more exclusive routes into the highest-status postsecondary institutions (for example, schools that offer Advanced Placement as well as "regular" college-preparatory courses in many subject areas). This differentiation affects the content, pace, and quantity of instruction, culminating in distinct programs that position students for different postsecondary chances, such as preparation for high-status four-year universities versus lower-status or two-year colleges, and preparation for high-status and high-paying technical careers versus low status–low pay skills training.[52]

The newer forms of tracking continue to mask an essential problem of teaching any group of twenty to thirty-five people. Such instruction always requires, and should require, a variety of teaching strategies. Not all students will benefit from the same tasks, materials, and procedures, even if the school grouped them because of their similarities. Multiple criteria for success and rewards benefit all students, regardless of grouping practices. Unfortunately, conventional grouping practices and the illusion of homogeneity deflect attention from these instructional realities. Yet when such unimaginative instruction fails, the problem is too often attributed to the child or perhaps to a wrong placement.

Contemporary forms of tracking continue to shape students' identities, status, and expectations for themselves as well as adults' expectations for them. Labels such as "gifted," "honors," "accelerated," "regular," and "learning disabled" still convey or certify students' overall ability and worth, and they cannot be seen as productive for any students. These labeling effects still permeate the school and social culture. Nevertheless, it is quite common to see these powerful life-shaping phenomena trivialized in popular discourse by the charge that educators care more about creating "feel good" environments where "self-esteem" rules than they do about acknowledging merit or fostering academic excellence, even though the more thoughtful gifted education advocates acknowledge their pernicious effects. The lesson for students is that if the school identifies them as less than fully capable, they should not expect to do well. Teachers still talk about high and low classes as "my best kids" and "my worst." Few students or teachers can defy these identities, expectations, and differences in the tangible schooling opportunities that tracking continues to structure.

As I will explain more below, the most important reason tracking today is so unchanged in its effects is that today's grouping practices take place within a normative and political context that is largely indistinguishable from the context of twenty years ago.

The Reform Battleground: Mend It or End It?

A third battleground in the tracking wars, the terrain of reform, has been especially contentious and confusing. It hinges on whether the harms associated with tracking are inherent in the structure of tracking or whether they stem from an ill-advised implementation of an otherwise neutral schooling structure.[53] I subtitled *Keeping Track* with the words *How Schools Structure Inequality*. By emphasizing the structural nature of tracking, I hoped to make clear that tracking exists not because it is a commonsense way of organizing schooling, but because it is embedded in a society that expects schools to sort, stratify, and treat students unequally. Tracking is the structural manifestation of a complex web of norms (beliefs and assumptions) and power (politics) that makes it anything but neutral.

Defenders of tracking claim that the rough edges of tracking *practices* have been or can be mended in spite of those obstacles. Loveless, for example, argues that research is so equivocal that local communities should decide whether to detrack or maintain tracked schools. He cautions against detracking, however, asserting that it risks both student achievement and community support. That said, he also advises schools to monitor their low-track classes to be sure that low-track students are being pushed to excel.

To say that tracking's structure systematically perpetuates inequality does not mean that tracked classes can't be improved. Some researchers who have documented and acknowledged tracking's many problems have suggested a menu of fixes to mitigate harms caused by tracking; for example, improve the quality of low-track classes, make the course placement processes fairer, and provide students with heterogeneous and equitable opportunities outside the classroom. These researchers may see eliminating tracking in U.S. schools as far too politically ambitious, or they may worry that implementing high-quality untracked classes is too difficult. However, the fact that equitable tracking has only rarely been documented is sobering evidence of just how politically and professionally challenging (or impossible) ending equality within the structure of tracking would be.

CAN TRACKING BE FIXED WITHIN THE CONTEXT OF A TRACKED SYSTEM?   The sociologist Maureen Hallinan acknowledges the evidence of tracking inequalities and notes that schools' responses to calls for detracking have been mixed. She cautions that many educators favor detracking, but detracking may not be feasible because so many parents, politicians, and other educators resist. She also suggests that teaching in a detracked school is far more difficult than in a tracked school, and that detracking requires reallocating teachers and administrators, modifying the curriculum, and providing professional training that may be prohibitive. Detracking, she asserts, is also problematic because parents of high-ability students tend to prefer rigorous, homogeneous classes, and parents of other students remain unconvinced about the benefits of heterogeneous classes. In the end, she concludes that schools should fix the problems in their tracking systems rather than dismantle tracking altogether.[54]

Hallinan has herself provided evidence of some problems resulting from tracking.[55] But her view is that the well-documented negative effects of tracking result from educators' failure to enact tracking theory faithfully (that is, in ways that benefit students in all tracks). Tracking's unintended consequences, she argues, are what impede its intended goal of enabling students at all levels to learn more than they would in mixed-ability classes. Some of these unintended consequences, she explains, are inherent to tracking, while others represent an implementation failure. For example, tracking's race and social class segregation may be inevitable, given the unfortunate coincidence of "low ability" with low-income and minority status, but the diminished outcomes are not, since they result from a flawed enactment of tracking's theory.

Hallinan advocates a tempered response that calls upon schools to improve their tracking practices and tracking's inherently negative features with more positive practices beyond the classroom, such as extracurricular activities in which diverse groups of students participate together. Further, she argues that educators could make tracks more homogeneous by basing students' placements on the most "objective" measures of ability and achievement and by frequently reassessing and reassigning students. The educational discrepancies among tracks could be remedied with a beefed-up low-track curriculum. In addition, the lamentable impact of students' social status, motivation, and effort could be circumvented if schools altered their reward structures in ways that extend higher status to low-track students. Tracking's segregative effects could be counterbalanced by mixing students by race and social class in their untracked classes and by creating a nonracist school atmosphere.[56]

Similarly, the sociologist Adam Gamoran, whose work has illuminated how tracking widens achievement inequality between high- and low-track students, has sought ways to fix tracking so that the low-track disadvantage can be eliminated while the high-track advantages are preserved. He was prompted to pursue this goal when he found that some tracking systems are better than others. That is, schools with tracking systems that permit greater mobility among tracks and that allow more students to take high-track classes seem to produce higher overall achievement and create smaller achievement gaps among tracks. Gamoran recommends that schools reduce tracking and that they make the tracking they retain more effective. Like Hallinan, he advocates that tracked schools must improve instruction in low groups. He also recommends that schools regularly reassess students' capabilities and take new information into account when making assignment decisions, so that students are not locked into their track assignments. He argues that schools should offer tutorials during the school year or the summer so that students can make up curricular material they may have missed by being in a low-track class. That way, they can learn what they need and would not be prevented from moving up in the tracking system by lack of curriculum coverage.[57]

What's wrong with these suggestions for improving tracking? Frankly, nothing. If schools could actually do the things that Hallinan and Gamoran suggest, tracking wouldn't be the problem it has been and remains today. But it wouldn't be tracking either. Hallinan and Gamoran are, in fact, recommending a massive redistribution of resources; yet tracking is a structure designed not on educative principles but rather on the exact distributional principles that Hallinan and Gamoran disdain.

Nearly all educators are well aware that low-track students consistently have lower-quality opportunities to learn than their peers in higher tracks. They also acknowledge that persistent inequalities in access to knowledge, instructional resources, and well-qualified teachers combine to create a nearly insurmountable obstacle to sustained improvement of curriculum and instruction for low-track classes. Many educators have spent their careers trying to beef up the low-track curriculum, to adopt a more positive disposition toward the capacities of low-track students, and to alter the reward systems that work against these students. Gamoran himself acknowledges that high-quality low-track classes are rare and very difficult to create. In his study, he found only two low-track classes from among all classes in twenty-five middle and high schools in which low-track students made progress at rates similar to their higher-track counterparts, and both were at Catholic schools.[58]

Why is creating good tracking so difficult? The answer lies in the deep connections between schooling and the larger social structure. Tracking is certainly a schooling technology often implemented with good intentions, but it may entail messy human decision making and unintended negative consequences. My research over the past two decades has persuaded me that tracking also reflects deep cultural and political tensions in American society. It manifests a web of cultural assumptions about what is true—what is "normal"—and cultural values about what constitutes appropriate action given particular "truths."[59] For example, tracking embodies the largely unquestioned assumption that students' individual needs and capacities differ enormously and in ways over which schools have little influence. It also reflects an extensive list of American biases around race, language, and poverty to cast doubt on the learning capacities of African Americans and of Latino immigrants. Tracking's opportunity inequalities both reflect and perpetuate these assumptions. Its "improvers" seldom acknowledge the deep, entrenched passions these cultural dimensions embody, hoping instead that incremental progress can lessen the salience of schooling inequalities around race, language, and poverty.

Tracking also reflects racial and social class stratification outside of school. Its inequalities perpetuate that stratification by facilitating (and helping to rationalize) the intergenerational transfer of social, economic, and political status and constraining social and economic mobility. The tracking debate is almost always argued in terms of its effectiveness as related to academic achievement. Certainly, this is a concern. Unspoken is tracking's clear connection to sorting, preparing, and certifying students for very different roles in society. Advantaged families are well aware of this function of tracking, so students' track placements become part and parcel of their quest for comparative advantage in the distribution of school resources, opportunities, and credentials that have exchange value in the larger society.

In sum, tracking is far more than a neutral curriculum structure that can be adjusted to eliminate the inequalities it creates. I am not suggesting that educators are engaged in a conscious conspiracy to make poor, minority students ignorant or to keep them at the bottom of the social and economic structure. However, I do remain persuaded that the results of tracked schooling—widening inequalities in achievement and aspirations—make for a compelling logic in a society marked by huge inequalities by race in economic and social power.

We saw these cultural tensions at work in the three *Matchmaking* schools. The greater number and quality of the high-track classes at affluent Washington High were not simply a matter of having greater resources available at the school, although this was the case. Rather, parents, educators, and the high-track students themselves at the more advantaged school believed that rigorous courses, supported by sufficient resources, would naturally be available. Because these opportunities had been available throughout these more privileged students' schooling, and students assumed that they deserved them, there could be no reason for such advantages to stop. The broad assumption of stability in students' intellectual capacity and motivation led educators to view their job as providing curriculum and instruction that continued a trajectory of excellent schooling begun long ago. Their job was to *accommodate* rather than change students' abilities and needs. Each school strove to offer courses that matched its view of its students. The affluent white school thought most of its students required advanced academics and highly technical vocational education such as computer programming languages and computer-assisted drafting. The less affluent minority and mixed schools felt they would meet more students' needs with lower-level academic classes and lower-tech vocational offerings such as cosmetology, typing, and woodshop. (To be fair, these are not always determinations made at the school level but may be reinforced by pressures and resources from the district.) Without question, cosmetology, typing, and woodshop could be incorporated within up-to-date, technology-rich learning environments with career-savvy, industry-tested, and fully credentialed teachers. Perhaps that's what tracking supporters have in mind when they suggest improving low-track opportunities. But few such programs are in place or on the horizon.

Track mobility, when it occurs, is usually downward—often because students lack the prerequisites to move up. But, as we saw in the *Matchmaking* schools, this is also because few teachers really expected students to get smarter. After a fashion, it might be said that the very lowest track is the one that is no longer in school. Dropout data and follow-up of dropouts is so inadequate that it is difficult to know precisely who drops out of school and what their school experiences were. It might be fairly construed, however, that for some the low track is a last chance to remain in school, and for a great many others it is a trajectory out of school prior to graduation.

At each of the *Matchmaking* schools subtle processes worked to limit the opportunities of the least-advantaged students. Within the schools, racial groups were identified with particular tracks. Asians and whites were identified mostly with high-track college preparation; Latinos (and to a lesser extent African Americans) were identified with low-track academics and vocational classes. At their most extreme, these judgments reflected stereotypical views about differences between racial groups. Many faculty spoke about group differences in family support, motivation, and interest. While Asians were almost uniformly considered highly motivated and hardworking and therefore well suited to academics, Latino students suffered the most negative judgments about their culture's impact on school effort and motivation and, as a consequence, on their class placements. Educators at all three schools characterized Latinos as having poor basic skills and low interest in school and as being culturally disinclined to aspire to postsecondary education. One teacher said, for example, that Latinos, "as a result of the way they were raised, don't want to learn and only view school as something to get away from."

The transcripts of the seniors at each school revealed course-taking patterns consistent with educators' perceptions. Negative assumptions about the culture and dispositions of African American and Latino students shaped counselors' advice to students and teachers' recommendations for course placement—advice that worked against students taking high-track classes.[60] In some cases, counselors and teachers responded quite differently to comparable achievement scores, with the result that Asians and whites secured placements in advanced classes when comparably scoring Latinos did not. It is hard to imagine a scenario that would leave tracking in place and simultaneously penetrate the biases and dispositions of a school and broader culture that find it normal to view African American and Latino students as less capable than white students.

We also saw the political dimensions of tracking at work in the *Matchmaking* study. At all three schools, the high-achieving, affluent (largely white and Asian) parents and students were the group that faculty reported as most willing to "push the system." White and middle-class parents more often lobbied schools and gained their children's admission to upper-track classes, even when their past performance would not ordinarily qualify them. Their political maneuvering gave some students far greater access to high-track classes than would be expected given their achievement levels. They had considerably more opportunities to exercise their "choices" than did other students.[61] The low-achieving and midrange students (often nonwhite or of lower socioeconomic status) frequently had less-involved parents and were less willing to challenge the system. To the extent they did, they often met resistance and skepticism.

The response of schools to calls for fair track placements—as a fix for unfair tracking—tends to be closely examined by parents. Not surprisingly, some of those parents (wealthier and in the main white and with more formal education) respond with speed and power. Savvy, high socioeconomic status (SES) parents use their political capital on behalf of their own children, and educators should be neither surprised nor disappointed by this. However, educators should be aware that lower-SES and minority students, whose ascribed characteristics already work against them in their initial track placements, tend to have families who are precluded from such political maneuvering by their timidity or unfamiliarity with how to manipulate the school's response to their own children. A placement system that facilitates greater inequities, grounded in the social and political capital of each student's parents, is inconsistent with broader American ideals of fairness and opportunity.[62]

By way of analogy, we might look to our national initiative to correct the ill effects of smoking cigarettes. We can demand warning labels, prohibit smoking in public places, mount media campaigns to educate, apply filter tips, bring litigation against those who make false claims, and so on. And indeed, these are all worthwhile steps in a comprehensive approach that will likely reduce overall smoking damage and affect the culture. Perhaps, after generations, many fewer people will smoke. Yet smoking today remains a widespread, damaging practice, and we recognize that mitigating some of the most egregious effects is still not adequate to protect the most impressionable and vulnerable among us: children. All states prohibit selling cigarettes to children because, in spite of various "improvements," there is no way to make smoking "safe enough."

Similarly, tracking can be improved, but it remains tracking. The harm to children is revisited each new school day and will continue as long as we wait for the practice to wither away. Suggestions to improve tracking simply beg the question. We are asked to believe that the inequities of tracking are somehow different from tracking itself. In fact, schools can no more remove those inequities from tracking than corporations can remove carcinogens from cigarettes.

WOULD DETRACKING DO MORE HARM THAN GOOD?   If improving tracking seems to be untenable, and detracking mobilizes powerful normative and political tensions and combativeness, what course might reformers, researchers, policymakers, educators, and communities take? In my view, this struggle must continue on many fronts, but an important place to start is to disarm the fears and misinformation held by powerful groups who see detracking as necessarily diminishing their children's advantages. Although tracking's most vociferous defenders warn of irremediable harms, there is no evidence to support claims that detracking puts students at risk—high achievers or low. On the contrary, over the past two decades, we've learned a great deal more about how to create high-quality, heterogeneous classrooms. We've also gained insights about the benefits that accrue from increasing students' access to the advantages of high-track classes.

Warnings about the likely harms of detracking emerged in the early 1990s, as advocates of separate programs for gifted students argued that heterogeneous grouping would be devastating for gifted students. They worried that students would be bored by the slow pace of instruction; that they would be exploited by teachers asking them, in the name of cooperative learning, to spend their time teaching lower achievers instead of challenging themselves; and that their achievement would fall dramatically. In the spring 1993 newsletter of the National Center for Gifted and Talented Education, for example, James Kulik warned,

American education would be harmed by the wholesale elimination of programs that group learners for instruction by ability. . . . Bright, average, and slow students would suffer academically from elimination of such programs. The damage would be greatest, however, if schools, in the name of de-tracking, eliminated enriched and accelerated classes for their brightest learners. The achievement level of such students falls dramatically when they are required to do routine work at a routine pace. No one can be certain that there would be a way to repair the harm that would be done if schools eliminated all programs of enrichment and acceleration.

More recently, Loveless voiced concerns that detracking would both undermine achievement and drive advantaged parents away:

Detracking is a gamble. . . . [T]he risks of the gamble are being assumed disproportionately by urban schools, low-socioeconomic-status schools and schools with low achievement. This should cause great concern. Some of society's most disadvantaged children are now part of an educational experiment, with the outcome completely unknown. . . . High-achieving minority students in low-income urban schools are most at risk of suffering from the abolition of tracking. . . . Educators should also assess the political costs of detracking. . . . Researchers have described schools where parents threaten to transfer their children if tracking is abolished.

Cautioning that detracking should wait until studies have documented its likely impact, the researcher Laura Argys told an *Education Week* reporter, "Somebody's going to pay for the choice to go to detracking, and it's either the low-skilled or the high-skilled students. That's a decision society is going to have to make."[63]

WHAT IS THE EVIDENCE FOR THESE CLAIMS?   Tracking advocates generally rely on analyses of large national databases that use self-reporting (by principals or teachers) to distinguish types of classrooms. Using such databases, a researcher may compare learning outcomes in classes described as composed of either (1) a wide range of student ability or (2) homogeneous groups at different ability levels. These analyses have typically found that low achievers do better in the mixed-ability classes than in the low track. But they have usually also found that high achievers do worse than in high-track classes. The researchers may therefore conclude that although detracking is likely to boost the test scores of students in the bottom tracks, it will hurt average and high-achieving students.[64]

I have already noted some limitations of these national databases. They show only a very small percentage of students enrolled in classes with widely varying ability levels. They are based on self-reporting. A class that a researcher may identify as tracked may be labeled "mixed ability" by a principal or teacher, or vice versa. Differences between schools, classrooms, and approaches will be washed out, telling us little about successful or unsuccessful approaches to teaching homogenous or mixed-ability classes. In part for these reasons, extrapolating from studies grounded in these databases to make predictions about likely outcomes for schools engaged in detracking reform is speculative at best. Just as the more positive findings in the *Keeping Track* schools— about the opportunities and resources in heterogeneous classes, com- pared to low-track classes—could provide only the most tentative pro- jections about the benefits of detracking, these studies say little about the actual risks. It's a real stretch to assert that they bear any resem- blance to the outcomes of purposeful detracking reform.

Loveless wanders even further in his search for harm. He suggests that the publication of *Keeping Track* in 1985 and the growing enthusi- asm for detracking might have some connection to the post-1985 wid- ening gap in achievement scores and the SAT. For that to be true, substantial numbers of schools would actually have had to have de- tracked after 1985, which, of course, they did not. Loveless's suggestion would also require us to discount many far more reasonable analyses that trace the widening gap to the decline of desegregation and the dismantling of resources to support disadvantaged minority students that had occurred by the mid-1980s.[65]

Whatever the merits of these warnings about detracking, many well-meaning educators and parents have been cautious about detrack- ing out of concern that there are no well-specified, proven alternatives to tracked schools. Some even doubt the *possibility* of curriculum and instruction in heterogeneous classes that won't leave slower students behind or force quicker ones to wait—a concern rooted in norms that essentialize the idea of faster and slower students who can be accommodated only by faster and slower versions of the curriculum.

It is true, as detracking critics charge, that there have been no experimental or statistically controlled studies comparing tracked and detracked schools. However, over the past two decades, the evidence has been accumulating about the efficacy of mixed-ability classes when educators use strategies that presume classroom heterogeneity and provide "multi-ability" instruction. This evidence should allay the fears of those who assume that detracking reform will necessarily harm high-achieving students, even as it benefits low achievers. I provide just a sampling of the evidence in what follows.

Some of the detracking policy initiatives described at the outset of this chapter have increased students' outcomes. For example, the *High Schools That Work* intervention has proven to be a promising approach to making the essential concepts from the college preparatory curriculum accessible to all students. Independent evaluations of the impact of the SREB reforms, using an exam developed by the Educational Testing Service to match the National Assessment of Educational Progress, compared the achievement of students at schools with "high implementation" of the reform to those where the levels of implementation were low. The schools that had implemented the reforms had significantly higher student achievement in reading, mathematics, and science as compared to students at low-implementation schools, and the gaps between African American and white students were smaller at high-implementation schools than at low-implementation schools.[66]

The College Board reports significant gains from its *Equity 2000* project. Their internal monitoring of the data about project students' course taking, grades, and other college preparation behaviors found that, by 1996, all six pilot sites dramatically increased student enrollment in Algebra I by the ninth grade; in three pilot districts all ninth graders took Algebra I. The percentage of students passing algebra did not decline significantly; and in some cases rose, as more students from the discontinued lower tracks enrolled in algebra classes. Moreover, participation in PSAT, SAT, ACT, and AP programs increased significantly; the percentage of students indicating that they plan to attend college after graduation from high school was substantially higher; and significantly greater numbers of students enrolled in higher mathematics such as second-year algebra, trigonometry, precalculus, and calculus than the national enrollments. These positive outcomes led the College Board to integrate the *Equity 2000* strategy into its core work with high schools across the nation, including working with schools to eliminate tracking and provide supplementary educational experiences for students beyond their regular academic courses.[67]

A longitudinal study of Mary Catherine Swanson's AVID program by the sociologist Hugh Mehan and his colleagues found that the four-year college attendance rates of AVID graduates outpaced both San Diego and national averages (50, 37, and 39 percent, respectively). Particularly impressive, AVID minority graduates' rates far exceed those of their African American and Hispanic peers (44 percent of the AVID Hispanic group, compared with 25 percent across San Diego, and 29 percent nationally; 50 percent of the AVID African American group, compared with 35 percent in San Diego, and 33 percent nationally). Mehan and his colleagues documented additional social benefits accruing to AVID participants. In particular, Hispanic and African American participants developed what Mehan terms a "reflective system of beliefs, a critical consciousness . . . about the limits and possibilities of the actions they take and the limitations and constraints they face in life." That is, AVID taught students they could achieve if they were motivated and studied hard. Even so, AVID students did not adopt a belief that their hard work would automatically bring success. Neither did they abandon their cultural identities. Rather, they maintained "dual identities" and adopted the view that, even though they would continue to face considerable discrimination and inequality, they could succeed if they developed "certain cultural practices, notably achieving academically, that are acceptable to the mainstream."[68]

Other new evidence comes from research studies showing the positive impact of mixed-ability classrooms. For example, the Stanford professor Jo Boaler studied British schools, examining the impact of traditional instruction (whole-class, textbook-based, with frequent tests) in a highly tracked school and of multidimensional instruction (open-ended projects and a variety of teaching strategies) in an untracked school. Boaler followed three hundred students over three years, amassing a comprehensive database from observations, interviews, questionnaires, and assessments that show the ways students' beliefs and mathematical understandings were shaped by the various approaches to mathematics teaching. Three times as many students in the school with heterogeneous, multidimensional instruction as those in the tracked groups in the textbook school attained the highest possible grade. They also developed a different type of mathematical knowledge that allowed them to adapt what they had learned to fit new and demanding problems.[69]

In a follow-up study in three U.S. high schools, Boaler monitored approximately seven hundred students over four years. She reports the incredible success of one of the schools, Railside High. Classes at Railside were heterogeneous. Teachers worked collaboratively to design the curriculum, drawing from different "reform" curricula. Mathematics was organized into the traditional sequence of algebra, geometry, advanced algebra, and so on, but the students worked in groups on longer, nontraditional problems. At the end of four years, Railside's diverse population of lower socioeconomic status students achieved more, enjoyed mathematics more, and stayed with mathematics to higher levels than at the more traditional schools she studied. Moreover, the achievement differences that were in place between students of different ethnic groups at the beginning of high school were reduced in all cases and disappeared in some. Studies of other detracked schools have yielded equally encouraging findings.[70]

Similar results were obtained in a researcher-designed heterogeneous classroom intervention called QUASAR (Quantitative Understanding Amplifying Student Achievement and Reasoning), which was designed to raise low levels of student participation and performance in mathematics. Based in urban middle schools, this demonstration project of the University of Pittsburgh's Learning Research and Development Center sought to help all students acquire a deeper, more meaningful understanding of math ideas and to demonstrate their proficiency in mathematical reasoning and complex problem solving. Schools in the project eliminated most forms of academic tracking and implemented programs to develop deeper student understanding and high-level thinking and reasoning skills. All project sites received extensive professional development and teacher support. Evaluation data show that students in the program performed as well as others on basic and traditional items from 1992 NAEP math assessment and outperformed others on less-traditional middle school math content.[71]

Also notable is the mounting evidence in the past twenty years of the positive effects of certain kinds of cooperative, small-group learning. Perhaps the most sophisticated and most rigorously studied form of cooperative learning is complex instruction, a strategy developed and rigorously tested by the sociologist Elizabeth Cohen. The theoretical and empirical knowledge base of complex instruction is the result of many years of programmatic research in heterogeneous classrooms at the elementary and middle school levels. In complex instruction, teachers use cooperative group work to teach at a high academic level in diverse classrooms. They also use multi-ability curriculum materials, assign open-ended, interdependent group tasks, and organize the classroom to maximize student interaction around major ideas and concepts. Explicit teacher interventions aim at reducing the status differences that exacerbate disparities in students' academic expectations for themselves and each other. In one careful study of the implementation of complex instruction, middle-grade teachers proved to be enormously skillful in adapting old curriculum materials to the new strategies. Moreover, students displayed sophisticated intellectual competencies in these classrooms.[72] Not one of these program evaluations and studies suggests that the highest-achieving students were harmed by these interventions.

Over time, some researchers specializing in the education of gifted students have endorsed strategies very similar to those employed in these detracking interventions. In doing so, they parted company with those warning of the damage that would be done to high-achieving students in mixed ability classes.[73] In part, the discourse about gifted students requiring separate classes has softened with a growing consensus that mainstream classrooms with accommodations probably provide the best settings for most students with special needs. In part, as IQ has become discredited as a single criterion for identification of giftedness, and as a wider range of more relevant criteria are included, "gifted" students themselves are becoming a more heterogeneous group both racially and in the type and range of their skills. In part, however, the research and discussion on detracking have resonated with those researchers of gifted education who have looked carefully at the evidence about the harms of tracking and the potential benefits of mixed classrooms.

Joseph Renzulli, director of the National Center for Gifted and

Talented Education, argues that gifted students can be served in regular classrooms containing students of varying ability so long as classroom teachers have special training in teaching gifted students or access to specialists who can come into the classroom to provide assistance. Under Renzulli's directorship, the center focuses its research on ways to provide "high-end learning" opportunities for all of America's students—opportunities that challenge the highest levels of learning and creativity. The center promotes high expectations, rigorous standards, and greater engagement with subject matter for all students, not simply those currently identified as gifted. Carol Tomlinson, a noted researcher of gifted education, has written a number of books and articles showing that the heterogeneous classroom can meet the needs of gifted learners, and she provides teachers with strategies for differentiating instruction within classrooms to challenge advanced learners.[74]

Finally, my most recent study of tracking and detracking has added evidence about the positive effects that are possible. My UCLA colleagues and I have worked over the past seven years with a group of thirty young people, who as ninth graders were not placed in the college preparatory track at their diverse comprehensive high school.[75] Although the school had a stellar record in preparing many white and Asian students for elite universities, it historically had sent very few students of color to four-year colleges. Partnering with the superintendent, the principal, and a handful of teachers, we designed and tested an intervention aimed at interrupting the schooling trajectories that were firmly in place for these thirty African American and Latino students. The students enrolled in courses that would prepare them for four-year colleges and universities, including some honors and advanced placement classes for some, and we provided them with a program that combined academic and social support (typical of college access programs like AVID) with opportunities for the students themselves to become researchers of the sociology of schooling. Our hypothesis was that this combination could help the students learn to navigate their high school successfully, develop a college-going identity, and move on to four-year colleges.

These high school students became research collaborators, rather than simply subjects, in our study. As members of a new sort of research community—high school students, teachers, and university researchers—they investigated schooling, social stratification, and educational equity. In their social studies class and in summer seminars at UCLA, these students (called the Futures students) produced original research examining such topics as tracking, schools' relationships with families, student resistance, and inequalities between schools in affluent and low-income communities. The classes, supports, and summer seminars were sustained from grades nine through twelve, during which time the students presented their research to a broad array of critical audiences: school and community groups, civil rights attorneys, graduate students and faculty at several universities, and directors of college access and university outreach programs. Initially, the Futures students associated their courses, their status at school, and their treatment by teachers with their track placements, and they had taken this status to be a natural and inevitable outcome of their social and personal worth. This changed as they studied these phenomena and drew connections between their personal experiences and the structures, practices, beliefs, and politics that sustain or disrupt patterns of inequality in the schools.

In spring 2000, all but one of the Futures students graduated from high school. Twenty-five had college acceptances in hand. In 2001, sixteen enrolled in four-year schools, and eight others went to two-year colleges. They far outpaced the high school graduation and four-year college-going rates of a matched comparison group of African American and Latino students who began ninth grade with the Futures students, but who did not participate in Futures. Although most students from both groups went on to college, the percentages attending selective four-year schools and less selective two-year schools differed significantly—53 percent and 26 percent, respectively, for the Futures, compared with 15 and 67 percent for the comparison group. Moreover, only 14 percent of the Futures students attend college part-time compared to 48 percent of their non-Futures peers. They all had a strong sense of themselves as young intellectuals who both belonged in college and hoped to return ready to contribute to their home communities.

As of this writing, the Futures participants are three years beyond high school graduation. Using their experience as members of a powerful research and action network in high school, many are now building similar networks in their colleges as they continue to draw upon their fellow Futures students for academic, political, and spiritual support. Their college persistence rate is laudable. As of spring 2004, 89 percent of those who started at any institution of higher education are still in school. Of the eight students who entered community college in fall 2001, three will transfer to four-year universities in fall 2004. These figures compare favorably to national averages showing that 59 percent of African Americans and 68 percent of Hispanics who enrolled in an institution of higher education (four-year, two-year, or a vocational education program) in 1995–96 either attained their degree goal or persisted three years beyond initial enrollment.[76] Like many students, however, few will earn a bachelor's degree within four years. Moreover, like other low-income, first-generation college students, they continue to struggle. Nevertheless, they have defied those who judged them as ninth graders to be unsuited for four-year college preparation.

What Happens When Schools *Begin* to Detrack?

The Futures project was not a naturally occurring school-based event, but what we termed a design experiment to generate ideas and test hypotheses. Although we gained important insights about tracking, it was not, principally, a detracking study. Over the past two decades, however, I have studied reforms expressly designed to detrack. I wanted to understand better why tracking persists in the face of the evidence against it. What happens when local policymakers and educators seek to reduce or eliminate tracking in diverse schools? What lessons might we derive from their experiences? In brief, my research and that of others demonstrates that, although equity reforms are technically difficult, the most powerful forces maintaining the status quo of unequal schooling, and most threatening equity reforms, are the deeply entrenched beliefs about low-income students and students of color and the competition among parents to make sure their children get the "best" education (and the life chances that follow). The next chapter tells the stories of these schools.

12

Democracy's Canaries

In 1990, Rockville Centre School District, a diverse, suburban school district located on Long Island, New York, began replacing its tracked classes with mixed-ability classes and teaching everyone the curriculum formerly reserved for the district's high-track students.[1] Previously, the high school had three tracks—school level, Regents, and honors—and the middle school had two or more in each subject. As in many districts, African American and Latino students were enrolled disproportionately in the lower track. Superintendent William H. Johnson's and the Rockville Centre Board of Education's ambitious goal was to have 75 percent of high school graduates earn a New York State Regents diploma and to close the district's racial and social class gaps. Achieving the superintendent's goal meant that students must pass at least eight examinations in mathematics, laboratory sciences, social studies, English Language Arts, and foreign language, examinations tied to the curriculum in the higher-track courses. Tracking stood in the way.

The district decided that all students would study the accelerated middle school math curriculum, since the Regents math test posed the greatest challenge. So the middle school put mixed-ability groups in the math class formerly reserved for the district's highest achievers. It provided support classes and after-school tutoring to help struggling students keep up. The results were astonishing. The following year, over 90 percent of the incoming freshmen, excluding the special education students, entered the district's South Side high school having passed the first Regents math examination. The achievement gap dramatically narrowed, as the percentage of African American or Latino students passing the algebra-based Regents exam in the eighth grade tripled, rising to 75 percent. The percentage of white or Asian American regular education students who passed the test at the end of the eighth grade also increased dramatically—from 54 percent to 98 percent. Not satisfied with those results, the district pushed further. The following year, the special education students were included as well; detracking expanded to other subjects, and in 1999 it followed students into the ninth and tenth grades. Enrollment in South Side's Advanced Placement (AP) and International Baccalaureate classes was opened up to everyone who wanted to enter them.

During the decade of detracking reform, the school became a U.S. Department of Education Blue Ribbon School of Excellence and one of *Newsweek's 100 Best High Schools in the United States*. By 2003, the gap among Rockville Centre graduates had nearly disappeared. Eighty-two percent of all African American or Latino and 97 percent of all white or Asian-American graduates earned a Regents diploma. In 2004, the overall Regents diploma rate increased to a remarkable 94 percent, with 30 percent of the graduating class also earning the International Baccalaureate diploma. In sum, detracking raised the bar for all students. Every group improved at the same time that the achievement gap narrowed dramatically at Rockville Centre.

Such remarkable success is difficult and rare. Rockville Centre has gotten closer than most to embodying the historical conviction that American society has a deep store of egalitarian potential waiting to be mined. From the beginning, the public school has been charged with educating future citizens, an endeavor on which the fate of a democracy depends. And at least since the *Brown vs. Board of Education* decision in 1954, schools have been charged with providing such an education to all on equal terms. Rockville Centre's dismantling of the tracking structure reveals, first, the need for adequate resources, fresh attitudes, and refined teaching skills; and second, the importance of communities that have the patience, willingness, and vision to recognize their democratic responsibilities for all their children.

However, few communities and educators have welcomed reform that challenges the structures of educational stratification. The accounts of detracking schools that follow make clear that, when those structures are threatened, school and community resistance often creates an environment that is toxic to equity-minded reform and reformers. From these schools' successes and failures, we have learned to recognize some danger signs—early warnings, if you will—of far deeper, more profound obstacles to the quest for healthy and democratic communities. The course of detracking reform tells us as much about ourselves, our communities, and our democracy as about our schools.

In the nineteenth and early twentieth centuries, coal miners took canaries down the mineshafts with them. When the air was safe, the canaries would chirp and sing. Rising levels of toxic gas, however, silenced the birds and gave an early warning to abandon the mine. We are reminded of those canaries as we observe detracking schools. Although some have thrived, the equity reform landscape is littered with dead initiatives, and communities and educators are timid about entering the terrain.

Social and cultural reproduction theorists help us understand the ever-present toxicity. American public schools mirror a highly inequitable economy. For the past century, at least, schools have provided students with separate, different, and unequal schooling experiences, as was seen to be appropriate for that economy. Citing students' differential merit, differential schooling has been deemed to be both fair to students and compatible with democratic capitalism. After all, as adults, students will occupy very different positions in the highly differentiated workforce. That such schooling consistently reproduces race and social class inequalities in educational and life chances is usually judged as regrettable, but it has not undermined the legitimacy of schools' sorting and certifying role.

Detracking schools, then, challenges not only school structures but also the broader economic and class structures that are foundational to tracking. These schools venture out ahead of more cautious reformers, testing the safety of our social atmosphere. They challenge deeply rooted values and assumptions about merit and fairness, and they disrupt the accepted distributional patterns of educational resources and opportunities. As they do, they become vulnerable to stifling cultural and political pressures. Their victories, like the canaries' singing, help the rest of us to know what is possible in our democracy. Their struggles forecast the dangers facing schools and society alike. We can learn a great deal from their stories—their songs and silences—about the possibilities and limits of equity reform.

Some people might think of detracking as a dangerous experiment, putting our students at risk in the name of some utopian idea. But this assumes that the current, tracked structure of schooling is natural and safe. In fact, as the evidence in the previous chapters makes clear, tracking places students at great peril. Only when we see our students thriving under a different system—like that at Rockville Centre—will the dangers of the current system become fully clear.

Beyond Sorting and Stratification

In the early 1990s, my then-colleague at UCLA Amy Stuart Wells and I launched a national study of nascent detracking efforts in racially mixed secondary schools.[2] We selected ten schools—six senior highs and four middle schools—in which the faculty had begun shifting from tracked to heterogeneous grouping. The schools ranged from big city schools under court desegregation orders (but not court detracking orders) to those in small communities where everybody went to the same middle or high school. They varied in size from more than three thousand to fewer than five hundred students. They were widely dispersed across the nation—one in the Northeast, three in the Midwest, one in the South, two in the Northwest, and three in various regions of California. They enrolled quite different mixes of white, African American, Latino, Native American/Alaska Native, and/or Asian students. Over three years, our research team visited the schools regularly, interviewing educators, students, parents, and other community members; we observed in classrooms; and we attended lots of school and public meetings. Our longitudinal, case study methods allowed us to examine in depth, first-hand, and over time the schools' activities and their communities' responses. We considered changes in the curriculum and teaching as well as whether the schools' detracking efforts reshaped norms, values, and relationships within schools and communities.

We found clear patterns across the ten schools' experiences, and I focus on those patterns in what follows. However, the stories we uncovered were unique to each place. The course that educators took and the way others responded to them were deeply affected by the local community culture and politics as well as by national patterns of race, social class, and home language.[3]

Seeking Educational Justice

In each of the schools we studied, educators (and, in some places, community members) took a critical look at school regularities and the part schooling plays in social inequality.[4] In each of the schools, a critical mass of people—in various combinations of numbers and status—could no longer abide by the existing gap between the ideals and reality of schooling. For example, at Union High a former school board member expressed the district's equity intentions when it initiated plans for the new, consolidated school: "I guess we just had a feeling that all kids could learn given the right opportunities, that really there weren't great differences in intellect between rich kids and poor kids, or it was just a matter of exposure."

Similarly, educators at highly regarded Liberty High chafed at the realization that, for all its National Merit Scholars and graduates attending elite universities, the school's record of failure with low-income students of color was equally impressive. As Liberty High Principal Evan Payne put it, "If you're in the 'haves' group, it's one of the best places in America to go to high school. If you're in the 'have nots,' it's like a lot of places—it's full of failure."

Grant High's reform was also driven by a concern for equity. As one teacher put it, "The teachers I most connect with are the ones who really sense that we can't afford to waste anybody. We just can't afford to say that we have this group of kids [the high achievers] that will carry us. You know, they'll be our leaders. . . . I'm convinced we don't live in a world like that anymore. We can't afford to lose those [other] kids."

At each of these schools, educators came to see tracking as a major impediment to their equity goals. At Rollinghills Middle School, for example, Assistant Principal Jane Griffen counseled the most alienated youngsters. Her work often took her to the South Side homes of bussed-in African American students, where she encountered the caring and high aspirations of families far less advantaged than those in the Rollinghills neighborhoods. Griffen came to believe that these students' inferior opportunities at school were at the root of most of the discipline problems she grappled with, and she chafed at white parents' efforts to exclude black students from the higher-level classes: "Part of my responsibility is to be respectful, but I have a hard time dealing with a racist. . . . Sometimes I want to say [to white parents] ' . . . you dare to sit there and put down children who may not have all the advantages that your child has but who are here working despite their disadvantages. You're sitting here telling me that they are not worthy to be in class with your child.' This is a real personal issue with me."

Bearfield Junior High School's principal also made clear his awareness that tracking limits students' access to knowledge: "You know when you don't teach a kid anything but two plus two is four, then you give him a test and he has no idea why the one train doesn't catch the other train, we think that he's stupid. He's not stupid. Who the hell are we to decide who gets access to what learning?" And that tracking has long-term social effects: "Detracking issues are really the salvation of America. I mean, we can't build a high, medium, and low America. . . . I mean, we really can't say to a kid in second grade, 'You've been elected to low America. You're just—we're not going to give you access to learning, like we do to everybody else.'" A Bearfield teacher we spoke to explained that white parents' resistance to eliminating honors is grounded in norms about race: "Quite frankly, I think the reason we have honors is parental pressure. It's a racial issue. An honors group is a white group."

Finally, in the wake of the Rodney King verdict and civil disturbance in 1992, Grant's high school students (several states away) targeted segregated classes as one of the major problems at the school. Reform-minded teachers and student leaders used this very public discussion about the racial composition of honors and regular classes as a mandate to detrack the school. These examples from a few of the ten schools in our study illustrate the commitment to educational justice fueling many change agents' detracking efforts.

Creating New Structures, Curriculum, and Pedagogy

Within three years of Principal Evan Payne's arrival at Liberty High School, he and a cadre of strong teacher leaders had made considerable progress toward detracking. The school's entire ninth-grade class was enrolled in heterogeneous two-hour English/history "cores" taught by partnered teachers, and many ninth-grade college preparatory math classes were heterogeneous. Each of the core classes was attached to one of the seven Liberty High School "families" composed of an administrator, a counselor, and a secretary. This arrangement—spurred in part by Liberty's involvement with the Coalition of Essential Schools— provided a greater degree of connectedness for the students and teachers. Students who would have traditionally been placed in a low-track English class because of low scores on the state's reading and writing proficiency exam were assigned to an English "backup" class designed to support learning in the core English classes.

Liberty's ninth-grade detracking was made possible by four tangible changes in the allocation of school resources, schedule, and registration practices: class sizes were limited to twenty students; backup classes with tutoring provided lower-achieving students with a double dose of instruction; common planning time was offered for teacher-teams who shared core classes; and "self-scheduling" was replaced with counselors' deliberately balancing sections of the core classes. Professional development promised to boost teachers' knowledge and skills about developing thematic curriculum and thereby to buttress the English and social studies departments' collaboration. These changes began to support Liberty's goal of giving all of its ninth graders access to high-quality, high-status, heterogeneous courses.

Educators in each of the ten schools took advantage of then-current reform initiatives to help them change their schools to better serve low-income, nonwhite kids. Two joined the Coalition of Essential Schools, two affiliated with networks of middle schools implementing Carnegie's *Turning Points* reforms, and two became part of their state's project providing funding for "restructuring" schools. Two others had been charged by their districts to develop special magnet programs, and two had reorganized as a consequence of district consolidation. Educators used these more comprehensive reform contexts as a framework and sometimes a shelter for altering tracking.

The ultimate goal at each of the schools was to provide greater access and academic achievement for low-track (disproportionately minority) students, while maintaining quality for traditionally high-achieving (mostly white) students. Each of the schools made changes in basic school structures to prompt fundamental changes in curriculum, instruction, and learning in heterogeneous classes. In addition to reducing or eliminating the number of track levels in academic subjects, the schools did such things as create new schedules, reorganize teachers into teams, balance class enrollments, and provide all students access to honors programs. Others permitted students to double up classes in particular subjects or take summer classes that allowed them to "jump" to a higher track. Most found ways for students previously in low tracks to get extra help to master the standard curriculum, for example, by providing backup classes that gave students an extra hour of instruction so they could keep up with the more demanding content and pace of detracked classes.

In addition to these organizational changes, some teachers at each of the schools adopted new classroom strategies they believed would permit students to show their ability in previously unrecognized ways—for example, Socratic Seminars and curriculum that emphasized active learning, such as project-based science and interactive math; reduced reliance on textbooks; and increased use of cooperative small-group learning. Other teachers created assignments that would challenge students of varying ability levels. Some developed new assessment techniques to identify a broader range of student strengths and needs. Many explored multicultural curricula to make knowledge more engaging and accessible for all students.

Challenging Beliefs and Assumptions that Sustain Inequality

The strongest force behind Bearfield Middle School's detracking efforts was its charismatic principal, Ben McCall, who had formerly been the principal at an all-white junior high school in the same community. McCall worked diligently and skillfully to convince his faculty that detracking (and the team structures and multicultural curriculum he thought necessary to support it) was essential for equality in their newly consolidated, racially mixed school. But even for McCall, the idea that detracking was a "sensible" reform did not come easily. As McCall described his conversion from a "tracker" to a "detracker," it became clear that adopting this reform challenged deeply felt convictions he held about how schooling should proceed:

I really liked [a former district administrator], but she and I were at totally different ends of the spectrum. She was anti-grouping and tracking and I was a tracker and a grouper. I was just finishing my degree so I was at [the university] all the time. She just laid all this research on me that was anti-tracking and I said

"Well, where's the research on my side of the fence?" She said, "Ben, there isn't any." . . . I looked one whole weekend at [the university library] and I couldn't find anything to support it and then [the administrator] and I went out to lunch that lasted till about six o'clock at night. She was right and I was wrong. When the light finally went on it was like holy shit! I was wrong.

None of the ten schools found its organizational and instructional changes easy to implement. There were technical glitches along the way, but these did not present the biggest problems. Far more serious difficulties arose when changes conflicted with the communities' conventional wisdom about what secondary students are like and what good schools should be like. Moreover, because these changes were re-distributive—that is, they fundamentally altered how the schools allocated their most precious resources, including time, teachers, materials, and high-achieving students—they challenged traditional ways of thinking about "merit" and which students "deserve" the best that schools have to offer. At each of the ten schools, change agents grappled with conventional norms that prevented them and others from having high expectations for all students and from creating structures that press all students toward high levels of academic competence. Each school's reform effort was jeopardized, not only by those who actively resisted reform but also by well-intentioned educators whose everyday commonsense actions unwittingly reinforced and reconstructed the logic behind traditional grouping practices. In the process of implementing structural and technical changes, they confronted (mostly) taken-for-granted conceptions of intelligence and ability, racial differences and merit, and deeply entrenched traditions of what is valued curriculum and appropriate practice at the schools.[5]

Educators attempting to build commitment for detracking struggled with increasingly outmoded conceptions of intelligence, some of which reflect deep-seated racist and classist attitudes and prejudices. These conceptions played out in school as educators interpreted the skills and knowledge that educationally and economically privileged parents pass on to their children as innate intelligence—interpretations that guide decisions about track placements and the learning opportunities afforded to students in different tracks. Once these differences in "innate intelligence" were identified, bureaucratic efficiency dictated that the best way to accommodate these differences is to sort students into separate classes and provide them with differentiated curricula.

Detracking challenged all of these norms. Laura Miller, a veteran teacher at Rollinghills Middle School, was the parent of children in the school district's Enriched Program as well as the teacher of "regular" students. Miller was unhappy with the cliquishness and an uninspired academic curriculum that her own "enriched" children experienced at school, and she was enormously saddened by the disheartened and self-deprecating attitudes of her regular students, whom she saw as far more capable than they saw themselves. In her search for better pedagogy, Miller regularly attended summer workshops on Gifted Education at the University of Connecticut. There, she learned that neither Rollinghills's rigidly exclusionary grouping practices nor stodgy, enriched curriculum in the special district program conformed to the best thinking in gifted education. A gifted educator from another state first suggested to her that gifted youngsters could be served better in high-level, heterogeneous classrooms—a message she brought back to Rollinghills.

As educators in each of the schools worked to change structures and instructional techniques, they simultaneously challenged themselves and their colleagues to adopt the view that all students could achieve at very high levels and to communicate through the schools' structures and practices that they expected them to do so. Changed beliefs alongside changed structures helped educators make better sense of both.

"Challenge" projects at Green Valley High, for example, often provided students with several options as to what they might do to complete the requirement. All students experienced the core lessons and then had a chance to tailor further work to their interests and skills. Appealing both to higher- and lower-achieving students, the challenge projects allowed all students to advance without separating anyone from the class for "special" treatment. During a *Romeo and Juliet* lesson, for example, a student could earn challenge credit by reciting part of the play, writing a contemporary script for the play, or researching the fashion of the time and submitting a portfolio of drawings and text. According to one teacher, these opportunities have enabled some of Green Valley's "nongifted" students and its traditionally lower-achieving Latino students to prepare elaborate responses to their experiences with the play: "Oftentimes they're really quite adept at drama. They like it a lot. So they enjoy going in front of their peers, performing. And that's generally the one they will choose—something that's a performance. They also like memorizing. The kids who can't do well on tests for example—I find it quite odd, and I'd like to do some research on this sometime—have wonderful memories. They will take a speech and do a dramatic interpretation of a speech."

Educators at a number of schools used new theories about the multidimensional nature of intelligence (though not always with great fidelity to the theories) to explain and dignify racial differences in students' academic performance and school behavior. This new understanding led teachers to see diverse instructional strategies as legitimate ways to press all students to achieve. At some schools, educators put greater emphasis on hard work and persistence, as opposed to conventional conceptions of ability that favored students who caught on quickly at an acceptable, if sometimes superficial, level. One Plainview teacher, for example, told us about her view of intelligence, associating it with motivation and confidence: "A student who has more faith in his or her ability, or more confidence, that student is going to be a higher achiever." A team of Bearfield teachers decided that intense effort ought to qualify students for awards for being outstanding students. They agreed to nominate a student who is not perfect but works industriously. At the same time, this group decided not to single out a higher-achieving student who got by without hard work.

Creating structures and school cultures that develop more inclusive definitions of high achievement and that make honors possible for every student is a challenge to powerful school norms. Educators did not agree on these matters. Despite some teachers' efforts to reconceptualize intelligence as multidimensional, developmental, and manifest equally across racial groups, traditional conceptions retained a firm hold. Grant's experience was quite typical. Many teachers held fast to a traditional view of students' abilities and stubbornly resisted changes on that basis. But even Grant's reform-minded language arts teachers struggled with ways to judge the work of students who may be very intelligent, but who have not learned how to *jump through the hoops*, traditionally expected of top students. As one teacher told us, "Some people give me real fine indications of their intelligence, but they're not getting the grade because the grade is the reward for the hoops. As a teacher, it would be nice to just say, 'God, you're a really smart person. I'd like to give you an "A."' But that would then degenerate into 'I like you, so I'm gonna give you an "A".' . . . I'm not sure, when the grading comes out, I'm not sure how I'm gonna handle this, really." Teachers at several of the schools did not entirely reject a nativist view of intelligence but proposed that learning required more than an inherent gift. For instance, one King Middle School administrator commented that the school's open structure and climate work best for students "*who have the work ethic,* and are not just *innately bright and lazy.*" A Bearfield teacher described high-achieving students at the school: "Few of them have a lot of *native intelligence.* Most of them are quote, unquote 'good kids'—ones who will study without you telling them to."

Teachers who entertained newer developmental and multidimensional conceptions of intelligence had to withstand the scrutiny of skeptical parents who feared their children had much to lose if traditional conceptions were altered. For instance, a Plainview High English teacher created a heterogeneous American Studies class after reading research that persuaded her that neither society nor schools really understand intelligence, how to measure it, or how to make use of it in schools. When she presented her research to parents—at the principal's request—her message was not well received, particularly by those parents whose children were in AP classes. According to the teacher, "If you were raised under the system that said you were very intelligent and high achieving, you don't want anyone questioning that system, OK? That's just the way it is." She said that what parents were most threatened by was how this research was going to be used by the school, and whether it would undermine advanced classes.

Confronting Racial Stereotypes

Stereotypical views of minority students' ability and motivation for academic work also remained salient in schools and communities. In all schools, some educators drew connections quite openly between students' abilities and race and social class. Often, their analyses began with a status quo description—that African Americans and Latinos tended to be lower achieving—perhaps uttered with a sense of sympathy and frustration, but with no indication that they would ever move beyond regret. It was not part of their normal discourse to look to the school's role in creating and maintaining what they were describing as students' deficits. Many teachers, parents, and others were open to the *idea* of reform as long as it did not require that they change their perceptions of children. For example, one educator lamented, "We're getting fewer honors kids, and that's just demographics." Another told us, "The percentage of academically capable . . . African American students versus the percentage of white students is very disproportionate." In a third school we heard, "They [Native American students] don't have the support at home, and they don't have the ability."

In many cases, racial differences in achievement are part of a complex interaction with (and attributed to) differences in background and culture. For example, a powerful and prevailing understanding of Central High's Latino population was that students were unmotivated because of their culture. One social studies teacher said, "It's hard though! 'Cause there's only so much you can do with the kids. We don't get really well-motivated, well-educated kids. Most come from not ideal family situations. They're not very well-motivated . . . and it's really hard to do anything in that situation. No matter what you do as teachers, there's just some kids, nothing is going to help them, or nothing is going to solve your problems."

Similarly, Green Valley had what some teachers called a *pear-shaped* academic population—light on high and middle achievers and heavy on low achievers. More than one Green Valley teacher attributed this to the racial makeup of the community. According to one, the preponderance of low-achieving students at the school was "a function of where we live." This teacher and many others believed that the school's and community's demography made the college preparatory track inappropriate for everyone. Similar views about the relationship between race, culture, and achievement were voiced by a few teachers at nearly every school. One Plainview AP teacher, for example, gave the following explanation of the black-white achievement gap at the school: "You know, every time we do something, I think, how will we deliver to Afro-American students? I don't think that a lot of teachers here really know where these kids come from, and I don't think they've seen the houses that they live in. I mean, maybe they have, but . . . I guess it's really hard to realize that somebody's mother might have been 15 when they were born, and they live with granny, and there's no books in the house. You can't give . . . that kid doesn't have an equal chance against the kid whose mother and father are both working and have a nice home with a stereo." Another explained, "You know, groups of African

Americans go through the normal solid high school program, but it's rare to find one that . . . has an ambition to start off with the Freshman Biology, and wants to get that extra science in. Again, I'm not sure why. Part of it, I think, is skills. Part of it, I think . . . has to do with attitude towards excelling or ambitions for the future. I think most of the African Americans I talk to have much more limited ambitions."

At Explorer Middle School, many Native American students had been identified as "communication disordered," an official school classification which is not a learning disability but refers to a constellation of perceptions about Native students' verbal ease. Native teachers and families told us, however, that the classification ignored a number of factors such as Native students' preferences not to speak out, compete for attention, upstage peers, or expose themselves to the negative judgments about what they might say or who they are. Teachers at Union were also mindful of how classist and racist stereotypes present in the community influenced judgments about what type of opportunities were appropriate for African American students. Several told us they had to contend with comments like, "Why'd they build such a nice school for those students?" These culturally and racially specific views of the inability of students of color (especially those from low-income families) to profit from educational opportunities were echoed in the voices of some educators, parents, and community members we interviewed at each of the ten schools. Reformers seeking to counter educators' and the community's resistance to detracking reforms had to address the very practical (technical) difficulties of rethinking pedagogy and school structures in the midst of contradictory, often hostile norms around middle-class definitions of valued knowledge and intelligence.

Confronting the Politics of Inequality

Reformers met resistance from parents and some of their faculty colleagues who feared that detracking would jeopardize the benefits they enjoyed under tracking. Savvy parents who wanted their children enrolled in the "best" classes mounted the greatest opposition; and teachers who preferred teaching those classes were also a powerful obstacle.

Schools need political support from these parents and teachers, and it does not come easily. Tracking policies that advantage more privileged children are offered by the school in exchange for the political support that more advantaged and involved parents bring to a school.[6] Nearly all the schools we studied had previously operated competitive systems, permitting only a small percentage of student slots in high-track classes. Indeed, most of the schools had long anchored their achievement culture on the existence of and competition for top classes, where the best educational resources are found. Nearly everywhere, placement in the high track had meant assurance of an experienced, fully credentialed teacher and a richer, more complex curriculum as well as the normative and shorthand assumptions behind the mantle of "honors" or "accelerated." It may be impossible to disentangle parents' preferences for the empirical advantages of the concrete resources from the less-tangible status of high-track placement. However, that high-track classes have carried with them an assurance of the "best" certainly explains part of this group of parents' resistance to detracking reform. Such reforms ask such parents to undergo major shifts in their notions of what is good for their children. Although it may not be enough to convince the ones focused primarily on status, educators must certainly demonstrate to parents that detracked classes bring with them the concrete resource and opportunity advantages their children enjoyed in high-track classes.

Parental resistance was particularly contentious among parents who felt their school was neglecting "gifted" students or that it was diverting resources "meant" for one group to another group of "less deserving" students. This belief was especially salient among a group of white parents at Liberty High, nicknamed the "Mothers of Excellence." According to one, "Liberty overlooks how very important it is to academically orient kids to get an academically stimulating education. Sometimes in Liberty it gets treated as a luxury. Oh, these kids are bright, they're going to do fine anyway. Well in reality, that's not true. A lot of these kids, if they're not stimulated, are going to fall back . . . losing these kids, losing any kids is a tragedy. And it bothers me when, somehow, the district acts like losing a bright kid is not as tragic as losing the kids at the bottom."

Similarly, some white parents in the Bearfield community felt that their tax dollars were wrongly used to supplement the education of the African American community's children: "People from Allison Park, there's whites in there and there's blacks in there. It's mostly black. . . .

First of all, they don't pay taxes like we pay taxes out in Dalton. And I don't think that's right that I have to pay those kind of taxes when they don't but they still go to our school. . . . [I]t has brought down our school system and I don't feel that it should. . . . I'm not a racist, but I am—I don't want my school being brought down because of a lower caliber."

Central High's faculty proposed a new "custom calendar" so that students could earn course credit at a more individualized pace. The school year would be divided into nine-week quarters, followed by two-week intercessions. During the intercessions, students could make up lost credits or repeat classes. The custom calendar was touted as complementing detracking, because it would allow lower-achieving students to make up work or get ahead during the intercession. Central's principal reasoned, "The paradigm here is that it takes every student . . . 180 days to learn Algebra 1, and my question is, how valid could that be? Aren't there some students who might need a couple more days to do that? Now is it better to tell that student that they're a failure and can't learn because they can't learn it in 180 days, or is it better to give them a few extra days to do it?" The custom calendar had features created with the special needs of migrant students and other at-risk students in mind. Migrant students often were away from the school for long periods of time; and if the custom calendar had been adopted, they would be able to complete classes within nine-week quarters. The parents who spearheaded the move to defeat the custom calendar initiative did so on the grounds that the majority of students were well served by the existing calendar and the custom calendar was designed to benefit only a few. While most Central faculty favored the custom calendar, the proposal was denounced by powerful parents in the community and by more conventional teachers. An assistant principal realized only later that, although the calendar was not framed as a redistributive policy, it was seen as a symbol of policymaking aimed at helping students traditionally disadvantaged by the system (at this school low-income, limited-English-speaking Latino students) and taking from those who benefit from the status quo. He felt the custom calendar was used as a symbol of a liberal ideological effort to take away from the haves and give to the have-nots.

Even in Green Valley, where parent opposition to detracking was mild, one district administrator claimed that the high school loses a fair amount of disillusioned white, middle-class students to private schools:

"If they [white parents] don't feel that there's a program here that is giving their child every opportunity, they pull their kids out and put them in private school. . . . I keep saying, 'The educational opportunities are there if your child chooses to take advantage of them.' I think parents . . . are saying, 'All of the emphasis is on giving kids a second chance, a third chance, a fourth chance.' . . . The teachers are draining themselves trying to nurture kids who come to school with nothing. The other [parents] are saying, 'What's in it for my child?' "

One important constant that emerged from our detracking study was the strong sense of entitlement exhibited by many parents of students in high-track classes. These parents expressed the belief that their children are entitled to more—more resources, more teacher time, more challenging curriculum, better instructional strategies, and so forth—because they are more intelligent and talented than other students. We also found a related sense of the parents' own entitlement; that is, they had worked hard, enabled themselves to move to certain neighborhoods, and paid taxes, and their children merited advantages comparable to the parents' own effort and resources. Deeply embedded in this sense of entitlement is the social construction of intelligence and the white, middle- and upper-middle-class cultural capital inherent in such a construction.[7]

A counselor at Central High School, for example, noted that parents of honors students would not take the time to listen to teachers' or administrators' pedagogical reasons for doing away with the honors track. She said they are simply "not as concerned with the whole [school] as much as they should be." Explorer Middle School's coordinator of "gifted" programs told us she was shocked to learn that her students' parents seemed far less interested in the rich substance she could offer their children in heterogeneous settings than they were in maintaining the status that came with a more visible, separate program. An assistant principal at Liberty High noted that "many upper-class, professional parents hold occupational positions in which they work toward equity and democracy, but expect their children to be given special treatment."

In part these fears are understandable, given the higher education system in the United States and how it forces high schools to differentiate between various courses and, ultimately, between the students in those courses. We have seen how in the schools the demands of competitive, high-status universities and politically powerful parents who want their children to attend these institutions drive K–12 educators to use differentiated credentials as exchange value for students in separate and distinct tracks. Given that the parents most likely to influence curriculum policymaking at the school level are those who are college-educated themselves, the symbiotic relationship between tracking and stratification at the secondary level and the college admissions process again perpetuates the intergenerational transmission of advantage.

Most parents who attended universities, particularly high-status ones, had a clear image of what their children's high school transcripts should look like to assure them a seat in the college of their choice. In several of the senior high schools, parents understood how the College Board's AP courses, with strict entrance requirements and an academically rigorous, test-driven curriculum, were absolutely critical to making their children competitive for slots in the best colleges. This parental pressure existed alongside the concerns of educators at these schools, who were hard-pressed to retain the status offered by AP at the same time they struggle to provide access to high-level, engaging subject matter and inquiry-based learning experiences that are not necessarily a priority in AP curricula.[8]

FEAR OF BRIGHT, WHITE FLIGHT   Parental opposition understandably led to a fear among educators that white, wealthy parents would abandon the schools, taking the schools' political credibility with them. This fear compelled even reform-minded individuals to proceed with caution and sometimes retain programs they found problematic. Rollinghills Middle School had initiated new, more rigid tracking practices in the wake of its countywide, court-ordered school desegregation plan. Many educators and parents told us that the district created a four-track structure expressly to appease fearful white parents, who, according to one Rollinghills teacher, *"wield a big stick."* Consequently, detracking at Rollinghills proceeded slowly and strategically, with educators knowing, as Assistant Principal Griffen put it, that for many white parents, "part of their agenda is 'I want a challenging academic program for my child,' and part of their agenda is that it can't be that way if there are twelve black children in the classroom with them."

At Plainview, the prior experiences of Principal St. John at nearby

Hamilton High School had convinced him that the AP course offerings are essential to maintaining the white student population. Under a desegregation plan, Hamilton had shifted from all-white and upper-middle-class to all-black, lower-middle-class to poor in a matter of ten years. Mere mention of Hamilton and "what happened there" served as an object lesson of the need to appease white parents. Consequently, Plainview's principal and many teachers felt they must encourage minority achievement within the present tracked system, rather than attempt to disassemble tracking.

Bearfield's superintendent was also deeply concerned about the potential "white flight" that might ensue if the white community perceives that schools are catering to the African American community. As he put it, "If we're going to start talking about all kinds of other things like equity in schools, how are we going to train the parents to understand what we're even talking about? Because what's going to be perceived is 'You're just trying to give me a bunch of mumbo-jumbo so you can take care of those black kids.' . . . We're going to upset people and spend a lot of money . . . and what'll happen is the white people will leave the system."

Schools and districts respond to parental resistance by reigning in the reform with a number of informal and sometimes formal strategies. Bureaucratic unresponsiveness, gradualism, staff reassignments, and so forth are all ways of discouraging reform without explicitly ending it.

SILENCE OF THE LESS POWERFUL   The political influence of uncomfortable high-track parents was only rarely balanced by other voices. At most schools, parents of lower-achieving and minority students had relatively little political clout and were mostly silent. For example, Native American parents were largely uninvolved at Explorer Middle School. Some felt the school had not approached the Native community in an appropriate manner. Others blamed an ugly racial history in the community. Adults in the community remembered Natives being beaten in school for speaking their language, and many being sent away to boarding schools. Native parents and community members told us that when they were young, stores and businesses in the town posted signs that read "No Natives or dogs." Only two Natives worked at Explorer, and many community members blamed racist hiring practices. The last superintendent, who had discontinued a process begun by his predecessor of working with the Native community to address student problems, angered and further alienated the community.

At Rollinghills, African American parent voices were also much quieter than those of whites, and Rollinghills Vice Principal Griffen told us, "They do not have the same powerful network as the white parents do." Only one African American sat on the school board, largely because of the gerrymandered downtown subdistrict. One Rollinghills teacher told us, "The African Americans who are principals and superintendents . . . are afraid to speak out because their jobs may be in jeopardy."

We heard various reasons from educators for this silence. Some teachers at Grant High School said that they have trouble contacting parents of failing students. Teachers at Grant and Bearfield told us they don't have time for all their students, so they concentrate on those who seem to have concerned parents. One Bearfield teacher stated that he focuses on students who have two parents because he fears his efforts might be wasted on single-parent children. Many minority parents told us that the school makes little effort to reach out to them and that they feel uncomfortable at the school. This problem may be exacerbated at schools that draw their minority populations from outlying areas. For example, a major problem at Rollinghills is the school's uneven dissemination of information about the heterogeneous program. Although the teachers meet yearly with parents of prospective sixth graders at all neighboring feeder schools, many parents from the city were uninformed about the programs available at Rollinghills, especially the heterogeneous program. Efforts to reach out to city parents have enjoyed minimal success. Central and Green Valley, both of which had large numbers of Spanish-speaking parents among their student populations, find that this language barrier also inhibits efforts to generate support for their reform efforts.

GOING IT ALONE   At many schools, parental dissatisfaction caused nervous district office personnel to "pull in the reins" on school reform efforts. Reformers at Liberty, Union, Explorer, and Central high schools all confronted strong skepticism or opposition from their district offices. And although the Bearfield district had a written policy denouncing tracking, district officials made no attempt to enforce it. Some were clearly uncomfortable with Bearfield's detracking efforts.

In the spring of 1993, Bearfield found that their Comprehensive Tests of Basic Skills (CTBS) scores had dropped slightly in some areas (study skills, for example), although they remained steady or even improved in others. This slight decline was used by district-level officials as "proof" that heterogeneity was negatively impacting achievement. Bowing to pressure from the district office, Bearfield focused during the 1993–94 school year on lessons targeted specifically at raising test scores—a focus that most of the faculty felt was misguided: "Our CTBS did not [go up]. . . . And so [district officials] were riding Ben [the principal] last year. We could feel it when we came back to school this year. That the stress was there, we need to get these scores up. And it was not like Ben. And we spent so much of this year worrying about tests, standardized tests. And . . . uh, it's unfortunate. It's unfortunate because that's not what we're about and that's not what we should be about." Union also was hampered by equivocation by its district administration. According to the vice principal, "What little support we have for the program is being eroded. Then our program will be gutted, and they'll come in here and build walls in those centers upstairs, and the chairs in their rows, and it will be business as usual. . . . It will be some external force that causes us . . . not to be able to do what it is we're trying to do here. . . . We've seen some of that already. Chinking away at the armor here and there." As a consequence of such ambivalence toward reform at the district office, few change agents believe they have support or buffering, and most feel they face enormous community pressures alone.

What Did These Schools Achieve?

At a structural level, the efforts made at the ten schools we studied must be judged to have been successful. All of the schools reduced some, and many eliminated all, of their basic or remedial courses. Most provided all students with access to the schools' most challenging or "honors" curriculum, and several developed a common curriculum in key academic subjects at some grade levels. All became far more attentive to providing greater curricular access and richer learning opportunities to low-income students of color. In fact, in several instances we found detracking actually convinced educators that low-track students are far more capable of engaging with higher-level curriculum and instruction in heterogeneous groups than they had previously thought. As one middle school counselor put it, "Heterogeneous grouping has made teachers think differently about all kids. They see more potential in kids; they will work harder with them and their needs." Other educators' comments affirm that this has indeed been the case. For example, one told us, "The program has done amazing things for standard-track kids."

Moreover, a number of teachers across the ten schools suggested specific mechanisms through which detracking enabled them to improve the quality of student work in their classrooms. One attributed the change to an atmosphere of higher expectations in heterogeneous classes: "All of a sudden somebody says, 'You can do this!'" Another credited the greater access to knowledge: "Heterogeneous grouping helps to stimulate, motivate students because of just the exposure that the students have." Others suggested that heterogeneous grouping makes more salient to teachers the need to employ a broader array of teaching strategies, and the greater opportunities that result enable former low-track students to achieve. A senior high school English teacher suggested how this greater exposure might take place: "[The student] who normally wouldn't succeed does succeed because the teacher is using strategies that appeal to various learning modes. Roles change, reverse. More time is spent on concepts, themes, thinking about things, projecting, making predictions, connections between the works read."

At Plainview Senior High, several states away, another teacher echoed this view as she told us how she set up her heterogeneous class to permit a lot of independent student learning as well as dynamic class discussions that engage students of different backgrounds and academic strengths. In doing so, this teacher believed she created a learning environment in which more students find what she called "the genius within them." Her multidimensional classroom, she explained, allows students to develop insight into their own ways of knowing and learning, and when they do that, they become highly motivated students in the broader sense of the word, thirsty for a greater understanding of the world around them.

Several teachers told us that a more individualized, yet interdependent approach to teaching and learning may be particularly helpful in racially and socioeconomically mixed schools in which students bring different ways of knowing to school. Some of the schools made headway in ameliorating racial tensions in their schools. For example, by emphasizing themes such as "Building a community of friends" and "Different is not deficient," and owing in no small part to Principal McCall's own unrelenting good will, Bearfield Middle School defused the racial disharmony rampant in the surrounding community and harmoniously brought the African American and white communities together under their school's roof.

However, in contrast to the Rockville Centre reform described at the outset of this chapter, none of the schools achieved nearly the extent of detracking that reformers sought originally, and several worried that old patterns of inequality were being replicated within their schools' new, detracked structure. Most were caught unprepared when the process and the shape of their equity-minded reforms called into question—often in very public ways—the norms and politics concerning race, home language, and socioeconomic status. Many felt battered and bruised by their efforts to reform, and some did not survive as school leaders.

In response to normative and political pressures, all the schools—intentionally or unintentionally—left some classes out of the reform, ensuring that the highest-achieving students can still get some sort of "special" treatment: separate honors, advanced, AP, or Regents (in New York) classes exist at all ten schools. These elite classes aided several of the schools in maintaining the delicate balance between satisfying the demands of an important parental power base and mitigating some of the most egregious instances of inequitable opportunities. Most of the students and families who "benefit" from these compromises are white.

For instance, the parents of the relatively small number of "gifted" students in the Green Valley community were dissatisfied with the ninth- and tenth-grade heterogeneous English curriculum. However, they agreed to tolerate these classes because separate honors classes were offered to eleventh and twelfth graders. Similarly, at King Middle School, the parents of gifted students, who were generally satisfied with the rich "standard" curriculum offered to all in the sixth and seventh grades, were willing to accept the heterogeneity of those classes partly because their children were promised selective "Regents" classes in the eighth grade.

Grant High's effort to eliminate separate language arts honors classes was particularly difficult because of the districtwide tradition of offering self-contained gifted classes at the elementary and middle school level. Some parents who were accustomed to this special treatment argued that their children could not be well served in an integrated system. Thus, while Grant's principal initially condoned the changes being made by the language arts department, he was influenced later by a small but vocal group of parents of "gifted" children. On the basis of their complaints, the principal refused the department's request to eliminate separate honors classes for ninth graders in the 1994–95 school year. Consequently, the department once again offered a choice of two honors opportunities—either a conventional honors class or a heterogeneous "regular" college-track class at the ninth-grade level, in which students could select to earn an "honors" designation on their report card if they completed an enriched set of course requirements.

Green Valley High School's "gifted" parents were also accustomed to separate programs in the elementary and middle schools. They, too, expressed considerable discomfort about the absence of special treatment at the high school. Many Explorer Middle School parents pushed to resume pull-out programs; some advocated separate all-day classes for gifted and talented and special education students. Plainview High School's active parent group, with a tightly knit leadership of almost all white parents, met monthly with the principal to serve as his sounding board. One teacher noted that there is "such great community support for tracking . . . there's absolutely no way (and the administration would never want to do this anyway) that they would ever get rid of AP."

Because of these pressures, educators who were committed to change often tried to straddle the fence between pleasing powerful parents and giving low-achieving students more access by reducing the number of tracks but not dismantling the track structure. For example, Rollinghills Middle School offered parents a choice between tracked and detracked classes (called combined teams) for their children. However, the shortage of African American families choosing Rollinghills's combined teams was striking. Most teachers were not clear whether African American parents lacked good information about the combined teams or whether they had unspoken reasons for choosing not to participate. Some, particularly the small number of African

American teachers, believed that the bussed-in African American children were deliberately excluded in order to keep the combined teams whiter than the rest of the school. Most years, the principal assigned a handful of African American students to the detracked teams to balance the large number of white choosers.

Although such strategies enabled the schools to modify their tracking system, they continued a hierarchical structure that offered a way for white, wealthy parents to maintain very separate classrooms for their children. This persistent tracking structure, albeit with fewer and ostensibly "higher" tracks, continued ongoing curriculum differentiation that supported unequal expectations and inevitably unequal standards for students of different racial, social class, and cultural backgrounds. As Bearfield's principal put it bluntly, "As our business manager in the superintendent's office once told me, the power is neither black nor white; it's green—as in money. And that's where the power is. Rich people have clout. Poor people don't have clout."

Becoming Good American Schools

In a second national study that paralleled our study of the ten detracking schools, our UCLA research team followed the course of detracking in sixteen middle schools in California, Illinois, Massachusetts, Texas, and Vermont over five years.[9] Unlike several of the ten schools in the first study that were working primarily on their own, the sixteen middle schools were part of Carnegie's *Turning Points* reform. Here, too, our research team made regular visits; interviewed educators, students, parents, and other community members; observed in classrooms; and attended lots of meetings. As in our study of the ten detracking schools, we sought to understand the practical dimensions of the middle schools' reforms—for example, reworking schedules, teaching in teams, integrating curriculum, and developing pedagogy for heterogeneous groups of students. In this study, too, we wanted to understand the normative and political factors that enabled or impeded detracking reform.

Our five years of data from this study revealed that state reformers and local educators worked tirelessly to create the inclusive, caring, and genuinely participatory classrooms that would provide fertile ground for untracked teaching and learning. Our findings were consistent with what we'd learned from the ten other detracking schools. All the schools made significant changes in their structures and practices.

All of the schools attempted to change the way students were grouped for instruction, both between and within classrooms, in the explicit attempt to make their schools more inclusive. Given their concerns about the uneven access to school success that tracking brought, even all-white schools tackled it as an equity issue. Several moved solidly away from tracking in academic subjects by eliminating or decreasing the number of tracks, although none grouped heterogeneously across all classes and subjects. Some focused on including Special Education students in regular classrooms; one, Madison Middle School in Massachusetts, integrated its bilingual program into what had been its English-only teams. Some schools adopted multicultural projects, hoping both to battle norms of exclusivity and racial tensions in classrooms and to make the substance of schooling inclusive of the full range of American cultures and subcultures. They crafted multidimensional assignments to challenge students of varying abilities. Many teachers adopted approaches recommended for "gifted and talented" in their heterogeneous classes to permit a wide range of students access to higher levels of achievement. Some developed new forms of assessment to provide all students in a diverse classroom with useful information and inclinations to work hard and successfully.

As in the other detracking schools we studied, when changes threatened prevailing norms and beliefs about students, teaching, and learning (as was required for meaningful change), they were often resisted or reworked to fit those norms and beliefs. In nearly every school, for example, teachers' and parents' perception that students have fundamentally different and fixed capacities to learn shaped attitudes toward heterogeneous classrooms and made these reforms extraordinarily difficult to implement. One Horace Mann Middle School teacher spoke for many when he told us that slogans like "Everyone can learn" are meaningless because "There are, of course, some kids who can learn, some [who] won't learn, and some [who] can't. . . . They've reached their capability; they've reached their potential. They just cannot go any further in terms of academics."

In these schools, too, when the changes threatened the exclusivity or privileges of the high-track classes, parents of high-track students mounted powerful political opposition. The reformers' difficulties underscored deeply rooted contradictions in American culture that make equity-minded school reform so formidable. Beyond the considerable technical challenges of creating new structures and practices, such reforms evoked deep tensions about race, social class, and culture in the schools and their communities.

In racially mixed schools, grouping reform was more than doubly difficult. Educators invariably ran headlong into community values and politics around race and social class that combined with beliefs and ideologies about intelligence. In all of the racially mixed schools with significant numbers of middle-class or more affluent white families, these parents battled heterogeneous grouping. For example, in Texas, Townsend Middle School's concerted effort to bring "gifted and talented" curriculum and instruction to all students was met with significant parent protest against heterogeneous grouping. The outcry from this group led the district to require that all schools maintain honors-level and regular-level courses but allowed parents to override placement recommendations and elect an honors placement for their child. When Townsend implemented this option, a handful of parents of high-achieving students complained to a district administrator that the academic rigor of honors classes was compromised, and Townsend teachers were subjected to an embarrassing review of their teaching by district personnel.

Parents and teachers also contested the cooperative learning strategies that many schools used in heterogeneous groups, fearing that the curriculum would become less challenging and that the pace of study would be slowed. A Townsend teacher summed up this argument by stating that cooperative learning "hurts some of the smarter kids because they're always having to remediate someone else in the group." Mountain View parents argued that cooperative learning allowed students to do less challenging work than they would if they worked alone. Even so, Mountain View's efforts to make their school more inclusive by integrating special education into regular classes and making all classes heterogeneous proceeded as smoothly as any such effort we saw at the sixteen schools. While Mountain View's reform fell short of its goals and skeptics continued to raise questions, most teachers prided themselves on the inclusive community they created.

Legal Rights, Local Wrongs

Taking a slightly different perspective on detracking issues, Kevin Welner and I studied detracking in San Jose, California; Rockford, Illinois; and Woodland Hills, Pennsylvania.[10] Unlike the other detracking reforms we studied, the impetus behind detracking in these three areas was not educators seeking more equitable school practices, although certainly there were equity-minded educators committed to detracking in all three of these school systems. Rather, members of each of these communities turned to litigation within the federal court system to prompt the reduction or elimination of ability grouping in classrooms. They believed that the districts' tracking practices, purportedly intended to target curriculum and instruction to students of different designated levels of ability, had been used discriminatorily against African American and Latino students. Before turning to litigation as a policy tool, the reformers in these communities first considered and attempted other, more grassroots reform strategies. But these bottom-up attempts to bring about change starting at the local, grassroots level came up empty.

Welner and I returned to the San Jose Unified School District to study their implementation of a detracking decree that had been issued by the court in accord with the district's settlement with the plaintiffs in their federal desegregation suit. We also studied the progress of the detracking remedy in Woodland Hills, a small, predominantly white community on the outskirts of Pittsburgh.[11] The San Jose and Woodland Hills superintendents had invited me to examine their practices as the districts worked to make the schools both desegregated and equitable according to their agreements with plaintiffs. In both districts, we studied documents and interviewed students, educators, parents, and community members. In Woodland Hills, we also did statistical analyses of the changes in course-taking and achievement during the district's detracking reform, and we conducted systematic classroom observations. Welner and I also returned to Rockford after that district's detracking order—in this case at the request of the plaintiffs, who wanted to know if progress was being made.[12] In Rockford, as in Woodland Hills, we examined computerized records of course offerings, students' placements, and their achievement over the five years of detracking.

Like the other detracking schools we studied, the schools in Woodland Hills, Rockford, and San Jose changed as a result of the reform initiatives. With the court mandates backing them up, dedicated individuals in these school communities spent years of hard work to make their schools better places for low-income students and students of color. The reformer-educators in these districts were similar in their ideas and commitment to those in the districts where detracking was locally initiated. However, they were in the political minority; they could not move the reform forward until the courts stepped in. The courts enabled detracking not so much by diffusing resistance as by boosting some of the tools and resolve of reformers who were already working on the local level to overcome obstacles to equity-minded change.

In Woodland Hills, the superintendent and other school leaders instituted considerable detracking, particularly in the district's English courses, thereby enhancing the educational opportunities of students who had for years been disadvantaged by district policies. Many teachers responded to the challenge of heterogeneous classes by making significant changes in their teaching. All students in these classrooms saw greater use of what some researchers call "authentic" instruction and assessment and more lessons designed to develop higher-order thinking.[13] San Jose schools participated in a variety of innovative reforms, including Henry Levin's Accelerated Schools and the College Board's *Equity 2000*. Classrooms did indeed become more integrated, and remedial classes were eliminated. Today, San Jose stands as a model in California of how school systems can make the college preparatory curriculum the default option for all high school students. Even Rockford, where high-level policymakers were particularly hostile toward the reform, saw the lowest tracks eliminated and the highest tracks no longer reserved for white children. The tracks also became less rigid, allowing some upward movement. In all three cases, the court forced real change.

However, as in almost all the other detracking schools we've studied, tracking's strongest supporters in these districts, whether teachers, students, or parents, focused their attention on preserving the quality of high-track classes; detracking was perceived as a threat to some of the most valuable aspects of a high-track child's education. Notably, no one in these districts defended the poor-quality education routinely offered in low-track classes. In fact, most parents who denounced their local schools' efforts to detrack would no doubt have fought ferociously to keep their own children out of those schools' lower tracks. Tracking's benefits, if they exist, adhere to those outside the lowest tracks.

Among the key lessons we learned from these communities is that districts and schools that initiate detracking reforms without preparing to overcome normative and political obstacles are likely to see their efforts at change substantially undermined. In San Jose, Rockford, and Woodland Hills, detracking reforms met enormous obstacles. The courts could embolden and buttress the reformers, but the court orders offered no direct mechanism to counter resistance, which often expressed itself in relentless and exhausting micro interactions around every aspect of the districts' workings—from policy decisions to parent support to teacher "buy-in." Moreover, the hard-won changes were far from the ideal that the reformers had envisioned.[14]

Futures

Finally, I've learned even more about detracking as our UCLA team has worked with the Futures project described in chapter 11. We had two questions in mind as we developed our intervention to help young people of color navigate the college track successfully, even though they hadn't been judged by their school to be "college material." The obvious question was, would it work? We can answer that question with a resounding yes, as the account in chapter 11 made clear. The second question was whether the presence of our project on campus and the evidence of the students' success in the college track would spur the school to reconsider and get rid of some of the tracking that had so disadvantaged its African American and Latino students. Here, too, the school has made notable progress.[15]

During the mid-1990s, the school's principal galvanized interest in equity reform, and at her urging, the "two schools" problem (her framing) became the central focus of reform at the school. Through a process of faculty inquiry and experimentation with new, more inclusive practices, the school made considerable progress. A significant number of Latinos and African Americans (among them, several Futures students) began participating in student government; and a small but significant number enrolled in honors and AP classes (again, including a fair number of Futures students). The students' successes led the school administration to commit to a default college preparatory curriculum for all students and eliminated many courses not meeting four-year college entrance requirements. The counseling department was completely restructured, the counselors were trained, and the focus of counseling shifted to ensure that all students had better information and access to meeting college eligibility. The school implemented a summer bridge program for underrepresented students challenging themselves with AP classes for the first time, and it committed to doubling the size of the AVID program. The district office expanded the college access program to one middle school and another high school. At the end of five years of work, the school's African American and Latino students were more likely than in previous years to earn college-eligible grades and to apply for and enroll in four-year universities.

Despite these successes, and despite the absolute lack of any evidence that the opportunities or outcomes for advantaged students were in any way compromised, a substantial group of parents, nearly all white, wealthy, and with considerable power in the community, launched a campaign to add another track to the school's curriculum structure—what they called a "mid-honors" track. Using the school's traditionally white PTA, an electronic mail Listserv, and informal contacts with school board members, they argued that the mid-honors track would better accommodate those who wanted more challenge than the regular track (by this point, the regular track was also college preparatory) but would prevent "unqualified" students from compromising the honors and advanced-track classes. We were seeing at this school much the same dynamic as had occurred in the other schools we had studied.

The principal held the objectors at bay until she retired. Her replacement was a popular former principal of the highly tracked middle school in the wealthy section of town. Nevertheless, impressed with the evidence that, even as the school had softened its tracking, it had maintained its rigorous, high-quality programs and that as many graduates as before were entering elite colleges, she and the superintendent have committed to pushing ahead with reforms. The plan, just now being implemented, is to restructure the high school into heterogeneous small "houses" where all students are supported to complete college preparation and all have access to honors and AP courses. Only time will tell just how the powerful, still-nervous segments of the community will respond, or how far this plan will really move the school away from tracking.

What Can We Learn from These Miners' Canaries?

This chapter began with the remarkable success story of detracking in Rockville Centre, New York. Yet, even in this highly successful case, the reform path was not entirely smooth. Some parents were vocal in their opposition to the reform. Their concerns generally reflected the beliefs about the efficacy of tracking traditionally voiced by tracking's defenders, but a few parents' racial and social class prejudices were only thinly disguised. Reflecting on her experience leading and studying Rockville Centre's reforms, Carol Burris has come to believe that "tracking persists because of three potent 'Ps'—power, prestige, and prejudice." Burris and her colleagues experienced firsthand the power of savvy parents who pressure schools to place their sons and daughters in prestigious high-track, high-status classes. She also saw the effects of deeply engrained prejudices that questioned the intelligence of low-income students and students of color.[16]

Although issues of equity were paramount to the Rockville Centre school leaders, they also understood that parents would be more concerned about the learning, achievement, and life chances of their own children. Consequently, these educators ensured (and made very public) that the curriculum in the heterogeneous classes was rigorous and that support classes for struggling learners allowed the instruction in heterogeneous classes to remain challenging. They consistently collected, analyzed, and communicated data about their remarkable achievements. This helped reassure parents of high achievers that the schools were maintaining their children's high-quality education, and it moved the discussion about the merits of detracking from worried opinion to fact. Fortunately, in the end, Rockville Centre was a school community willing to engage with the reformers about legitimate educational concerns, willing to trust educators to ensure a high-quality education, and willing to suspend opposition pending the results of their ambitious reforms. They've not been disappointed.

The stories of detracking schools both inspire and give pause. That tracking has been identified as a problem and detracking has been the central focus of reform at even a modest number of schools is in itself striking. This is a very substantial shift from fifteen years earlier, when most schools seemed not to notice there was anything at all questionable about their sorting practices. Equally striking is that educators, students, and parents—acting alone or together—have labored mightily against the educational stratification that creates such inequalities, and at times they have altered it or changed its course.

Yet, consistently, educators committed to creating high-quality schooling for all students confront the persistent American dilemma of inequality as it rears its head under the contemporary rubric of school reform. These educational reformers proceeded on their conviction that discriminatory beliefs and schooling practices are at odds with basic American values, and that therefore Americans will, if given the opportunity, naturally move away from past racist practices.[17] They were thus ill-prepared to deal with objections that, although often raised as matters of educational quality, just as often represented perceived threats—both educational and social—from race and social class mixing. Such concerns catch most equity-minded educators off guard. As one of the principals in our study of ten detracking schools said, reflecting on her decision to detrack English classes at her middle school, "If I look back at it now, I would never, ever make such a radical change. You know why? Because I thought everybody would just think like I did, that it would just make such sense. It was so democratic and fair. And when I look back at it now, I think how could I have been so stupid? How could I have thought that there were people out there who would not want the good for everybody? I mean, I was very idealistic."

It's true enough that today's racial practices are quite different from those of the past: rigid tracking replaces Jim Crow segregation; test-, counseling-, referral-based tracking replaces rigid IQ-based tracking. Yet, as critical social theorists have helped us understand, even seemingly neutral schooling practices interact with race and social class differences in ways that mirror and help reproduce social, political, and economic inequalities outside of school.[18]

Many of the leaders we studied were reasonably well versed in the educational change literature, and they relied on its precepts as they detracked their schools. Yet, detracking differs in fundamental ways from many other contemporary reforms that seek changes that are primarily technical. The major issue around detracking reforms is not which grouping strategy "works" best in the conventional sense.

While grappling with new schedules, new curriculum, new pedagogies, and new support programs, reformers were struggling to break free of the pull of social stratification. Powerful parents focused on gaining access to prestigious universities worried that democratizing the high-status curriculum would jeopardize their children's chances for a place at the top of the social structure. White, middle-class parents in our study often associated their daughters' and sons' increasingly scarce opportunities with the "problems" caused by minority students in their schools, most of whom were poor. In sum, detracking created a struggle between more- and less-privileged families over scarce resources; and it entailed an ideological struggle over the meaning of race and culture as they are enacted in schools. Most fundamental, it threatened the delicate balance that schools have struck between the conflicting demand of educating a democratic citizenry and preparing a highly differentiated and unequal workforce.

Detracking reformers found little in the change literature to help them with these political and normative challenges. The literature is virtually silent on confronting deep-seated beliefs about race and social class and about the politics of altering the distribution of access and achievement. In the absence of attention to these underlying issues, the inequalities currently associated with tracking inevitably resurface in a new organizational guise. Even when reformers are successful in convincing others, their goals can be transformed or subverted as they make their way into the cultures and political milieu of particular schools. Those reformers we studied learned important, if painful, reform lessons not taught by the school change literature. Strategies for dealing with the normative and political challenges of detracking do not emerge neatly from these stories. However, these stories do offer some powerful insights.[19]

First, reformers should affirm the democratic values that detracking efforts embody and openly acknowledge that this reform has both a moral as well as an empirical grounding. They must share the empirical evidence about tracking's inequities and the promise of detracking for making schooling more equitable in order to reassure anxious parents and skeptical colleagues that principled actions also have firm grounding in educational research. Bearfield's principal, Ben McCall, is only one of many who have found the research compelling as they struggle with decisions about what is right for their schools.

Second, emphasize the educational high ground on which detracking rests. In addition to the social justice basis for reform, educators can argue with legitimacy from the evidence that detracking can leverage higher-quality teaching and learning for all students. Such an argument has considerable validity, since those teaching strategies and learning experiences that seem to work best for heterogeneous groups—those that actively engage students in rich and complex concepts and problems—are also those recommended for meeting the needs of gifted and talented students and raising academic standards generally. As such, detracking can be positioned as reform aimed at benefiting all students.

Third, aim for the ideal of completely detracked schools, and eschew the labeling and ranking of students on global categories related to their intelligence or merit. Although reformers will probably need to proceed incrementally and slowly, they must keep clear on these ideals. They should promise worried parents that, as they change the grouping structure, they will also find ways to accommodate any child whose intellectual "gifts" are so extreme or whose disabilities are so severe that they require different schooling arrangements on a case-by-case basis, but not with new ways of differentiated grouping for particular classifications of students.

Fourth, cultivate a climate of learning and inquiry among faculty and parents, acknowledging that it takes serious investigation of all of these issues for educators and parents to take risks with practices that society has taught us work to our children's advantage. They must challenge explicitly the existing norms of intelligence, student ability, and what is valued as knowledge. School faculties should use at least some of their professional development time to consider detracking in order to examine the relationship between commonsense conceptions of intelligence, student ability, and valued knowledge and social factors—for example, race, class, and home language. The growing bodies of literature on the developmental and multidimensional nature of intelligence and learning and about the relationship between culture, social context, and cognition can help ground these discussions of values, beliefs, and "common sense."

Fifth, marry serious inquiry with real changes in teaching practices in heterogeneous classrooms and provide systematic evidence of the effectiveness of the changes they've made. Only then will their carefully framed arguments be educationally justified or politically salient. As the educators at Rockville Centre learned, there may be nothing as powerful as careful documentation and reporting of the results of detracking. Although good data may not assuage white, middle-class parents' anxieties about increased racial and social class mixing at school or their child's access to prestige and comparative advantages, it rightfully moves the argument away from the contention that detracking reforms sacrifice the needs and interests of high-achieving children in the interest of equity. As in the case of Rockville Centre, monitoring and reporting the effects of reform focus the reform discussion on facts, rather than on opinion and fear.

Sixth, look for "top-down" support. Top-down support can be found in the widespread federal and state policy focus on having all students meet rigorous academic standards and in pressing schools to "leave no child behind." Nothing in schools leaves children behind more systematically than tracking and ability grouping. Top-down support can also be found in calls from policy and research groups to expand college preparation and access to all students. For example, the Pathways to College Network is an alliance of thirty national organizations and funders working collaboratively to promote college access for underserved students at national, state, and local levels. Notably, the network's first priority is to "encourage schools to make a rigorous college preparatory curriculum the standard course of study for all students, so they will have the skills and knowledge they need to be successful in both postsecondary education and the workplace."[20]

Top-down support can also be found in the explicit calls for ending tracking that have come from some of the nation's most respected research institutions. For example, in the past five years, two research syntheses produced by the National Research Council—the research arm of the prestigious National Academy of Sciences—have documented strong negative effects of low-track classes and recommended that they be abolished. These reports provide the most trustworthy accounts of what the past decades of research have found and the implications of these findings for policy and practice. The Ford Foundation, Bill and Melinda Gates Foundation, Lumina Foundation for Education, James Irvine Foundation, W. K. Kellogg Foundation, and the David and Lucile Packard Foundation have all lent their name and philanthropic dollars to expanding college going and making it more equitable.[21]

In some states, top-down support is also provided by policymakers who have taken up the issue of expanding access to the college preparatory track in high school. In New York, all high school students are now expected to take Regents-level classes and obtain Regents high school diplomas. Rockville Centre's reforms benefited from this state mandate. In California, all students must take and pass algebra, and, in 2004, State Superintendent of Education Jack O'Connell and State Senator Richard Alarcon sponsored legislation making the course requirements for entry into the state's university system the "default curriculum" for all of the state's high school students. The legislation failed, but the call for high school reform that provides all students access to the college track has become a major theme in the state. Such top-down support allows local educators to undertake reforms that could not be entertained politically without them. Accompanied by the commitment of appropriate resources and support, top-down calls for detracking can translate into serious opportunities to create successful detracked schools.

Seventh, look for "lateral" support from other schools and related school reform initiatives. These can range from informal alliances found through word of mouth to well-organized networks such as the Coalition of Essential Schools. Over the past two decades, educators have found powerful ideas and examples as well as helpful advice from their peers who are also confronting the technical, normative, and political challenges of detracking. Lateral support can also be gained by placing detracking in the context of other widely recognized reforms. Currently, the "small high schools" movement sweeping the country carries with it the considerable clout and funding of the Gates Foundation and the vocal support of many of the nation's most respected educators, such as Deborah Meier. Small high school reform, done right, is extraordinarily compatible with and supportive of detracking. In fact, it's pretty difficult logistically to maintain tracking when high schools and middle schools enroll fewer than eight hundred students.

Eighth, and perhaps most critical, cultivate "bottom-up" support. Neither top-down calls for detracking nor even the best support from like-minded colleagues will enable educators to withstand the objections of anxious parents and communities. Because detracking shifts the most consequential reform decisions away from educators' professional discretion and into the public arena, schools seeking to detrack should make sure that *all* voices—not just those of the most powerful parents and community members—are represented and heard as schools deliberate how to proceed. Most important is the active engagement of low-track students' parents and communities—participation that is often missing in school reform discussions. This will probably require a tenacious effort to bring parents and community members from different racial groups and socioeconomic positions to the same table. On a practical level, each school should review the composition of its parent groups to ensure that they reflect enrollment. If they do not, the school should monitor agenda-setting practices, meeting times, locations, communications, outreach, and other procedures to increase the groups' accessibility to all members of the school community.

Bottom-up support can also be found by forging alliances with grassroots community-based organizations and advocacy groups. In the past few years, many such groups have taken up school reform as a focus of campaigns for social and racial justice. Large national organizations with hundreds of local chapters, such as ACORN (Association of Community Organizations for Reform Now) and local groups of organized parents and young people are often eager to join forces with progressive educators. Concerned about the "school-to-prison pipeline," limited college access for students in low-income communities, and other related problems, many such groups are eager to support educators seeking to detrack their schools, for example, New York ACORN, a group representing twenty thousand mostly low-income New Yorkers. ACORN took action against tracking when a 1995 report showing that African Americans and Latinos were dramatically underrepresented in the crown jewels of the New York City Public Schools: Stuyvesant and Bronx Science. Knowing that enriched academic experiences early on were key to qualifying for these selective schools, white and nonwhite ACORN parent "testers" visited about fifty New York City elementary schools to inquire about programs available to their young children. Finding that white parents were told more often about gifted programs than parents of color, ACORN called for a moratorium on gifted programs until the chancellor could verify citywide that the programs were not substantially segregated and that they were open to any children who could meet reasonable admission policies. ACORN also demanded that the chancellor evaluate the programs' content and approach. Of particular interest was finding out what gifted programs do differently from regular schools and why the approaches used in gifted programs could not be extended to all students.[22] Such activism on the part of community groups can pave the way for tracking reform.

So is detracking possible? Surely it is, as the stories in this chapter make clear. Is detracking possible in every community? Perhaps. Without doubt, it is worth trying. Detracking is an extraordinary reform to undertake; and for those who would commit themselves to take it on, it is the work of a career and not something to accomplish in the short term and then move on to the next challenge. The evidence runs deep that tracking is rife with problems and that detracking, if allowed to proceed, is good for students. What is less certain is whether America will allow it. There can be no question that detracking dramatically alters the way schooling takes place and how many students gain the best education schools offer. That's the whole point. On the other hand, there are plenty of proposals across the land that promise to similarly turn schools upside down and give them a good shake—vouchers and privatization, for example. Curiously, many of the very same critics who raise alarms about how detracking would abruptly and precipitously jeopardize American schooling are those who promote these latter ill-documented privatizing reforms that leave schools to float on the magic carpet of marketplace competition.

Is detracking enough? Certainly not. Public schools remain our best hope for achieving a free and democratic society in which all have decent lives and rich opportunities. That said, serious work toward such ends must surely go far beyond detracking. I began chapter 11 by noting that much has changed in the twenty years since the publication of *Keeping Track*. Those changes, despite today's "no child left behind" rhetoric, have brought little progress toward equality—in school or out. In fact, the early 1980s were more propitious than today, in terms of the equalizing potential of detracking. Today, not only have the gaps between wealthy and poor Americans widened, but neighborhoods and schools in most parts of the country are more segregated racially than they were in 1985.[23] Not surprisingly, the educational gaps, which had narrowed considerably by 1985 as a result of school desegregation and war on poverty reforms and resources, are now considerably wider.[24] Not only has the black-white test score gap widened over the past two decades, but the inequalities in students' access to high-quality teaching and well-resourced learning environments are as stark as ever.[25] Tracking reforms to equalize opportunity within schools won't touch these between-school inequalities, to say nothing of the horrendous inequalities outside of schools that shape children's lives.

Nevertheless, it is all the more important as social, economic, and educational gaps widen that we confront the myths about inequality that schools and tracking perpetuate. We must abandon the wishful thinking that advantaged Americans' wealth and happiness rest on a moral platform of merit, and that their children's advantages make them more deserving of schooling opportunities and life chances. We must struggle against the ruinous consequences of blaming the dire circumstances of those with the fewest advantages in school on their own lack of ability and effort or on their failure to take advantage of schooling. No mere structural changes—detracking included—can bear the weight of changing these powerful norms and the political arrangements that hold them in place. However, such reforms can prompt an honest, public dialogue about whether Americans are ready to extricate schools from the structural inequalities that permeate our lives and undermine our democracy. Detracking reform is surely not enough, but it is an auspicious place to begin.

Notes

Chapter 1

1. For good reviews of the research on grouping and student achievement, the reader is referred to the following: for the earliest studies, W. S. Miller and H. J. Otto, "Analysis of Experimental Studies in Homogeneous Grouping," *Journal of Educational Research*, 1930, *21*, 95–102; for more recent work, J. I. Goodlad, "Classroom Organization," in *Encyclopedia of Educational Research*, 3d ed., ed. Chester Harris (New York: Macmillan, 1960), pp. 221–25; D. Esposito, "Homogeneous and Heterogeneous Ability Grouping: Principal Findings and Implications for Designing More Effective Educational Environments," *Review of Educational Research*, 1973, *43*, 163–79; and R. D. Froman, "Ability Grouping: Why Do We Persist and Should We," paper presented at the annual meeting of the American Educational Research Association, Los Angeles, 1981. (Note the somewhat contrary conclusion drawn by C. C. Kulick and J. A. Kulick, "Effects of Ability Grouping on Secondary School Students: A Meta-Analysis of Evaluation Findings," *American Educational Research Journal*, 1982, *19*, 415–28.)

2. See Esposito's review (1973) for a more complete discussion of self-concept and tracking.

3. K. A. Alexander, M. Cook, and E. L. McDill, "Curriculum Tracking and Educational Stratification: Some Further Evidence," *American Sociological Review*, 1978, *43*, 47–66; B. Heyns, "Selection and Stratification within Schools," *American Journal of Sociology*, 1974, *79*, 1434–51; J. E. Rosenbaum, *Making Inequality* (New York: Wiley, 1976).

4. W. E. Shafer and C. Olexa, *Tracking and Opportunity* (Scranton, Penn.: Chandler, 1971).

5. W. Findley and M. Bryan, *The Pros and Cons of Ability Grouping* (Washington, D.C.: NEA, 1975).

6. Heyns, "Selection and Stratification"; R. A. Rebert, and E. R. Rosenthal, *Class and Merit in the American High School* (New York: Longman, 1978).

7. B. Bloom, *All Our Children Learning* (New York: McGraw-Hill, 1981).

8. For a good critical discussion of testing and student placement, see C. H. Persell, *Education and Inequality: A Theoretical and Empirical Synthesis* (New York: Free Press, 1977).

9. Ibid.

10. For a fascinating look at the attempts to link IQ, race, and class, see S. J. Gould, *The Mismeasure of Man* (New York: W. W. Norton, 1981).

11. *Larry P. v. Wilson Riles*, 495 FS 975.

12. *Educational Measurement: Issues and Practices*, 1982, 1.

13. A. V. Cicourel and J. I. Kitsuse, *The Educational Decision Makers* (Indianapolis: Bobbs-Merrill, 1963).

14. Persell (1977) reviews this literature as well.

15. J. E. Rosenbaum, "Track Misperceptions and Frustrated College Plans," *Sociology of Education*, 1980, 53, 74–88.

Chapter 2

1. L. A. Cremin, *The Transformation of the School* (New York: Random House, 1964).

2. D. B. Tyack, *The One Best System* (Cambridge, Mass.: Harvard University Press, 1974).

3. Tyack, *The One Best System*.

4. C. W. Eliot, "Shortening and Enriching the Grammar School Course," in *Charles W. Eliot and Popular Education*, ed. E. A. Krug (New York: Teachers' College Press, 1961), pp. 52–53.

5. A good discussion of Eliot's view and the committee's work can be found in H. M. Kliebard, "The Drive for Curriculum Change in the United States, 1890–1958" *Curriculum Studies*, 1979, 11, 191–202.

6. Tyack, *The One Best System*.

7. Cremin, *The Transformation of the School*.

8. Ibid., p. 72.

9. Samuel Capen cited in M. Lazerson, *The Origins of the Urban School* (Cambridge, Mass.: Harvard University Press, 1971), p. 33.

10. Eric Goldman, *Rendezvous with Destiny* (New York: Random House, 1952).

11. Herbert Spencer, *Social Statistics* (London: J. Chapman, 1851).

12. Cited in Goldman, *Rendezvous with Destiny*, p. 93.

13. L. F. Ward, *Pure Sociology*, as quoted in Cremin, *The Transformation of the School*, p. 93.

14. John Dewey, *The School Journal*, 1897, 54, 77–80, cited in Cremin, *The Transformation of the School*, p. 100.

15. G. Stanley Hall, *Adolescence: Its Psychology and Its Relations to Physiology, Anthropology, Sociology, Sex, Crime, Religion and Education*, 2 vols. (New York: D. Appleton, 1905).

16. Hall, *Adolescence*, p. 510.

17. Eliot, cited in Kliebard, "The Drive for Curriculum Change," p. 195.

18. Eliot, *The Fundamental Assumption in the Report of the Committee of Ten*, as quoted in Kliebard, "The Drive for Curriculum Change," p. 195.

19. Goldman, *Rendezvous with Destiny*, p. 29.

20. Ellwood P. Cubberly, *Changing Conceptualizations of Education* (Boston: Houghton Mifflin Co., 1909), pp. 15–16.

21. J. Riis, *How the Other Half Lives* (New York, 1890).

22. Goldman, *Rendezvous with Destiny*, pp. 61–62.

23. F. W. Tylor, *The Principles of Scientific Management* (New York and London: Harper & Bros., 1919).

24. Tyack, *The One Best System*.

25. Cremin, *The Transformation of the School*.

26. Cited in R. E. Callahan, *Education and the Cult of Efficiency* (Chicago: University of Chicago Press, 1962), p. 15.

27. *The Ladies' Home Journal*, November 1912, 39, p. 9. as quoted in Callahan, *Education and the Cult of Efficiency*, p. 51.

28. National Education Association, *Report of the Committee on the Placement of Industries in Public Education*, 1910, pp. 6–7.

29. M. Lazerson and W. N. Grubb, *American Educational and Vocationalism* (New York: Columbia University, 1974).

30. Massachusetts Board of Education, *Report on Manual Training* (Boston, 1893), cited in Lazerson, *Origins of the Urban School*.

31. R. J. Becker, "Education and Work: A Historical Perspective," in *Education and Work*, ed. H. F. Silberman, eighty-first yearbook of the National Society for the Study of Education (Chicago: University of Chicago Press, 1982).

32. Cremin, *The Transformation of the School*.

33. Ibid.

34. Cited in J. H. Spring, *Education and the Rise of the Corporate State* (Boston: Beacon Press, 1972).

35. Ibid., p. 110.

36. Ibid., p. 111.

37. E. P. Cubberly, *Changing Conceptions of Education*, pp. 18–19, as

quoted in D. A. Cohen and M. K. Lazerson, "Education and the Corporate Order," *Socialist Revolution*, 1972, 2, p. 53.

38. Boston, *School Documents*, 1908, no. 7; p. 53, cited in Lazerson, *Origins of the Urban School*, p. 189.

39. *Report to the Commission on National Aid to Vocational Education together with the Hearings Held on the Subject*, U.S. House of Representatives, 63rd Cong., 2d Sess., Doc. no. 0004 (Washington, D.C.: U.S. Government Printing Office, 1914), 1:12, as quoted in Becker, "Education and Work," p. 3.

40. Cited in Spring, *Education and the Rise of the Corporate State*, p. 111.

41. W. B. Pillsbury, "Selection—An Unnoticed Function of Education," *Scientific Monthly*, January 1921, 12, p. 71, as quoted in Cohen and Lazerson, "Education and the Corporate Order."

42. Cited in S. Bowles and H. Gintis, *Schooling in Capitalist America* (New York: Basic Books, 1976), p. 192.

43. L. Terman, *Intelligence Tests and School Reorganization* (New York: World Book Co., 1923), pp. 27–28.

44. Ibid., as cited in Bowles and Gintis, *Schooling in Capitalist America*, p. 123.

45. C. J. Karier, "Elite Views on American Education," in *Foundations of Education: Dissenting Views*, ed. J. J. Shields and C. Geer (New York: Wiley, 1974), p. 47.

46. Cohen and Lazerson, *Education and the Corporate Order*, p. 53.

47. An excellent discussion of the conceptualization of the idea of measurable intelligence and the social and political uses of this idea can be found in S. J. Gould, *The Mismeasure of Man* (New York: W. W. Norton, 1981).

48. Charles A. Prosser, as cited in Kliebard, "The Drive for Curriculum Change," p. 279.

49. J. Conant, *The American High School* (New York: McGraw-Hill, 1959).

50. H. M. Kliebard, "The Drive for Curriculum Change," makes this point citing J. D. Koerner in his article "The Tragedy of the Conant Report," *Phi Delta Kappa*, 1960, 42, 121 as a "lone voice" of criticism.

Chapter 3

1. For more detailed information about A Study of Schooling generally and more specifics about the methodology used, see the final report of the study, John I. Goodlad, *A Place Called School* (New York: McGraw-Hill, 1981); the following technical reports of the study will be helpful: J. I. Goodlad et al., *A Study of Schooling: Series of Introductory Descriptions* (1979–1980), Technical Report no. 1; and B. C. Overman, *A Study of Schooling: Method-*

ology, Technical Report no. 2, both available from the ERIC clearinghouse on teacher education.

2. Ibid.

3. W. Findley and M. Bryan, M. *The Pros and Cons of Ability Grouping* (Washington, D.C.: National Education Association, 1975).

Chapter 4

1. Administrators at the Newport schools prohibited the collection of race or ethnicity data about individual students. They did, however, provide us with the percentages of different groups that constituted their schools' populations.

2. The analysis of the distribution of white and nonwhite students into high- and low-track classes in six multiracial schools yielded a chi-square significant at the .001 level with 1 df. See J. Oakes, *A Question of Access: Tracking and Curriculum Differentiation in a National Sample of English and Mathematics Classes*, A Study of Schooling Technical Report no. 24 (Los Angeles: University of California, 1981), available from the ERIC clearinghouse on teacher education, for a complete presentation of this analysis.

3. The findings presented here are the results of discriminant analyses conducted separately for each construct in each subject area at each of the two levels of schooling. For a detailed presentation of these analyses and precise definitions of the variables and summary statistics, see the report cited above.

4. J. H. Spring, *The Sorting Machine* (New York: David McKay, 1976).

5. J. I. Goodlad, *What Schools Are For* (Bloomington, Ind.: Phi Delta Kappa, 1979).

Chapter 5

1. The term *opportunity to learn* has come to mean different things to various educational researchers. Carroll, for example, in his model for school learning, used the term to mean the specific content covered during instruction (J. B. Carroll, "A Model for School Learning," *Teachers College Record*, 1963, *64*, 723–33).

2. See R. Barr and R. Dreeken, *How Schools Work* (Chicago: University of Chicago Press, 1983), for an excellent discussion of the interrelatedness of group composition, variation in instructional conditions, and student learning outcomes at the elementary level.

3. For example, see J. Stallings, M. Needels, and N. Stayrook, *The Teaching of Basic Reading Skills in Secondary Schools, Phase II and Phase III* (Menlo Park, Calif.: SRI International, 1979).

4. D. Wiley and A. Harnischfeger, "Explosion of a Myth: Quantity of

Schooling and Exposure to Instruction, Major Educational Vehicles," *Educational Researcher*, 1974, 3, 7–12.

5. W. C. Frederick and H. J. Walberg, "Learning as a Function of Time," *Journal of Educational Research*, 1980, 73, 183–94.

6. See, for example, F. Welch, "Black White Differences in Returns to Schooling," *American Economic Review*, 1973, 53, 893–907; and Carnegie Council on Higher Education, *Giving Youth a Better Chance* (San Francisco: Jossey-Bass, 1979).

7. See J. Stallings, "Implementation and Child Effects of Teaching Practices in Follow-Through Classrooms," *Monographs of the Institute for Research in Child Development*, 1975, 40 (Serial No. 163); and N. Karweit and R. E. Slavin, "Measurement and Modeling Choices in Studies of Time and Learning," *American Educational Research Journal*, 1981, 18, 157–71.

8. See, for example, the discussion of this issue in B. V. Rosenshine and D. C. Berliner, "Academic Engaged Time," *British Journal of Teacher Education*, 1978, 4, 3–16.

9. B. V. Rosenshine, "Academic Engaged Time, Content Covered, and Direct Instruction," *Journal of Education*, 1978, 3, 38–66.

10. Karweit and Slavin, "Measurement and Modeling Choices."

11. For a report of observational procedures used, see P. Giesen and K. A. Sirotnik, *The Methodology of Classroom Instruction in A Study of Schooling*, A Study of Schooling Technical Report no. 5 (Los Angeles: University of California, 1979), available from the ERIC clearinghouse on teacher education.

12. For a fuller discussion of this issue and a more comprehensive look at time and learning in A Study of Schooling, see K. A. Sirotnik, *The Contextual Correlates of the Relative Expenditures of Classroom Time on Instruction and Behavior: An Exploratory Study of Secondary Schools and Classes*, A Study of Schooling Technical Report no. 26 (Los Angeles: University of California Laboratory in School Community Education, 1981), available from the ERIC clearinghouse on teacher education.

13. B. S. Bloom, "Time and Learning," *American Psychologist*, 1974, 29, 682–88.

14. Carroll, "A Model for School Learning."

15. B. V. Rosenshine and N. Furst, "Research on Teacher Performance Criteria," in *Research in Teacher Education: A Symposium*, ed. B. O. Smith, AERA (Englewood Cliffs, N.J.: Prentice-Hall, 1971).

16. D. E. Wiley and A. Harnischfeger in "Determinants of Pupil Opportunity," in *The Analysis of Educational Productivity. Vol. 1: Issues in Microanalysis*, ed. R. Dreeben and J. A. Thomas (Cambridge, Mass.: Ballinger, 1980), assert that recently developed models of school learning have these understandings in common.

17. W. Doyle, "Paradigms for Research on Teacher Effectiveness," in *Review of Research in Education*, ed. Lee S. Schulman, 1977, 4, 163–98.

18. A considerable amount of research effort has established that student responses prove to be both reliable and realistic measures of classroom environments and teacher effectiveness. See, for example, the work of M. Eash and H. C. Waxman, "Students' Perceptions of Effective Teaching in Different Subject Areas," paper presented at the annual meeting of the American Educational Research Association, Boston, April, 1980; and J. Stallings, M. Needels, and N. Strayrook, *How to Change the Process of Teaching Basic Reading Skills in Secondary Schools, Phase II and Phrase III* (Menlo Park, Calif.: SRI International, 1979).

19. Throughout this section, even though track-level scores are not given for the various teaching behaviors discussed, the relationships considered important have satisfied two criteria during our data analysis process. First, track-level differences were statistically significant at the .05 level, and second, the *actual size* of the differences between the mean scores for track levels indicated they were of substantive importance as well. In other words, we wanted to be satisfied the differences between tracks were large enough to be meaningful in students' experiences as well as not likely to occur merely by chance.

Chapter 6

1. H. J. Walberg, ed., *Educational Environments and Effects* (Berkeley, Calif.: McCutcheon, 1979).

2. R. H. Moos, "Educational Climates," in *Educational Environments and Effects*.

3. H. J. Walberg and G. Anderson, "Properties of the Achieving Urban Classes," *Journal of Educational Psychology*, 1970, 69, 381–85.

4. R. P. McDermott, "Social Relations as Contexts for Learning in Schools," *Harvard Educational Review*, 1977, 47, 198–213.

5. McDermott, "Social Relations," p. 191.

6. Moos, "Educational Climates."

7. Ibid., p. 199.

8. Bowles and Gintis, *Schooling in Capitalist America*.

9. Ibid., p. 12.

10. Ibid., p. 129.

11. See, for example, M. W. Apple and L. Weiss, eds., *Ideology and Practice in Schooling* (Philadelphia: Temple University Press, 1983); R. B. Everhart, *Reading, Writing and Resistance* (Boston: Routledge & Kegan Paul, 1983); and P. Willis, *Learning to Labour: How Working Class Kids Get Working Class Jobs* (Lexington, Mass.: D. C. Heath, 1977).

12. K. A. Sirotnik, "What You See Is What You Get: Consistency, Per-

sistency, and Mediocracy in Classrooms," *Harvard Educational Review,* 1983, 53, pp. 16–31.

Chapter 7

1. Bowles and Gintis, *Schooling in Capitalist America.*
2. R. Rist, "Student Social Class and Teacher Expectations: The Self-Fulfilling Prophecy in Ghetto Education," *Harvard Educational Review,* 1970. 40, 411–451.
3. Bowles and Gintis, *Schooling in Capitalist America,* p. 129.
4. Ibid., p. 108.
5. J. Karabel and H. Halsey, "Educational Research: A Review and an Interpretation" in *Power and Ideology in Education,* ed. J. Karabel and H. Halsey (New York: Oxford University Press, 1977), p. 25.
6. See D. Esposito, "Homogeneous and Heterogeneous Ability Grouping: Principal Findings and Implications for Designing More Effective Educational Environments," *Review of Educational Research,* 1973, 43, 163–79; K. A. Alexander, M. Cook, and E. L. McDill, "Curriculum Tracking and Educational Stratification: Some Further Evidence," *American Sociological Review,* 1978, 43, 47–66; Heyns, "Selection and Stratification Within Schools"; J. E. Rosenbaum, *Making Inequality* (New York: Wiley, 1976).

Chapter 8

1. I. Berg, *Education and Jobs: The Great Training Robbery* (Boston: Beacon Press, 1971).
2. H. F. Clark and H. S. Sloan, *Classrooms on Main Street* (New York: Teachers College Press, 1966).
3. B. Duncan, "Dropouts and the Unemployed," *Journal of Political Economy,* 1964, 72; M. Plunkett, "Schools and Early Work Experience of Youth, 1952–1957," *Occupational Outlook Quarterly,* 1960, 4, 22–27.
4. R. C. Young, W. V. Olive, and B. E. Miles, *Vocational and Educational Planning: Manpower, Priorities and Dollars* (Columbus: Center for Vocational Education, Ohio State University, 1972).
5. A. P. Garbin et al., *Worker Adjustment Problems of Youth in Transition from High School to Work* (Columbus: Center for Vocational Education, Ohio State University, 1970).
6. J. T. Grasso, "The Contributions of Vocational Education, Training and Work Experience to the Early Career Achievements of Young Men" (Ph.D. diss., Ohio State University, 1972).
7. W. N. Grubb and M. Lazerson, *American Education and Vocationalism* (New York: Teachers College Press, 1974); W. N. Grubb and M. Lazerson, "Education and the Labor Market: Recycling the Youth Problem," in *Work, Youth, and Schooling,* ed. H. Kantor and D. B. Tyack (Stanford, Calif.:

Stanford University Press, 1982). This overall lack of return to students in vocational programs has been found even for many students enrolled in public postsecondary vocational programs. W. W. Wilms and S. Hansell, "The Dubious Promise of Post Secondary Education: Its Payoff to Dropouts and Graduates in the U.S.A.," *International Journal of Educational Development*, 1982, 2, 43–60, for example, found that few students who studied for upper-status jobs (accountant, computer programmer, and electronic technician) attained these kinds of jobs. Graduates of training programs for lower-status jobs *were* more likely to find work and eventually have higher earnings than program dropouts. But this finding must be seen in the light of an overall 60 percent drop-out rate in programs at public schools. Relevant here, too. is the fact that disproportionate percentages of low SES and black students were among those who dropped out. These findings together suggest that while postsecondary programs may show a greater likelihood of return to students than do secondary programs, this may be partly a function of the elimination from programs (and from the statistics) of those students least likely to profit from their training in the labor market.

8. Bowles and Gintis, *Schooling in Capitalist America;* M. Carnoy, *Education as Cultural Imperialism* (New York: David McKay Co., 1974); Cohen and Lazerson, "Education and the Corporate Order"; R. Collins, "Functional and Conflict Theories of Education Stratification," *American Sociological Review*, 1971, *36*, 1002–19.

9. J. D. Anderson, "The Historical Development of Black Vocational Education," in *Work, Youth and Schooling*, ed. H. Kantor and D. B. Tyack (Stanford, Calif.: Stanford University Press, 1982).

10. R. N. Evans and J. D. Galloway, "Verbal Ability and Socioeconomic Status of 9th and 12th Grade College Preparatory, General and Vocational Students," *Journal of Human Resources*, 1973, *8*.

11. Of the seven white senior highs, one school enrolled 80 percent white students; the other six were 90 percent or more white. Each of the mixed senior highs enrolled approximately 50 percent nonwhite students. Each nonwhite school enrolled more than 95 percent nonwhite students. The white schools represent an enrollment of 6,728 students, the nonwhite schools 5,708 students, and the mixed schools 5,318 students (2,623 white and 2,695 nonwhite). The white junior highs had an enrollment of 95 percent or more white students. Mixed junior highs each had approximately 50 percent nonwhites enrolled. Nonwhite junior highs enrolled 95 percent or more nonwhite students. The white junior high schools enrolled a total of 4,055 students, the nonwhite schools, 2,540 students, and the mixed schools, 3,515 students (1,664 white and 1,851 nonwhite).

12. This total was divided by the number of teacher hours required of full-time teachers at the school. The resultant score was determined to be

the number of full-time teaching positions or their equivalents (FTEs) allocated to vocational programs at the school. These FTEs were used as a measure of vocational teacher resources at each of the schools which could be
compared to teacher resources in other subjects at the same school or with
those in vocational education programs at other schools in the sample.

13. On the average, similar percentages of FTEs were found at the two
categories of schools.

Allocation of Teacher Resources to Vocational Education and School
Race/Ethnicity

Senior High Schools		Junior High Schools	
Race/Ethnicity	X% FTES[a]	Race/Ethnicity	X% FTES[a]
White	23.14%	White	9.83%
Mixed and nonwhite	20.05%	Mixed and nonwhite	11.33%

[a]Full-time teachers or equivalents.

14. At one black/white junior high school, 74 percent of the students
enrolled in sampled classes were white; at another, 60 percent were white.
Vocational education courses were required for all eighth-graders at one of
these schools and for all seventh- and eighth-graders not enrolled in music
or foreign language classes at the other. Under these circumstances, an uneven enrollment of nonwhite students in vocational education is unlikely to
occur. At a third junior high, five vocational classes were studied, with a total
enrollment of 25 students. Of these, however, only five (20 percent) were
white. It does not appear that vocational education was required at this school.
At the fourth mixed junior high, we were prevented from asking about students' race. At one mixed senior high school, seventeen classes were studied
with a total student enrollment of 193. Of these, 52 percent were white,
nearly the same as the 53 percent white at the school as a whole. At a second,
five classes were studied with a total enrollment of 90 students. Whites made
up 29 percent of the total, a considerably smaller percentage than the 50
percent at the school as a whole. Three classes were sampled at a third school
with a total enrollment of 63 students. Of these, 29 percent were white in
contrast to 52 percent white in the total school population.

15. It should be kept in mind that this analysis is based on the number
of different course offerings available at a school and does not consider the
number of sections of a particular course that may have been offered.

16. Evans and Galloway, "Verbal Ability and Socioeconomic Status."

17. Interestingly, these results are parallel to those found in the mid-
1930s in a nationwide survey of federally funded vocational education oppor-

tunities for blacks. Then, as now, black enrollment was strikingly concentrated in courses leading to a limited number of low-skilled occupations. See Anderson, "The Historical Development of Black Vocational Education."

18. Wilms and Hansell, "The Dubious Promise of Post Secondary Education."

19. L. C. Thurow, "Education and Income Quality," *Public Interest,* 1972, *28 ;* 66–81.

20. C. C Maier, "What California Business Needs from Our Schools," *Los Angeles Times,* March 4, 1983.

21. R. Collins, *The Credential Society* (New York: Academic Press, 1979).

22. H. Gintis, "Education, Technology, and the Characteristics of Worker Productivity," *American Economic Review,* 1971, *61 :* 166–279; Thurow, "Education and Income Quality."

23. The National Commission on Excellence in Education, *A Nation at Risk* (Washington, D.C.: U.S. Government Printing Office, 1983).

Chapter 9

1. Brown v. *Board of Education of Topeka,* 347 U.S. 483 (1954).

2. J. S. Coleman et al., *Equality of Educational Opportunity* (Washington, D.C.: U.S. Government Printing Office, 1966); U.S. Commission on Civil Rights, *Racial Isolation in the Public Schools,* vol. 1 (Washington, D.C.: U.S. Government Printing Office, 1965); D. K. Cohen, T. F. Pettigrew, and R. Riley, "Race and Outcomes of Schooling," in *On Equality of Educational Opportunity,* ed. F. Mosteller and D. P. Moynihan (New York: Random House, 1972).

3. National Education Association, "Ability Grouping: Teacher Opinion Poll," *National Education Association Journal,* 1968, 53.

4. Excellent reviews of this literature include Heathers, "Grouping"; W. G. Findley and M. M. Bryan, *Ability Grouping: 1970, Status, Impact, and Alternatives, 3–12* (Athens: University of Georgia Press, 1971); D. Esposito, "Homogeneous and Heterogeneous Ability Grouping: Principal Findings and Implications for Evaluating and Designing More Effective Educational Evironments," *Review of Educational Research,* 1973, 43, 163–79; C. H. Persell, *Education and Inequality: A Theoretical and Empirical Synthesis* (New York: Free Press, 1977).

5. See W. R. Borg, *Ability Grouping in the Public Schools* (Madison, Wis.: Dumbar Educational Services, 1966); and Findley and Bryan, "Ability Grouping," for reviews of this literature.

6. See Persell, "Education and Inequality," for a comprehensive review of this literature.

7. *U.S. Constitution,* Amendment XIV, Section 1.

8. *Wisconsin v. Constantineau,* 400 U.S. 433 (1971).

9. *Goss* v. *Lopez*, 419 U.S. 565 (1975).

10. *Pennsylvania Association of Retarded Children* v. *Commonwealth of Pennsylvania (PARC)*, 334 F. Supp. 1257 (1971) and 343 F. Supp. 279 (1972).

11. *Mills* v. *Board of Education*, 348 F. Supp 866 (1972).

12. For an excellent discussion of this issue, see M. H. McCarthy, "Is the Equal Protection Clause Still a Viable Tool for Effecting Educational Reform?" *Journal of Law and Education*, 1977, 6, 159–82.

13. T. Shannon, "Chief Justice Wright, the California Supreme Court, and School Finance: Has the Fourteenth Done It Again?" *Nolpe School Law Journal*, 1973, 3.

14. *Serrano* v. *Priest*, 5 Cal. 3d 584 (1971).

15. *Serrano*, at 609.

16. *San Antonio Independent School District* v. *Rodriguez*, 411 U.S. 1 (1973).

17. *Rodriguez*, at 62.

18. *Rodriguez*, at 299.

19. *Plyler* v. *Doe*, 102 S. Ct. 2382 (1982).

20. *Plyler*, at 2397.

21. *Plyler*, at 2398.

22. J. E. Dick, "Equal Protection and Intelligence Classifications," *Stanford Law Review*, 1974, 26, 647–56.

23. *Trustees of Schools* v. *People ex. rel. Van Allen*, 87 Ill, 303 (1877).

24. *Peter Doe* v. *San Francisco Unified School District*, 60 Cal. 3d 814 (1976).

25. *Hobson* v. *Hansen*, 269 F. Supp. 401 (1967).

26. *Hobson*, at 514.

27. *Hobson*, at 515.

28. *Smuck* v. *Hobson*, 408 F. 2d 175 (1969).

29. For an excellent discussion of the *Hobson* case, see B. Bruno, *Poverty, Inequality and the Law* (St. Paul, Minn.: West Publishing Co., 1976).

30. *Moses* v. *Washington Parrish School Board*, 456 F. 2d 1285.

31. *Moses*, at 1342.

32. *McNeal* v. *Tate County School District*, 508 F. 2d 1017 (1975).

33. *McNeal*, at 1020.

34. *United States* v. *Gadsden County School District*, 572 F. 2d 1049 (1978).

35. *Gadsden*, at 1050.

36. *Gadsden*, at 1052.

37. *Larry P.* v. *Riles*, 343 F. Supp. 1306 (1972).

38. *Larry P.* v. *Riles*, 495 F. Supp. 926 (1979).

39. *Lora v. Board of Education of City of New York*, 456 F. Supp. 1211 (1978).

40. Dick, "Equal Protection."

41. *Washington v. Dairs*, 426 U.S. 299 (1976).

42. *Larry II*, at 975.

43. *Larry II*, at 976.

44. For a good discussion of this point, see A. Bloomdahl, "How Educational 'Tracking' Railroads Minority Students," *Human Rights*, 1980, *9*, 10–15.

45. *Hobson*, at 517.

46. *Brown*, at 495.

Chapter 10

1. Recently there has been some systematic inquiry into the effects of student attributes and classroom behaviors on how teachers behave. See, for example, G. Walriello and S. M. Dornbusch, "Bringing Behavior Back In: The Effects of Student Characteristics and Behavior of Teachers," *American Educational Research Journal*, 1983, *20*, 29–43.

2. Again, for good reviews of the research on grouping and student achievement, the reader is referred to the following: for the earliest studies, W. S. Miller and H. J. Otto, "Analysis of Experimental Studies in Homogeneous Grouping," *Journal of Educational Research*, 1930, *21*, 95–102; for more recent work, see J. I. Goodlad, "Classroom Organization," in *Encyclopedia of Educational Research*, 3d ed., ed. Chester Harris (New York: Macmillan, 1960), pp. 221–25; D. Esposito, "Homogeneous and Heterogeneous Ability Grouping: Principal Findings and Implications for Designing More Effective Educational Environments," *Review of Educational Research*, 1973, *43*, 163–79; and R. D. Froman, "Ability Grouping: Why Do We Persist and Should We," paper presented at the annual meeting of the American Educational Research Association, Los Angeles, 1981. (Note the somewhat contrary conclusion drawn by C. C. Kulick and J. A. Kulick, "Effects of ability Grouping on Secondary School Students: A Meta-Analysis of Evaluation Findings," *American Educational Research Journal*, 1982, *19*, 415–28.

3. For details of the statistical procedures used and tables showing the results, see J. Oakes, *A Question of Access: Tracking and Curriculum Differentiation in a National Sample of English and Mathematics Classes*, A Study of Schooling Technical Report no. 24 (Los Angeles: University of California, 1981), available from the ERIC clearinghouse on teacher education.

4. M. F. D. Young, *Knowledge and Control* (London: Collier-Macmillan, 1971).

5. M. Apple, "Ideology, Reproduction, and Education Reform," *Comparative Educational Review*, 1978, 22, 367–87.

6. P. Bordieu and J. C. Passeron, *Reproduction in Education, Society and Culture*, trans. Richard Nice (Beverly Hills, Calif., Sage Publications, 1977).

7. Bowles and Gintis, *Schooling in Capitalism America*.

8. Willis, *Learning to Labour: How Working Class Kids Get Working Class Jobs;* Everhart, *Reading, Writing and Resistance*.

9. B. Bernstein, *Class, Codes, and Control*, vol. 3 (London: Routledge & Kegan Paul, 1977).

10. Bowles and Gintis, *Schooling in Capitalist America*.

11. J. Karabel and H. Halsey, "Educational Research: A Review and an Interpretation," in *Power and Ideology in Education*, ed., J. Karabel and H. Halsey (New York: Oxford University Press, 1977).

12. Apple, "Ideology, Reproduction and Educational Reform."

13. Bordieu and Passeron, *Reproduction in Education*, p. 210.

14. I. Illich, *Deschooling Society* (New York: Harper & Row, 1973).

15. D. W. Johnson and R. T. Johnson, *Learning Together and Learning Alone: Cooperation, Competition and Individualization* (Englewood Cliffs, N.J.: Prentice-Hall, 1975).

16. D. W. Johnson et al., "Effects of Cooperative, Competitive, and Individualistic Goal Structures on Achievement: A Meta-analysis," *Psychological Bulletin*, 1981, 89, 47–62; S. Sharon, "Cooperative Learning in Small Groups: Recent Methods and Effects on Achievement, Attitudes and Ethnic Relations," *Review of Educational Research*, 1980, 50, 241–71; R. Slavin, *Cooperative Learning* (New York: Longman, 1983).

17. J. Oakes, *208 English Teachers*, A Study of Schooling Technical Report no. 11 (Los Angeles: University of California, 1980), available from the ERIC clearinghouse on teacher education.

Chapter 11

1. For a fuller discussion, see J. Hochschild and N. Scrovronick, *The American Dream and the Public Schools* (Oxford: Oxford University Press, 2003).

2. M. Adler, *The Paideia Proposal: An Educational Manifesto* (New York: Macmillan, 1983); D. Ravitch, *The Schools We Deserve: Reflections on the Educational Crisis of Our Time* (New York: Basic Books, 1987).

3. Tom Loveless coined the term in the title of his book *The Tracking Wars: State Reform Meets School Policy* (Washington: Brookings Institution, 1999), which itself has been a key weapon in the fray.

4. "Is Your Child Being Tracked for Failure?" *Better Homes and Gardens*, October 1988, 34–36; J. Rachlin, "The Label That Sticks," *U. S. News and World Report*, July 3, 1989, 51–52; S. Tobias, "Tracked to Fail," *Psychology Today*, September 1989, 54–60.

5. National Governor's Association, *Ability Grouping and Tracking: Current Issues and Concerns* (Washington: author, 1993).

6. See, for example, "Ability Grouping in Social Studies," Prepared by the Ad Hoc Committee on Ability Grouping Approved by NCSS Board of Directors, 1992 (*http://www.socialstudies.org/positions/ability*, last visited September 21, 2004); National Council of Teachers of English Position Statement on Tracking (Seattle: author, 1991) (*http://www.ncte.org/about/over/positions/category/profcon/107542.htm*, last visited October 23, 2004); National Council of Teachers of Mathematics, *Curriculum and Evaluation Standards for School Mathematics* (Reston, Vir.: author, 1989); California State Department of Education, *Caught in the Middle* (Sacramento: author, 1989); Massachusetts Department of Education, State Plan to Eliminate the General Track (Malden, Mass.: author, 1996).

7. The Carnegie Council for Adolescent Development, *Turning Points: Preparing American Youth for the 21st Century*. (New York: Carnegie Corporation of New York, 1989). See also A. Jackson and G. Davis, *Turning Points 2000: Educating Adolescents in the 21st Century* (New York: Teachers College Press, 2000); J. Oakes, K. H. Quartz, S. Ryan, and M. Lipton, *Becoming Good American Schools: The Struggle for Civic Virtue in Education Reform* (San Francisco: Jossey-Bass, 2000).

8. *Horace*, May 1992, 8 (*http://www.essentialschools.org/cs/resources/view/ces_res/9*, last visited September 22, 2004).

9. The College Board, *Equity 2000* (New York: author, 1989).

10. For an analysis of the evidence offered to the Wilmington court and the way this evidence was understood (and misunderstood) by the court, see K. G. Welner and H. Kupermintz, "Rethinking Expert Testimony in Education Rights Litigation," *Educational Evaluation and Policy Analysis*, 2004, 26(2), 127–42.

11. See, for example, the accounts of detracking schools in A. Wheelock, *Crossing the Tracks: How "Untracking" Can Save America's Schools* (New York: New Press, 1992).

12. See, for example, C-L. C. Kulik and J. A. Kulik, "Ability Grouping and Gifted Students," in *Handbook of Gifted Education*, edited by N. Colangelo and G. A. Davis, pp. 178–96 (Boston: Allyn and Bacon, 1991); J. A. Kulik and C-L. C. Kulik, "Synthesis of Research on Effects of Accelerated Instruction," *Educational Leadership*, 1984, 42(2), 84–89; J. F. Feldhusen, "Synthesis of Research on Gifted Youth," *Educational Leader-*

ship, March 1989, 46, 6-11; Susan Demirsky Allan, "Ability Grouping Research Reviews: What Do They Say about Grouping and the Gifted?" *Educational Leadership*, March 1991, 48, 60-65.

13. The following policy position, approved in 1991, still appears on the website of the National Association for Gifted Children: "The practice of grouping, enabling students with advanced abilities and/or performance to be grouped together to receive appropriately challenging instruction, has recently come under attack. NAGC wishes to reaffirm the importance of grouping for instruction of gifted students. . . . Strong research evidence supports the effectiveness of ability grouping for gifted students in accelerated classes, enrichment programs, advanced placement programs, etc. Ability and performance grouping has been used extensively in programs for musically and artistically gifted students, and for athletically talented students with little argument. Grouping is a necessary component of every graduate and professional preparation program, such as law, medicine, and the sciences. It is an accepted practice that is used extensively in the education programs in almost every country in the Western world. NAGC does not endorse a tracking system that sorts all children into fixed layers in the school system with little attention to particular content, student motivation, past accomplishment, or present potential. To abandon the proven instructional strategy of grouping students for instruction at a time of educational crisis in the U.S. will further damage our already poor competitive position with the rest of the world, and will renege on our promise to provide an appropriate education for all children. (Approved 11/91) (*http://www.nagc. org/Policy/abilgroup.htm*, last accessed September 23, 2004).

14. E. D. Fiedler, R. E. Lange, and S. Winebrenner, "The Concept of Grouping in Gifted Education: In Search of Reality—Unraveling the Myths about Tracking, Ability Grouping, and the Gifted," in *School Reform: The Critical Issues*, edited by W. M. Evers, L. T. Izumi, and P. A. Riley (Stanford: Hoover Institution, 2001).

15. T. Loveless, "The Tracking and Ability Grouping Debate" (Fordham Foundation, unpublished paper, 1998); Loveless, *The Tracking Wars*.

16. Loveless, *The Tracking Wars*.

17. J. F. Feldhusen, "Susan Allan Sets the Record Straight: Response to Allan," *Educational Leadership*, March 1991. J. A. Kulik, "Findings on Grouping are Often Distorted, Response to Allen," *Educational Leadership*, March 1991. For critiques of Kulik's own reviews see R. E. Slavin, "Ability Grouping and Student Achievement in Elementary Schools: A Best-Evidence Synthesis," *Review of Educational Research*, 1987, 57, 293–336. Loveless, *The Tracking Wars*, pp. 3, 12, 17, 16, 15.

18. Some research finds that, in comparison with the practices in most

NOTES TO PAGES 226–27   317

public schools, Catholic high school students enrolled in nonacademic tracks typically take more academic courses and fewer electives than their counterparts in public schools. See, for example, V. E. Lee and A. S. Bryk, "Curriculum Tracking as Mediating the Social Distribution of High School Achievement," *Sociology of Education*, 1988, 61, 78–94. Other researchers have found, in contrast to the national trends in public schools, that particular low-ability classes do have adequate facilities, a solid curriculum, and qualified teachers. Here, too, most of the examples are from Catholic schools. See, for example, L. Valli, "A Curriculum of Effort: Tracking Students in a Catholic High School," in *Curriculum Differentiation: Interpretive Studies in U.S. Secondary Schools*, R. Page and L. Valli, pp. 45–65 (Albany: SUNY Press, 1990).

19. The study examined science and mathematics curriculum, teachers, facilities, equipment, and learning activities at the school and within school (track) level using data from the National Science Foundation's 1985–86 National Survey of Science and Mathematics Education. Cross-tabulations, correlational analyses, and analysis of variance documented the distribution of these features of science and mathematics programs. Multivariate analyses sorted out the effects of school and classroom characteristics, and separate track-level analyses were performed on groups of similar schools. This juxtaposition enabled a policy analytic interpretation of whether and how the distribution of specific features of schools and classrooms is likely to affect the learning opportunities of various groups, and it permitted me to draw implications for changes in policy and practice. J. Oakes (with T. Ormseth, R. Bell, and P. Camp), *Multiplying Inequalities: The Effects of Race, Social Class, and Tracking on Opportunities to Learn Mathematics and Science* (Santa Monica: RAND, 1990); J. Oakes, "Can Tracking Research Inform Practice?" *Educational Researcher*, 1992, 21(4), 12–22.

20. Raudenbush, Rowan, and Cheong found that variation in teachers' emphasis on teaching higher-order thinking in four subjects (and most strongly in mathematics and science) was a function of hierarchical conceptions of teaching and learning related to perceived ability group (track). That is, teachers placed much greater emphasis on higher-order thinking and problem solving in high-track classes than in others. See S. W. Raudenbush, B. Rowan, and Y. F. Cheong, "Higher Order Instructional Goals in Secondary Schools: Class, Teacher, and School Influences," *American Educational Research Journal*, 1992, 30, 523–53. Gamoran and Nystrand found high-track students more often experienced "authentic" assignments and higher-order cognitive tasks. By authentic, Gamoran and Nystrand mean questions and assignments request information that is new to the

teacher, rather than requiring a prespecified answer. A. Gamoran and M. Nystrand, "Background and Instructional Effects on Achievement in Eighth-Grade English and Social Studies," *Journal on Research in Adolescence,* 1991, 1(3), 277–300. Reba Page's ethnographic account of differentiated English and social studies classes shows that lower-track classes were characterized by what Page called a "skeletal curriculum," in which academic topics from regular classes were covered in less depth; a basic skills curriculum, in which academic subjects such as history and literature were reduced to reading, largely to decoding; and a "therapeutic curriculum," in which practical or "relevant" topics such as drug or law education replaced traditional academics. R. Page, *Lower-Track Classrooms: A Curricular and Cultural Perspective* (New York: Teachers College Press, 1991).

21. Iris Weiss, *A Profile of Science and Mathematics Education in the United States: 1993* (Chapel Hill: Horizon Research, 1994), p. 20. Additional evidence comes from qualitative research showing that low-track classes exhibit greater student disruption, hostility, and alienation, and teachers' relationships with students tend more toward control. See, for example, Page, *Lower-Track Classrooms.*

22. See, for example, J. E. Talbert and M. Ennis, "Teacher Tracking: Exacerbating Inequalities in the High School" (Stanford: Center for Research on the Context of Teaching, 1990, *www.stanford.edu/group/CRC/publications.htm*); R. M. Ingersoll, "The Problem of Underqualified Teachers in American Secondary Schools," *Educational Researcher,* 1999, 28, 26–37.

23. See, for example, R. J. Coley, R. Ekstrom, J. Gant, A. M. Villegas, R. Mitchell, and S. M. Watts, *On the Right Track* (Princeton: Educational Testing Service, 1992); K. J. Meier, J. Stuart, and R. E. England, *Race, Class and Education: The Politics of Second Generation Discrimination* (Madison: University of Wisconsin Press, 1989). J. H. Braddock, "Ability Grouping, Aspirations and Attainments: Evidence from the National Educational Longitudinal Study of 1988," *Journal of Negro Education,* 1993, 62(3); C. Adleman, *Answers in the Tool Box* (Washington: U.S. Department of Education, 1999); R. Atanda, *Do Gatekeeper Courses Expand Education Options?* (Washington: National Center for Education Statistics, 1999); L. Horn, A. Nunez, L. Bobbitt, *Mapping the Road to College: First Generation Students' Math Track, Planning Strategies, and Context of Support* (Washington: U.S. Department of Education, National Center for Education Statistics [NCES], 2000) p. 153; X. Ma and J. D. Willms, "Dropping Out of Advanced Mathematics: How Much Do Students and Schools Contribute to the Problem?" *Educational Evaluation and Policy Analysis,* 1999, 21 (4), 365–83.

24. For a comprehensive discussion of Rossell's testimony and its methodological problems, see Welner and Kupermintz, "Rethinking Expert Testimony in Education Rights Litigation."

25. In contrast, other research has found that socioeconomic status (SES) has important effects on track placement above and beyond students' academic performance, with higher SES students more likely to be placed in higher tracks when compared to lower SES students with similar academic records (see, for example, A. Gamoran and R. D. Mare, "Secondary School Tracking and Educational Equality: Compensation, Reinforcement, or Neutrality." *American Journal of Sociology*, 1989, 94, 1146–83). Additionally, controlling for academic achievement, family income, and family structure, a study using the NELS 88/94 data by Horn, Nunez, and Bobbitt, *Mapping the Road to College*, found the "first-generation" students from immigrant families were less likely to participate in college-preparatory programs.

26. J. Oakes and G. Guiton, "Matchmaking: The Dynamics of High School Tracking Decisions," *American Educational Research Journal*, 1995, 32(1), 3–33; see also M. Selvin, J. Oakes, S. Hare, K. Ramsey, and D. Schoeff, *Who Gets What and Why? Curriculum Decision-Making at Three Comprehensive High Schools* (Santa Monica: RAND Corporation, 1989).

27. Other researchers have found that differences among schools—such as the size of various tracks, entry criteria for particular tracks, and scheduling practices—affect the likelihood of a student with particular characteristics being placed in particular classes. See, for example, A. B. Sorensen, "The Organizational Differentiation of Students in Schools as an Opportunity Structure," in *The Social Organization of Schools: New Conceptualizations of the Learning Process*, edited by M. T. Hallinan, pp. 103–29 (New York: Plenum Press, 1987); M. Garet and B. DeLany, "Students, Courses, and Stratification," *Sociology of Education*, 1988, 61, 61–77.

28. The results of these studies were reported in expert analyses presented to the court in conjunction with the school desegregation cases. In addition, however, these studies are reported in J. Oakes, "Two Cities: Tracking and Within-School Segregation," *Teachers' College Record*, 1995, 96, 681–90; and, most comprehensively, in K. G. Welner, *Legal Rights, Local Wrongs: When Community Control Collides with Educational Equity* (Albany: SUNY Press, 2001).

29. See, for example, S. Lucas, *Tracking Inequality: Stratification and Mobility in American High Schools* (New York: Teacher College Press, 1999); B. E. Vanfossen, J. D. Jones, and J. Z. Spade, "Curriculum Tracking and Status Maintenance," *Sociology of Education*, 1987, 60, 104–22.

30. For similar findings, see A. Gamoran, "Access to Excellence: As-

signment to Honors English Classes in the Transition from Middle to High School," *Educational Evaluation and Policy Analysis*, 1992, 14, 185–204; R. A. Mickelson, "Subverting Swann, First- and Second-Generation Segregation in the Charlotte-Mecklenburg Schools," *American Educational Research Journal*, 2001, 38, 215–52; Sean P. Kelly, "The Black-White Gap in Mathematics Course Taking," University of Wisconsin-Madison, unpublished paper, 2003.

31. S. R. Lucas and A. Gamoran, "Race and Track Assignment: A Reconsideration with Course-Based Indicators of Track Locations" (University of Wisconsin Working Paper, 1993).

32. One exception is a recent paper from the National Bureau of Economic Research that concludes there is no evidence that separating students into tracks harms disadvantaged students. The report also suggests that tracking can support diversity, in that separate gifted programs are likely to attract and keep students from higher-income families. D. Page and M. Figlio, "School Choice and the Distributional Effects of Ability Tracking: Does Separation Increase Equality?" (Washington: National Bureau of Economic Research, Working Paper no. W8055, 2000).

33. See, for example, R. S. Weinstein, "Reading Group Membership in First Grade: Teacher Behaviors and Pupil Experience Over Time," *Journal of Educational Psychology*, 1976, 68(1), 103–16; R. Barr and R. Dreeben, *How Schools Work* (Chicago: University of Chicago Press, 1983); A. Gamoran and M. Berends, "The Effects of Stratification in Secondary Schools: Synthesis of Survey and Ethnographic Research," *Review of Educational Research*, 1987, 57, 415–36; R. E. Slavin, "Ability Grouping and Student Achievement in Elementary Schools: A Best-Evidence Synthesis," *Review of Educational Research*, 1987, 57(3), 293–336; R. E. Slavin, "Achievement Effects of Ability Grouping in Secondary Schools: A Best Evidence Synthesis," *Review of Educational Research*, 1990, 60(3), 471–500; R. E. Slavin, "Ability Grouping in the Middle Grades: Achievement Effects and Alternatives," *Elementary School Journal*, 1993, 93(5), 535–52.

34. For details of this analysis, see Welner, *Legal Rights, Local Wrongs*.

35. See, for example, P. White, A. Gamoran, A. C. Porter, and J. Smithson, "Upgrading the High School Math Curriculum: Math Course-Taking Patterns in Seven High Schools in California and New York," *Educational Evaluation and Policy Analysis*, 1996, 18, 285–307; T. Madigan, *Science Proficiency and Course Taking in High School* (Washington: U.S. Department of Education, National Center for Education Statistics [NCES], 1997), pp. 97–838; M. T. Hallinan and W. N. Kubitschek, "Curriculum Differentiation and High School Achievement," *Social Psychology of Education*, 1999, 3, 41–62.

36. See, for example, A. Gamoran, "The Variable Effects of High School Tracking," *American Sociological Review,* December 1992, 812–28.

37. See, for example, J. Kulik, *An Analysis of the Research on Ability Grouping: Historical and Contemporary Perspectives* (Storrs, Conn.: National Research Center on the Gifted and Talented, 1992).

38. Resource differences among tracks may also include the resources that students bring (prior knowledge, enthusiasm for learning, an ethic of trying hard, etc.) as well as the resources that schools provide.

39. See, for example, V. E. Lee and A. S. Bryk, "A Multilevel Model of the Social Distribution of Achievement," *Sociology of Education,* 1989, 62(3), 623–45.

40. See, for example, L. M. Argys, D. I. Rees, and D. J. Brewer, "Detracking America's Schools: Equity at Zero Cost?" *Journal of Policy Analysis and Management,* 1996, 15 (4), 623–45.

41. See, for example, R. E. Slavin, "Achievement Effects of Ability Grouping in Secondary Schools: A Best Evidence Synthesis," *Review of Educational Research,* 1990, 60(3), 471–500; R. E. Slavin, "Ability Grouping in the Middle Grades: Achievement Effects and Alternatives," *Elementary School Journal,* 1992, 93(5), 535–52; see also Figlio and Page, 2000; F. Mosteller, R. J. Light, and J. A. Sachs, "Sustained Inquiry in Education: Lessons from Skill Grouping and Class Size," *Harvard Educational Review,* 1996, 66, 797–843.

42. A. Gamoran and R. D. Mare, "Secondary School Tracking and Educational Inequality: Compensation, Reinforcement, or Neutrality?" *American Journal of Sociology,* 1989, 94(5), 1146–83; Vanfossen, Jones, and Spade, "Curriculum Tracking and Status Maintenance"; F. Paul, "Academic Programs in a Democratic Society: Structured Choices and Their Consequences," *Advances in Educational Policy,* 2 (Philadelphia: Falmer Press, 1995).

43. See J. Braddock and M. P. Dawkins, "Ability Grouping, Aspirations, and Attainments: Evidence from the National Educational Longitudinal Study of 1988," *Journal of Negro Education,* 1993, 62(3), 1–13; S. Dornbush, "Off the Track" (Paper presented as the 1994 Presidential Address to the Society for Research on Adolescence, San Diego.

44. P. McDonough, *Choosing Colleges* (Albany: SUNY Press, 1997); F. Paul, "Academic Programs in a Democratic Society."

45. Atanda, *Do Gatekeeper Courses Expand Education Options?*; Horn, Nunez, and Bobbitt, *Mapping the Road to College.*

46. Argys, Rees, and Brewer, "Detracking America's Schools."

47. T. Loveless, "The Tracking and Ability Grouping Debate."

48. G. Orfield and F. Paul, *High Hopes, Long Odds: A Major Report on Hoosier Teens and the American Dream* (Indianapolis: Indiana Youth Institute Evaluative Report 142, 1994).

49. G. Guiton and J. Oakes, "Opportunity to Learn and Conceptions of Educational Equality," *Educational Evaluation and Policy Analysis*, 1995, 17(3), 323–36.

50. S. Yonezawa, A. S. Wells, and I. Serna, "Choosing Tracks: 'Freedom of Choice' in Detracking Schools," *American Educational Research Journal*, 2002, 39(1), 37–67.

51. See Lucas, *Tracking Inequality*.

52. Note the recent proliferation of AP classes. National Research Council Committee on Programs for Advanced Study of Mathematics and Science in American High Schools, *Learning and Understanding: Improving Advanced Study of Mathematics and Science in U.S. High Schools* (Washington: National Academy Press, 2002).

53. Later in this chapter I'll have more to say about the cultural and political tensions that make it impossible to address tracking as a strictly technical issue or to find credibility in suggestions that tracking is all about doing a good job of educating children.

54. Maureen Hallinan, "The Detracking Movement." *Education Next*, Fall 2004.

55. Hallinan wrote in 2004, "In studies published in 1986 and 1999, my colleagues and I found that students assigned to low-ability groups score lower on standardized tests than if they had been placed in mixed-ability or high-ability groups." Ibid.

56. Maureen T. Hallinan, "Tracking: From Theory to Practice," *Sociology of Education*, 1994, 67, 79–84.

57. Gamoran's 1987 analyses of nationally representative survey data documented that the gains bright students in higher-level tracks make in homogeneous groups are canceled out by the losses weaker students suffer by being placed in low-level tracks. A. Gamoran, "The Stratification of High School Learning Opportunities," *Sociology of Education*, 1987, 60: 135–55. A. Gamoran, "Alternative Uses of Ability Grouping in Secondary Schools: Can We Bring High-Quality Instruction to Low-Ability Classrooms?" *American Journal of Education*, 1993, 102(1), 1–22.

58. A. Gamoran, Public Lecture: "Standards, Inequality and Ability Grouping," April 9, 2002 (*http://www.ed.ac.uk/ces/conferences/Gamoran_Lecture.htm*).

59. The term *norm* is defined broadly here, going beyond a common but narrower definition of norms as formal or informal standards that prescribe acceptable action in a setting.

60. For similar findings, see Paul, "Academic Programs in a Democratic Society," and McDonough, *Choosing Colleges.*

61. The influence of middle-class parent interventions appears as early as middle school, as students vie for eighth-grade algebra placements. Useem, for example, found a strong relationship between parents' education levels and placement in middle school mathematics, with college-educated parents involved in school programs and parent information networks, intervening in placement decisions, and influencing their children's course choices. E. L. Useem, "Middle Schools and Math Groups: Parents' Involvement in Children's Placement," *Sociology of Education,* 1992, 65(4), 263–79. See also E. Brantlinger, *Dividing Classes.*

62. Oakes et al., *Good American Schools.*

63. J. A. Kulik, "An Analysis of the Research on Ability Grouping" (National Center for Research on Gifted and Talented Education, Newsletter, Spring, 1993) (*http://www.gifted.uconn.edu/nrcgt/newsletter/spring93/sprng935.html,* last visited September 27, 2004). Loveless, *The Tracking Wars,* p. 155; Figlio and Page, "School Choice and the Distributional Effects of Ability Tracking." Argys, Brewer, and Rees, "Detracking America's Schools."

64. See, for example, Gamoran, "The Stratification of High School Learning Opportunities."

65. Loveless, *The Tracking Wars,* p. 26. See, for example, D. Grissmer, A. Flanagan, and S. Williamson, "Why Did the Black–White Score Gap Narrow in the 1970s and 1980s?" in *The Black–White Test Score Gap,* edited by C. Jencks and M. Phillips (Washington: Brookings Institution, 1998).

66. P. Frome, *High Schools That Work: Findings from the 1996 and 1998 Assessments.* Prepared by the Research Triangle Institute for the Planning and Evaluation Service, U.S. Department of Education, Washington, 2001; P. Kaufman, D. Bradby, and P. Teitelbaum, *High Schools That Work and Whole School Reform: Raising Academic Achievement of Vocational Completers Through the Reform of School Practice* (Berkeley: University of California at Berkeley, National Center for Research in Vocational Education, 2000).

67. The College Board, "Equity 2000: A Systemic Education Reform Model" (*http://www.collegeboard.com/about/association/equity.html*). Note, however, Gamoran's caution: "In 1991 in this system, 31% of these kids were in algebra and therefore nearly 70% in watered down general math—moving up to 99% in 1997. So much greater uptake of academic programmes, but failure rates got worse, so 25% of kids were failing in 1991, 55% were failing in 1997. So it is very difficult to implement a programme

like this successfully. Great progress, but still many failures." A. Gamoran, Public Lecture: "Standards, Inequality and Ability Grouping," April 9, 2002, (*http://www.ed.ac.uk/ces/conferences/Gamoran'Lecture.htm*).

68. Hugh Mehan, L. Hubbard, and I. Villanueva, *Constructing School Success: The Consequences of "Untracking" Low Achieving Students* (London: Cambridge University Press, 1994), pp. 100, 105.

69. J. Boaler, *Experiencing School Mathematics* (London: Lea, 2002).

70. J. Boaler, "Promoting Equity in Mathematics Classrooms—Important Teaching Practices and Their Impact on Student Learning," *Proceedings of the International Congress on Mathematics Education* (Copenhagen, 2004). See, for example, C. C. Burris, J. P. Heubert, H. M. Levin, "Accelerating Mathematics Achievement Using Heterogeneous Grouping," forthcoming.

71. U.S. Department of Education, "Mathematics Equals Opportunity," *White Paper Presented for U.S. Secretary of Education Richard W. Riley* (Washington: author, 1997).

72. E. G. Cohen and R. A. Lotan, "Equity in Heterogeneous Classrooms," in *Handbook of Research on Multicultural Education,* edited by J. Banks and C. Banks, 2d ed. (New York: Teachers College Press, 2003). D. K. Cohen, M. W. McLaughlin, and J. E. Talbert, eds., *Teaching for Understanding: Challenges for Policy and Practice* (San Francisco: Jossey-Bass, 1992). See also Elizabeth Cohen and Rachel Lotan, *Working for Equity in Heterogeneous Classrooms* (New York: Teachers College Press, 1977).

73. Continued resistance to heterogeneous grouping can be found in *The Roeper Review.* Rather than a research journal, Roeper idenfies itself as follows: "Published by The Roeper School in Michigan, the Roeper Review applies the highest standards of peer review journalism to cover a broad range of issues—for professionals who work with teachers and psychologists, and for professionals who work directly with gifted and talented children and their families." For example, K. Rogers, "Grouping the Gifted and Talented," *Roeper Review,* 2002, 24(4), 103–07; C. Shields, "A Comparison Study of Student Attitudes and Perceptions in Homogeneous and Heterogeneous Classrooms," *Roeper Review,* 2002, 24(3), 115–19. The Roeper School is a day school for gifted and talented children located in Bloomfield Hills, Michigan, a suburb of Detroit.

74. The center's mission and work are detailed on its website: *http://www.gifted.uconn.edu/nrcgt.html,* last visited September 27, 2004. C. Tomlinson, *How to Differentiate Instruction for Mixed-Ability Classrooms* (Alexandria, Va.: Association for Supervision and Curriculum Development, 1995); C. Tomlinson, "Differentiated Instruction in the Regu-

lar Classroom: What Does It Mean? How Does It Look?" *Understanding Our Gifted*, 2001, 14(1), 3–6. Tomlinson also argues that most schools will need to provide a variety of services and learning options for the full range of learners, in addition to differentiated heterogeneous classrooms.

75. A. Collatos and E. Morrell, "Apprenticing Urban Youth as Critical Researchers: Implications for School Reform," in *Critical Voices in School Reform: Students Living Through Change*, edited by B. Rubin and E. Silva (New York: RoutledgeFalmer, 2002); J. Oakes, K. Rogers, M. Lipton, and E. Morrell, "The Social Construction of College Access: Confronting the Technical, Cultural, and Political Barriers to Low-Income Students of Color," in *Extending Our Reach: Strategies for Increasing Access to College*, edited by W. G. Tierney and L. S. Haggedorn (New York: SUNY Press, 2002); E. Morrell and A. Collatos, "Toward a Critical Teacher Education Pedagogy: Using Student Sociologists as Teacher Educators," *Social Justice*, 2003, 29(4), 60–71; A. Collatos, E. Morrell, A. Nuno, and R. Lara, "Critical Sociology in K–16 Early Intervention: Constructing Latino Pathways to Higher Education," *Journal of Hispanic Higher Education*, 2004, 3(2), 164–79; E. Morrell, *Becoming Critical Researchers: Literacy and Empowerment for Urban Youth* (New York: Peter Lang, 2004). The students as ninth graders happened to be taking the same ninth-grade humanities class.

76. L. Berkner, L. Horn, and N. Clune, *Descriptive Summary of 1995–96 Beginning Postsecondary Students: Three Years Later* (NCES 2000–154). U.S. Department of Education, National Center for Education Statistics. Washington: U.S. Government Printing Office, 2000.

Chapter 12. Democracy's Canaries
    Earlier versions of some of the material in this chapter appeared in the following: J. Oakes, A. S. Wells, S. Yonezawa, and K. Ray, "Change Agentry and the Quest for Equity: Lessons from Detracking Schools," in *The Sharp Edge of Educational Change*, edited by N. Bascia and A. Hargreaves (London: RoutledgeFalmer, 2000); J. Oakes, K. Welner, S. Yonezawa, and R. Allen, "The Norms and Politics of Equity-Minded Change: Researching the 'Zone of Mediation,'" in *The International Handbook of Educational Change*, edited by M. Fullan, A. Hargreaves, A. Lieberman (London: Klewer, 1998); K. Welner and J. Oakes, "The Limits of Conventional Reform Strategies," in *Bringing Equity Back In*, edited by J. Petrovitch and A. S. Wells (New York: Teachers College Press, 2004).

    1. A fuller account of the Rockville Centre experience is detailed in C. C. Burris, J. P. Heubert, and H. Levin, "Math Acceleration for All," *Educational Leadership*, 2001, 61, 68–71; C. C. Burris and K. Welner,

"Closing the Achievement Gap Through Detracking," *Phi Delta Kappan,* in press; C. C. Burris, J. P. Heubert, H. M. Levin, "Accelerating Mathematics Achievement Using Heterogeneous Grouping," forthcoming.

2. Amy Stuart Wells is now professor at Teachers College, Columbia University, where she continues to study race, education, and social stratification.

3. The results of this study are reported more comprehensively in the following publications: R. Cooper, "Urban School Reform from a Student of Color Perspective," *Urban Education,* 2000, 34(5), 597–622; R. Cooper, "A Promising Example of Urban School Reform: Detracking in a Racially Mixed High School," *Journal of Education for Students Placed at Risk,* 1999, 4(3), 259–75; R. Cooper, "Detracking Reform in an Urban California High School: Improving the Schooling Experience of African American Students," *Journal of Negro Education,* 1996, 65(2), 190–208; A. Datnow, *The Gender Politics of Educational Change* (New York: RoutledgeFalmer, 1997); A. Datnow, "Using Gender to Preserve Tracking's Status Hierarchy: The Defensive Strategy of Entrenched Teachers," *Anthropology and Education Quarterly,* 1997, 28(2), 1–26; A. Datnow and D. Hirshberg, "The Symbiosis of Heterogeneous Grouping and Multicultural Education: A Case Study of King Middle School," *Journal of Education for Students Placed at Risk,* 1996, 1(2), 115–34; J. Oakes, A. S. Wells, A. Datnow, and M. Jones, "Detracking: The Social Construction of Ability, Cultural Politics and Resistance to Reform," *Teachers College Record,* 1997, 98, 482–511; A. S. Wells and J. Oakes, "Potential Pitfalls of Systemic Reform: Early Lessons from Research on Detracking," *Sociology of Education* 1996, Extra Issue, 135–43; J. Oakes and A. S. Wells, "The Comprehensive High School, Detracking, and the Persistence of Social Stratification," in *The Comprehensive High School Today,* edited by F. M. Hammack (New York: Teachers College Press, 2004); A. S. Wells and J. Oakes, "Tracking, Detracking and the Politics of Educational Reform: A Sociological Perspective," in *Emerging Issues in the Sociology of Education: Comparative Perspectives,* edited by Carlos Torres and Ted Mitchell (Albany: SUNY Press, 1998); A. S. Wells and I. Serna, "The Politics of Culture," *Harvard Education Review,* 1996, 62(1), 93–118; S. Yonezawa, A. S. Wells, and I. Serna, "Choosing Tracks: How Students Structure Inequality," *American Educational Research Journal,* 2002, 39(1), 37–68.

4. I am indebted to Seymour Sarason for introducing me to the powerful concept of schooling regularities. See, for example, *The Culture of School and the Problem of Change* (Boston: Allyn and Bacon, 1982).

5. See Oakes, Wells, Datnow, and Jones, "Detracking: The Social Construction of Ability."

6. For a more complete discussion of this issue, see Wells and Serna, "The Politics of Culture."

7. For a more comprehensive discussion of this issue, see Oakes, Wells, Datnow, and Jones, "Detracking: The Social Construction of Ability."

8. See National Research Council, *Learning and Understanding* (2001), for a discussion of these weaknesses in the Advanced Placement curriculum.

9. J. Oakes, K. H. Quartz, S. Ryan, M. Lipton, *Becoming Good American Schools: The Struggle for Civic Virtue in Education Reform* (San Francisco: Jossey-Bass, 2000); see also the special issue of *Research in Middle Level Education Quarterly*, 1997, 20:1.

10. The phrase "legal rights, local wrongs" comes from the title of Kevin Welner's book detailing the studies reported in this section, K. Welner, *Legal Rights, Local Wrongs: When Community Control Collides with Educational Equity* (Albany: SUNY Press, 2001).

11. For a full report of this study, see J. Oakes, K. Welner, and S. Yonezawa, *Mandating Equity: A Case Study of Court-Ordered Detracking in the San Jose Schools* (Berkeley: University of California, California Policy Research Center, 1998). See K. Welner, J. Oakes, and G. FitzGerald, *Reforming for Excellence and Equity in Woodland Hills: A Progress Report on Detracking*, Report for the United States District Court for the Western District of Pennsylvania, the Commonwealth of Pennsylvania, the Woodland Hills School District, and the plaintiffs and other concerned parties associated with *Hoots v. Commonwealth of Pennsylvania*, No. 71–538, 1998.

12. J. Oakes, *Within-School Integration, Grouping Practices, and Educational Quality in Rockford Schools*, report prepared in conjunction with *People Who Care v. Rockford, IL. Independent School District*, 2000.

13. *Authentic instruction* is a term coined by Fred Neumann and Gary Wehlage at the National Center for Research on Organization and Restructuring of Schools and Professors of Curriculum and Instruction, University of Wisconsin–Madison. By "authentic," Neumann and Wehlage attempt "to distinguish between achievement that is significant and meaningful and that which is trivial and useless." See, for example, F. Newmann and G. Wehlage, "Five Standards of Authentic Instruction," *Educational Leadership*, April 1993, 8–12.

14. Welner, *Legal Rights, Local Wrongs*; K. Welner and J. Oakes, *Navigating the Politics of Detracking: A School Leaders' Guide* (New York: Skylight Publications, 2000); Oakes, Welner, and Yonezawa, *Mandating Equity*; Welner and Oakes, "The Limits of Conventional Reform Strategies."

15. J. Oakes and M. Lipton, "Struggling for Educational Equity in Diverse Communities: School Reform as Social Movement," *International Journal of Educational Change*, 2002, 3, 383–406.

16. C. C. Burris, personal communication, 2003; see also, C. C. Burris, "Commentary: When Excellence and Equity Thrive," *Education Week*, January 28, 2004.

17. G. Myrdal, *An American Dilemma: The Negro Problem and American Democracy* (New York: Harper and Brothers, 1944). J. Hochshild, *The New American Dilemma* (New Haven: Yale University Press, 1985).

18. The work of social theorists cited in chapters 6, 7, and 10 has been continued and developed over the past twenty years, both by those cited in the chapters and by others working in the tradition of critical scholarship.

19. For a fuller discussion of these reform suggestions, see Welner and Oakes, *Navigating the Politics of Detracking*. The publisher, Skylight, has graciously made this booklet available for free download online through UCLA's Institute for Democracy, Education, and Access (*www.idea.gseis. ucla.edu/publications/detracking/index.html*).

20. Pathways to College Website: *http://www.pathwaystocollege.net/ aboutus/index.html*

21. D. Stipek, *Engaging Schools: Fostering High School Students' Motivation to Learn* (Washington: National Academies Press, 2004); J. P. Heubert and R. M. Hauser, *High Stakes: Testing for Tracking, Promotion, and Graduation* (Washington: National Academies Press, 1999). For example, these foundations all contributed to a three-hour PBS documentary, "The College Track: America's Sorting Machine," which aired nationally in fall 2004.

22. New York ACORN Schools Office, "Secret Apartheid I: A Report on Racial Discrimination Against Black and Latino Parents and Children in the New York City Public Schools" (*http://acorn.org*, last visited December 7, 2004).

23. E. Frankenberg et al., *A Multiracial Society with Segregated Schools: Are We Losing the Dream?* (Cambridge: Civil Rights Project, Harvard University, 2003) (*http://www.civilrightsproject.harvard.edu/research/resego3/ resegregation03.php*).

24. D. Grissmer, A. Flanagan, and S. Williamson, "Why Did the Black–White Score Gap Narrow in the 1970s and 1980s?" in *The Black–White Test Score Gap*, edited by C. Jencks and M. Phillips (Washington: Brookings Institution Press, 1998).

25. See, for example, the special double issue of *Teachers College Record* devoted to *Williams v. California*, October and November 2004.

Index